SWEET FIGHTING MAN
(Volume II)

BY

MELANIE LLOYD

With best wishes
Melanie
x

SWEET TOUCH PUBLISHING COMPANY

Published by Sweet Touch Publishing Company

Cover design by Gomer Press Limited

Sweet Touch Publishing Company
Studio 221
61 Victoria Road
Surbiton
Surrey
KT6 4JX
United Kingdom
Tel: 07930 918 281
E-mail: melanielloyd@aol.com

ISBN 978-0-9556657-0-7

Printed by Gomer Press Limited

This book is dedicated to the memory of Johnny Bloomfield.

(12th May 1947 to 17th September 2004)

CONTENTS

BOXERS ON THE BILL

INTRODUCTION 7

1. GEORGE COOPER 9

2. CLINTON McKENZIE 37

3. TEDDY LEWIS 71

4. BOB 'B.F.' WILLIAMS 87

5. MICHAEL SPROTT 117

6. MARK ROWE 157

7. JANE COUCH 191

8. IVOR 'THE ENGINE' JONES 211

9. TONY BOOTH 241

10. COLIN JONES 271

THE LAST WORD 309

ACKNOWLEDGMENTS

I would like to thank the following people in order of appearance: Reg Gutteridge OBE, Sylvester Mittee, Alan Minter, George Cooper, Clinton McKenzie, Bruce Baker, Teddy Lewis, Betty Lewis, Johnny Winter, Bob 'B.F.' Williams, Shlomit Williams, Johnny Bloomfield, Michael Sprott, Colin 'The Dynamo' Dunne, Jim Evans, Jimmy Tibbs, Mark Rowe, Steve 'Columbo' Richards, Johnny Kramer, Bob Paget, Crawford Ashley, Jane Couch MBE, Tex Woodward, Simon Euan-Smith, Lenny Lee, Danny Gwilym, Mike Barrett, Ivor 'The Engine' Jones, Colin Lake, Charlie Magri, Peter Buckley, Tony Booth, Wally Walsh, Colin Jones and James Cook MBE.

I would like to pay my deepest respects to the memory of: Johnny Bloomfield, Harry Gibbs, Jack Fox, Jim Wicks, Joe Erskine, Freddie Mills, Patricia Walker, George Francis, Mavis Williams, Jim Williams, Eleoncio Mercedes, Fred Rix, Dudley McKenzie, Ernie Fossey, Harry Mullan, Eddie Thomas, Howard Winstone MBE, Vicente Saldivar, Tiny Ricci, Dennie Mancini, Max Schmeling, Solly Cantor, Wally Thom, Iris Lee, Llewellyn Jones, Danny Vary, Johnny Owen, Arthur Boggis, Pat Floyd, Eddie Futch, Bill Rowe and Ron Olver.

I would like to thank the following people in no particular order: Don Ewing, Harold Alderman, Tommy Eastwood, Jim Oliver, John Lloyd, Steve Holdsworth, Mandy Byrne, Barbara Cooper, Jim Dawson, everybody at the Boxing News (particularly Claude Abrams, Daniel Herbert and Tony Connolly), Brian and everybody at the Colindale Newspaper Library, Nigel James, Sandra Rowe, Debra Jones, Sally Bloomfield, John Stadnicki, Rebecca Harley, Christine Mitchell, Lloyd Dyer, Ray Caulfield, Julie & Graeme Oliver, Camelia Rizzacasa and Ronnie Moult.

Photographic acknowledgments:
Whilst every effort has been made to obtain copyright permission on all photographs, in some cases this has not been possible.

INTRODUCTION

> ***"When we're young we think we are invincible. It is only as we get older, when we look back, that we see the danger in what we do.***
>
> ***"Boxing is a dream and when it is over we must have a normality to return to. The higher you go, the longer distance you have to fall and the harder you fall.***
>
> ***"Each time we psyche ourselves up for a fight, it leaves a scar on us, a memory."***
>
> **(Sylvester Mittee)**

Sylvester Mittee came originally from the Caribbean island of St Lucia. He travelled to England in 1966 and ten years later he represented Great Britain in the Olympic Games at Montreal. The following year he turned professional. He went on to become Southern Area Light-Welterweight Champion and British & Commonwealth Welterweight Champion in the 1980s. Sylvester was as famous for his colourful post-fight interviews as he was for his manful boxing style. He was one of Frank Warren's first champions and he once told me, "Frank dressed me up in gold shorts, gold boots and he called me 'The Master Blaster.'"

Sylvester is one of the wisest human beings I have ever known, and his friendship is very important to me. Despite experiencing hardship in his own life, he is always there when I need him. I have benefited greatly from his knowledge and insight into what makes the world go round, and his careful advice has often given me the strength to stand my ground in the face of troubled times. Although, for his own reasons, Sylvester was initially reluctant to appear in this book, I am most delighted to report that he has graced several of the following pages in his own inimitable style, which puts me in mind of a wandering minstrel.

CHAPTER ONE - GEORGE COOPER

"This is so interesting because we all know about Henry and everything he achieved, but none of us really know very much about George." **(Alan Minter)**

They were known as, 'The Cooper Twins of Bellingham.' They were identical to look at and, in their era, they captured the imagination of the British boxing world. Henry Cooper is still a household name in Britain today and we all have big respect for Henry and everything that he achieved, but we seldom hear about his twin brother, who arrived into the world 20 minutes after Henry; the one who came as a surprise to everybody, including his mother!

When you say the name, George Cooper, most boxing fans will say something like, 'Oh yes, Henry's twin brother. He boxed under the name of Jim Cooper,' and that is often the entire extent of people's knowledge about this enigmatic and unpretentious man. But take a look at George's record and you will find the names of Dick Richardson, Brian London, Chic Calderwood, Johnny Prescott, to name but a few. George stood his ground with all of those men, beating Dick Richardson on points in a professional debut that saw George on the canvas twice in the first round. George was the first man to defeat Johnny Prescott as a professional, stopping the Birmingham hero in the second round. He drew with Chic Calderwood in Glasgow and toughed it out with Brian London to get stopped in the forth round of a most brutal fight. Although he topped the bill a few times himself, he often found himself fighting down the under-card, while Henry headed the show.

George's was a career that was racked with injury and, by the time he felt truly strong and fit, it was too late for him. By that stage, Henry was British, Commonwealth and European Champion and there was nowhere for George to go, other than to fight his twin, which was something he would never have done. On top of this, fights for George were scarce. Nobody wanted to box him for fear of beating beaten and thus denied a crack at Henry. So George decided to hang up his gloves and he took his place beside Henry to become his trainer, helping his brother successfully defend his British, Commonwealth and European Titles several times.

When I met George, his strong and solid demeanour made me think how lucky Henry was to have such a man behind him.

It was a few years ago when I interviewed George, and in those days I was still happily ensconced at the Foley ABC. My good friend there, Jim Dawson, was attending an amateur show in Kent and I learned that George Cooper was going to be present. That night, Jim approached George on my behalf to request this interview and I was over the moon when Jim Dawson rang me the next day to tell me that George had agreed. *'Sweet Fighting Man – Volume II'* was now officially on the way, and what a beginning!

The date of the interview arrived in February 2003 and George invited me to his home in Kent. Jim Dawson acted as my chauffeur that day and we got to the Cooper residence 40 minutes early. We sat outside in the car for a few moments to discuss our next plan of action and I then rang George from my mobile. His wife, Barbara, answered the phone. I explained who I was and that I was well aware that I was early. "Don't worry about that," came the kind reply, "Come on in and have a nice cup of coffee with us." As I stepped onto the driveway, the front door opened and George and Barbara stood on the doorstep in welcome. Barbara is sweet and petite and George towers over her. I was soon made at home in their sunny lounge that boasts a spectacular view across the fields yonder. The bungalow with its stone chimney is called 'Fourwinds' and George built it back in 1966 for him and Barbara to begin their married life. He proudly told me, "Marrying Barbara is the best thing I've done. I built this house while we were engaged. I didn't build it all myself, but I helped everyone do things."

Barbara disappeared into the kitchen, and George and I settled down with the tape-recorder. I was anxious that George immediately understood that this chapter was to be all about him. I told him that, although I might refer to Henry, both in the interview and the chapter, this chapter was to be written as a tribute to George's career and George's life. He simply nodded in bashful agreement, his hands in a prayer like pose beneath his chin. And so I made it my mission to lure this modest and peaceful man into the limelight, if only for a few hours. Before we got talking Barbara slipped into the room carrying a big tray of coffee and cakes. "You must try one of Barbara's famous fairy rock cakes," she implored me. "Let them cool down a little bit though, because I've just taken them out of the oven." I tried more than one of those cakes, and they were delicious.

George and Henry still look very similar, although these days George looks far more wiry than his twin. He confirmed, "I'm six foot, three. I'm an inch taller and I was always about four pounds heavier than Henry." I remarked that George looked pleasingly fit for a man who had, at that time, seen 69 summers and he chuckled, "Yeah, Henry's a bit tubbier than me now. I still go out and do a bit of plastering, see, not every day but two or three times a week."

George has blue eyes set deeply into the lean features of a face that can say a lot without the expression changing very much. "Blue, yeah, we're both the same." His words were spoken quietly and many years of living in the green and pleasant countryside of Kent have not eroded his London accent at all. He has a sometimes wry sense of humour and, when he recounts something that amuses him, his voice rises mirthfully in an almost singsong manner.

George and Barbara have three sons and one daughter. I had the pleasure of meeting Gavin and Alexander during my visit. George told me, "We've got three boys and one girl. Darryl's the eldest. Then there's Gavin. Alexander, he's out there now. He's into the theatre. He's the Stage Manager at the Miskin Theatre. Gavin plays the organ and Alexander collects them. We've got a cinema upstairs; I'll show you later. Then we've got our daughter, Beth. Beth and her partner just got engaged this weekend, as a matter of fact."

The Cooper twins were born at the Lying-In Hospital, Westminster on 3rd May 1934. "It comes under Lambeth actually. It's right opposite Westminster Hospital on the Westminster Bridge, but it comes under Lambeth so we're real cockneys. Me mum was Lily and me dad was Harry. When they met, me dad lived at the Elephant and me mum lived at Southwark, which wasn't far away, near London Bridge." Henry was born first weighing in at six pounds. George grinned, "Yeah, something like that. He was 20 minutes before me. I was a bit heavier."

George came as a complete surprise to Lily, who believed that she was only having one baby. She had decided that, if it was a son, she was going to call him Walter. "No, she didn't know she was having twins. By all accounts, Henry and George were family names, and one of the nurses said, 'Oh, a typical Henry and George,' and my mum said that the names just stuck, so she called us Henry and George." The twins had an older brother Bernard, who was born in 1930. "Yeah, he's four years older than us. Cory his wife came from Bargoed."

After George and Henry were born, they were taken home to Camberwell Green. It was in early 1940 that the three Cooper boys were evacuated. "Just for a year. We lived at Brixton then. We were about five. We went to Worthing, right by the Sussex coast. It was worse down there than what it was here! They had all mines and army blocks, because that's where they was expecting an invasion. All the Spitfires used to fly over. We used to see 'em on the South Downes, thousands of them, and then when they were going back, anything they had, they used to drop that way, you know? We was only there about ten months I think, and then we came home." For a London lad of such tender years I assumed that George might have been scared to be sent to a strange place, away from his parents. He looked at me as if he did not know what it was like to be scared. "Nah, we used to run out and think it was lovely. You don't think nothing of it when you're five years old. You don't think how terrible it was. We used to watch all the Spitfires fighting and we was all cheering."

While the boys were away, their house in London was hit by a German parachute mine. Thankfully, nobody was in it at the time. "They were living in Bellingham then and they used to go round my aunt's. One night, a land mine dropped on the corner and blew all the street down. It blew all the back of the house down. I mean, all the back and the doors went right through, but the front was all right. About half the street was completely demolished, because they were great big land mines on parachutes, and they used to explode and blow the whole bleedin' lot up. When we came back we went to live in Bellingham."

The twins attended Athelney School, which was about ten minutes walk away from where they lived. "Yeah, that's right, Athelney School. We stayed there all the time. When we went there, half the school had been bombed. There was only half the school there. We went there as juniors, and then it was the pilot scheme for secondary modern schools so we stayed there all the time. We never went anywhere else."

Apart from their schooling, the Cooper twins were industrious boys. Indeed, they needed to be. Without a father at home to bring the money in, their mother needed all the help she could get. "Because my dad had to go in the army then. He'd gone into the army because he was a reservist, you see. Just after the First World War he was in the army, and then, being a reservist, they called him up. He was 41 when they called him up and they said anyone over 40 wouldn't go into a war zone, but he did. They sent him to Burma. He was in the medical corps and he was there for about three years, so we never saw him. So, of course, things were a bit hard at home.

"We used to do everything, just to earn a few bob. We used to help the milkman. We all had paper rounds. We used to get up five o'clock in the morning to deliver papers. All of us used to work at Evans' down in Southend Lane, and we had to mark all our own papers, not like these days when they're all marked up already. Then we had to go and deliver them, and all for about ten bob a week, or it might have been seven and six, I can't remember. But it was a lot of money then and my mum could do with it, so we had to give it to her. She used to let us have two shillings or something. My mum had three boys and we used to break a pair of shoes in a fortnight, so she was always cleaning. She used to clean the gasworks. She did school dinners, a dinner lady she was. Doing charring. God, she had a hard old life."

But life wasn't all work and no play. For a brief period in their lives, George and Henry joined the Church Cubs. Unfortunately this was to be a short-lived association. The twins were asked to leave for being a little bit too lively. "Well, they used to have this game. I forget what it was called now, but you all had to line up and you all had to run through, and whoever stopped you, you had to help them to stop the rest. In the end it was left down to one. But, the thing was, me and Henry was a bit big and boisterous and we used to knock people over. They said we were too big and rough, so they slung us out after a week or a fortnight."

The lads also enjoyed participating in more organized forms of sport. They both enjoyed playing cricket, George being a particularly good batsman. "I was better at cricket than Henry was." Football was another favourite. "We always liked football. Henry was a good footballer. He played for Lewisham Schools. He was a good goalkeeper. I used to like football, but I was never as good as him. Then, when we got to about nine, we started concentrating on boxing.

"What we used to do, we used to round all the kids up and we used to say, 'Right, you and you box each other,' and we'd all stand round and watch. We had a green near us where a railway bridge used to go over it. They'd stopped using it as a bridge, and they had square areas down each side so we used to use that as a ring. We used to get all the kids sparring, and me and Henry'd be sparring, and there was a fireman who lived in one of the houses nearby. He'd see us and we used to drive him mad with the noise. Anyway, one day he come out and he says, 'You two, if you want to learn boxing, learn it properly.' Now, we'd all been brought up on boxing with my dad and my granddad, but my dad was away so this man took us to the Bellingham Boxing Club. Anyway, it was half a crown a year so we said, 'Oh, we can't go there.' So he paid out our first year's fee. Ron Hill his name was. He was the first one to take us to a boxing club, and he paid the fees because my mum couldn't afford it."

Before we embarked on the subject of George's boxing career, he had a last story to tell me on the subject of football. He once knocked himself out on a drainpipe while playing 'The Beautiful Game' and suffered concussion. "Oh yeah. We was rushing around, and they all dived out the way and I dived down and I hit this drainpipe. I landed on my temple and it gave me 24 hour amnesia. It was at the time when my dad was coming home, and Bernard and Henry, they tried me once. They said,

'It's good that dad's coming home,' and I said, 'Oh, is he?' and we'd been excited for months! Ten seconds later they said, 'Dad's coming home,' and I said, 'Oh, is he?' And they kept doing it, because it was a game to them. They thought it was funny. Anyway, I went to the doctor, and after 24 hours it went and I was all right. But I had a big lump on me forehead."

Up until this point, I was under the impression that George had never been knocked out like that in the boxing ring, but I was to be gently corrected. "Well, once I did. Dick Richardson knocked me out when I was an amateur. Spark out. Our second was Ernie Shackleton. He was the top amateur fighter at one time and they used to say he was the best amateur ever. Anyway, the bell went and I realized I didn't have me gum-shield in. I said, 'Quick, gum-shield.' I bent through the ropes for him to put me gum-shield in and I've turned around. The next thing I remember was waking up in the dressing room, because Richardson came running over and, as I've turned round, he's hit me on the chin and he's knocked me sparko!

"So the next fight I had, after about a month, I had Dick Richardson again, and I stopped him in one round. I didn't run over and hit him, but I stopped him in one round. We boxed five times, amateur and professional. It was three, two to me all together. We won one each as a professional; I beat him once and he beat me.

"Anyway, we started boxing at Bellingham Boxing Club and then, as we got better, we found out through our school friend, Johnny Gibson, about Eltham and District Club. Johnny's dad worked with Georgie Page in the foundry and he was a good amateur trainer at Eltham and District Club, so we started going there."

The Cooper twins left school when they were 15 years old. "Our first job was at Burnham's in Sydenham, unloading sheet metal from lorries. They used to make interiors for refrigerators and their main thing was signs. You used to see their signs everywhere. They was the biggest sign makers, and it was all done with sheet metal. It was sprayed with enamel and baked in a furnace, and it all came out in enamel. They used to say,

'There's ten ton of metal there. Shift that.' I know we were big for our age, but we had to wear leather mitten things to pick these sheets up because it was like a razor; it would cut your hands to pieces. You had to stack each sheet dead level on the next one because, if you didn't, you couldn't move them because they was so heavy, so you had to stack them just right. We got paid nine pence an hour. After about a year we heard the Gasworks was paying ten pence an hour, so we went there. Sydenham Gasworks was one of the biggest gasworks in the country at the time. Yeah, about thirty bob a week we used to get.

"Then, we got into plastering. There was this bloke at Eltham and District, Reg Reynolds. He used to help George Page in the corner. They were great friends and Reg owned his own plastering business. One day he said to me and Henry, 'Come and work for me and I'll give you time off when you want to go boxing. You can go any time you want', so we learned plastering with him." As if to complete the circle in this little tale, George married Reg's daughter, Barbara. "I used to see Barbara and her sister Mavis every morning, going off to school. Barbara was about eight years old then, and every morning I used to see her. We was 16 at the time." Barbara has never been a boxing fan. "No, no. We didn't get married until after I'd finished boxing. She never liked it. My mum didn't like it either.

"My dad did because his family were all into boxing. We were brought up on all these stories about my grandfather. He was a bare-knuckle fighter. He used to do all tours with Ted Pritchard, who was the old Middleweight Champion. In them days, they used to do exhibitions in theatres and they used to introduce my grandfather as someone as good as Pritchard, if he'd only stay off the barley wine! He used to like a drink, you know. My grandfather used to work at the Elephant and Castle, at the horse repository. They used to have the biggest horse repository in Europe at the Elephant, and he used to travel all over the world. They took the first British bloodstock to Russia for the Czars, and all the way he used to fight. They had this foreman who was a right bully and he had these lovely riding boots, what they called spring side boots. So they arranged for this guy to have a fight with my granddad. Anyway, my granddad knocked him out and, when he saw these boots, he said, 'I'll have those boots while I'm at it.' So while the foreman was unconscious, my granddad took his boots. But the foreman was a right bully by all accounts.

"They used to travel all through France and Belgium, and all through the countries they used to fight and do exhibitions, so we were brought up on all these stories." I put it to George that his grandfather must have lived his life a bit like a gypsy. "Well he did, yeah. And he could sing. He had a marvellous voice. That's how he died. A blood vessel broke in his throat while he was singing at a wedding. He beat Reg Gutteridge's granddad, big Arthur Gutteridge. He was the father of the Gutteridge twins, who were the seconds at the Sporting Club. So my old grandfather beat Reg's grandfather, and we always used to pull Reg's leg about it!" Reg Gutteridge OBE is a good pal of mine and, when I next saw him, I asked him about this legendary battle of the grandfathers. He gave me a stern, sideways look and replied, "Yes, they always said that, but they've never proven it mind!"

Although George and Henry were identical twins, George was right-handed and Henry was left-handed. However, they both fought from an orthodox stance. "Yeah, Henry's completely left-handed. I'm right-handed, but now I do lots of things left-handed. Like, if I use scissors, I use me left hand then; I couldn't use me right hand doing that. I plaster right-handed. Henry is completely left-handed, but I'm sort of ambidextrous. I write right-handed and I shoot a rifle right handed. If I pick a spoon up, I'll use my left hand. It's funny. I think it's a mental thing. When we were boxing, it was always, 'Left hand, left hand.'" George gave me a demonstration of a perfectly straight left jab to emphasize his point. "When we were nine years old, for hours we had to go, bomp, bomp." The jab flicked out again. "You had to learn not to lean forward, how to slip the left hand, and I think, because I was taught to use me left hand all the time, I gradually got used to using me left hand to do things. Then again, Henry, being completely left-handed, normally left-handed fighters always shape up southpaw, but Henry never did. He went straight, naturally into orthodox stance. He never went southpaw at all."

My research showed that George had 64 amateur bouts in all, winning 42. "I think I had more than that, near a hundred all together. There was a lot we couldn't remember, you know, as kids. We didn't have too many. That's why we were all right. We were big for our age and we used to go to loads of shows; we'd go to about three shows a week, and might not get one fight because they would say we were too big. They didn't have anybody for us to fight of our age. I suppose it might have been about 60 but I'd have thought it would have been more like a hundred.

"In my last amateur fight before I went in the army I fractured my thumb. Up until then, it was Henry knocking his bloke out with his left hand and me knocking my bloke out with my right hand. Who did it first, that was the question, Henry or me? Anyway, I boxed this fella, and I hit him on the top of his head and I fractured me right thumb. Well, of course, I lost the fight. I had to stop immediately. I went to Lewisham Hospital and they set it, and after a week I had to go back and they had to break it again and re-set it. I still have that big bump." He showed me. "I was out for weeks with that." The thumb never really healed properly and George was always aware of it. "Well, after breaking my thumb, I never used my right hand so freely. I still knocked a few people out with my right hand, but I never really used it the same. I always used to try to use me left hand, but I could still dig with me right hand, when I wanted to." The last sentence was spoken quietly, as if to himself alone.

I asked George if his memories of his amateur days are happy ones. "Yes, especially in the later years, when we was in the army. We did our National Service in the 4th Battalion, Royal Army Ordinance Corps, which was the boxing Battalion. We was there from 1952 to 1954, and that's when the British Army *was* the British Army. They had them in Malaysia, India, you name it and we had British troops there, and they all used to enter the team boxing championships. The 4th Battalion won it six years on the trot. Anyone who was anyone, George Eastlake, the Captain, used to try and get them on the 4th Battalion. So our Battalion team was like an international team. We had Joe Erskine, Nicky Gargano, Ron Hinson, Dennis Hinson, Eddie Woodard, Henry and me. We even had, like, a second string. Eddie Woodard was the second string light-heavyweight to Henry, and he was an international fighter. So when we used to go up against an ordinary Battalion, they used to be, like, 'Wow!' you know, and wallop and down they'd go. A lot of times you had hard fights, but a lot of them, they only volunteered to box to get off duty, and then they'd come up against us and they thought the end of the world had come!

"We were there for about four months and everybody started complaining, because we never did anything other than boxing. So they said, 'You've got to have a job now', but they used to give us time off in the mornings for training. We didn't have to report for work until half-past nine, so we did our training of a morning and then we cooked our own breakfast. We used to have eggs and bacon. Our Captain Eastlake, before the team championship he'd give us all eggs and sherry. Raw eggs and sherry, we had. Cor, he couldn't do enough. Once the season ended, he wasn't quite so happy with us, mind. But he'd do anything to win that team championship. He thought the world of that."

Another major force (if you will pardon the pun) in the twins' army life was Sergeant Major Cavanagh. He was the man in charge of the 4th Battalion boxers, but this was not the first time the Cooper twins had crossed his path. "Three months before we went in the army, we boxed a team from Liverpool with Eltham and District. They used to fill Eltham Baths up and we used to have great matches. Anyway, who did Henry box but Sergeant Major Cavanagh, so when we go in the army we suddenly get called. We've done our first ten weeks basic training and now we've got to go and see the Sergeant. And we're like, 'Jesus Christ, what have we done now?' Because when the Sergeant Major said he wanted to see you, I mean to say, a Lance Corporal could ruin your life for you. When we went in there, who is it? It's him! Sergeant Major Cavanagh, who Henry's beaten three months before we went in the bleedin' army, and he's our Sergeant Major! We're still friendly with him now. He's a lovely bloke. He's marvellous. But he loved it, you know. He was a lovely guy and he still is. He's in his eighties now.

"I remember we toured Germany and I boxed in the brilliant Olympic Stadium in Berlin. They didn't have anyone good enough in the Army team so they matched me with Wolfgang Engle. He was the European

Police Champion. He was a bloody great big bloke. Christ, he was about 18 stone. He couldn't come through a door! He was six foot, seven. The night we boxed there were mainly French soldiers in there for some reason, and they all went mad when I beat him on points. They was all cheering me and lifting me from the ring, and I thought, 'Oh, good Gawd!' Because the war had only been over a few years and they used to hate the Germans, the French did. So they liked me for beating him.

"I boxed Joe Erskine at the Albert Hall in the Army Finals. And, I mean, I won the bleedin' fight, and because he was the favourite ... He was the favourite to win the Light-Heavyweight Title but, when he weighed in, he was too heavy so they put him in the Heavyweights. Anyway, we both got to the final, and he was the favourite and they gave it to him. But you know, Peter Wilson of the Mirror, who was a great fan of Joe's, even he said he thought I won the fight, and so did I, but they give it to Joe."

That year Henry had stood down in the championships because he wanted to give George a chance. "My uncle, my dad's brother, he had 'Henry' tattooed on one arm the year he won the ABA Title, and then the year I was boxing in the final he had my name tattooed on his other arm, before I won the fight. And then they give it to Joe Erskine, so he had a tattoo of me, saying I was the ABA Champion, and I wasn't! But I could always handle Joe. When we were touring and fighting all the different teams out in Germany, we used to spar a lot. Joe wasn't a big puncher but he was a marvellous boxer. I used to like Joe."

When the twins were demobbed from the army, they decided to become professional boxers. The manager they chose to go with was Jim Wicks, a man whose bond with the Cooper twins would become a part of boxing folklore. "Well, before we went in the army, our amateur trainer took us to see Jim Wicks. What I liked about Jim was he never bought a fighter. In them days, they was offering thousands for fighters to turn professional. Jim never did that. He used to say, 'If you buy a fighter, you can't manage him properly.' I mean, our mate, Johnny Gibson, he had one professional fight and Jim said to him, 'John, my advice to you is to pack boxing up, because you're never going to make it as a professional,' and then he give him his contract back. And he did things like that. He said, 'Well if I'd have paid him £2,000, I would have put him in the ring until I got that money back. You can't manage a fighter if you buy a fighter.' So when we went to see him in 1952, before we went in the army, he didn't give us any money or anything. He just said, 'If you still want to turn professional when you come out of the army, come and see me.' So we had him in mind, and when we came out we turned professional with him. Because anyone who offered us money, me and Henry, we didn't like it. I suppose we was a bit suspicious. We used to think, if they offered you money, they were trying to get you for some other reason. And Jim had all the good local fighters at the time, so we went back to him after we came out and turned professional."

I was intrigued as to how Jim Wicks came to be known as 'The Bishop' and George enlightened me. "Well, that was because he looked like a Bishop. He weighed 19 stone, he was a big man and he used to wear a Homburg hat. Anyway, someone, I forget who it was, nicknamed him 'The Bishop' and it stuck." The tone of George's voice became gentle when he talked about his old mentor and friend. "Oh, he was like another father to you. He was different to all the other managers. I never met anyone like Jim. He took to me and Henry, and we were with him for years. I was a professional for ten years, Henry was a professional for 15 years, and we knew him socially as well. He used to live not far from here and, later on, when he was old and dying, I used to go round and see him and take stuff round to him. When his wife died, he was on his own. It's sad really.

"Jim was a born gambler. When he was younger he used to win loads of money, but he never told you what he'd won. He'd win £20,000 or £30,000 and we wouldn't know, but he'd lose thirty thousand quid and not tell you about that either. But, when he was old, he wasn't getting the money and he used to gamble every day, not in a bad way, but he had what they call 'the blower.' You know, when you go into a betting shop, you hear all the different races? Well, he had that put into his house and he used to gamble. And he'd double up, and when you need it you don't win it. I used to say, 'Jim, for Christ sake!' And he used to say, 'It's got to be done. The game has got to be played.' That was one of his famous sayings. 'The game has got to be played.'

"When we were boxing, you never knew whether Jim had won £60,000 or lost £60,000. He knew all the backgrounds of the horses. Just say the name and he knew who the mother and father were, and the brothers and the sisters. And, I mean, not only horses. Cards, he won £40,000 playing cards. What he won on the horses one day, he lost playing cards the next day, and you never heard him moan, but if we had half a crown on a horse he'd go bleedin' mad!

"So anyway, our manager was Jim Wicks and Danny Holland was our trainer. He was Jim's main trainer at the time. Danny was very good at cuts, and he was a good trainer in the respect that he knew how to get you fit. Danny knew the boxing game inside out, so he was a good conditioner, trainer and cuts man. We was the first ones to sign as professionals on television. BBC Sportsview." In July 1954 George and Henry appeared on the front page of the Boxing News, two bright eyed and bushy tailed young men, each with a mop of curls and big smiles, dressed in their tracksuits and looking as fit as a pair of butchers dogs. The headline read, *'Twins Turn Pro on TV'*. The Cooper twins had made their mark on television history and I asked George, "Were you nervous doing that on the telly?" He shook his head and pursed his lips, "No, not really. I mean, once you was used to fighting … I mean, we boxed in all the big halls. Although I never topped the bill at the big halls, I boxed at Wembley, Earls Court, Harringay; we had our first three fights at Harringay, which held about 10,000. I boxed in all the big places, the biggest places ever."

Before George could box as a professional he had to adopt a new ring name, because there was already a professional boxer around at the time named George Cooper, who incidentally came from Orpington. "Yeah, he used to box in the booths and things. So I took Jim Wicks' name, and it was easy to write the name 'Jim.' I thought it might bring me some luck, but it didn't! The trouble with me was, anything going, I got it. In 1957, I'd been a pro three years and I caught Scarlet Fever. And I kept getting cut eyes; I used to get badly cut. Every time I got three or four wins under me belt, I'd get stopped again on a cut eye. So then I had plastic surgery and, all the time I was out, Henry was going up and up and up. He became the Champion and then, when I came back, I had all my better fights. But I could never fight the Champion because that would have meant fighting Henry."

1954, the year the Cooper twins turned professional, was a time ripe with boxers who became true legends. Archie Moore was still around. So were Rocky Marciano and Ezzard Charles. But George most admired the great British boxers of the era. "Bruce Woodcock, I used to think he was a great British fighter, but he was unlucky. He fought Joe Baski and broke his jaw; he gave away about three or four stone then. He was always an under-rated fighter, I think. When we were kids, we all used to be dead nervous listening to the radio, listening to Woodcock and Mills. Freddie Mills, he was another one. We loved him. We knew him well. Before he died, we were with him doing a charity thing. And Johnny Williams, he'd finished when we started, but he was still fighting at the time when we started as amateurs and we sparred with him. Don Cockell was another one we sparred with."

George and Henry made their professional debuts on Tuesday, 14th September 1954. George beat Dick Richardson on points over six rounds at Harringay Arena. George's first fight in the paid ranks was a fierce one. Richardson had over half a stone in weight advantage and was a notoriously tough Welshman. "Yes, I was about 13 and a half stone and he was about 14 and a bit." I reminded George that Richardson knocked him down twice in the first round. He replied in a nonchalant fashion, "Did he? I can't remember. I liked Dick. He was always nice. He was rough. Oh he hit you with everything; elbows, knees, *everything*, but there was something likeable about him. At the Boxing Writers dinner we'd meet him, years afterwards, and it would be, like, 'Hello you old sod! You old bleeder!' I mean, we had right tussles."

Two months later, George forced Johnny Apee of Welling to retire after one round at Manor Place Baths in Walworth. "That was a charity do at Manor Place Baths, yeah. Apee had stepped in as a late substitute. I forget who I was gonna' fight now. I can't remember." Two weeks after that, George rounded off the year with a fight against Bob Gardner, brother of former British and European Heavyweight Champion, Jack. It was the man from Market Harborough's first visit to London as a professional boxer and he stopped George in one round at Harringay Arena. It was a right hook from Gardner that slashed George's eye and caused the fight to be stopped in 55 seconds. I asked George to describe his feelings on his first professional loss. "Well, I was cut again, and I thought, 'Oh my God, I'm cut again.' Harringay Arena was my favourite place to box. It was like a hexagon shape, like an old thrupenny bit. It held about 10,000 and, wherever you was in Harringay, you could see. I always had a soft spot for that place. That was the main place to fight."

George's first fight of 1955 was on the 15th March at Streatham, and this would be his final fight with old foe, Dick Richardson. The Welshman stopped George in two rounds, cutting his eye so badly that George was not allowed to continue. "Yeah, he was a lad! It was always a gruelling struggle with Dick. He was big and he was strong with it, and you had a right job with him all the time, you know. He'd go like that and he'd hit you with his bleedin' elbow. Not on purpose. It was never on purpose with him. He was just a big, strong, awkward ... He'd swing a punch and he'd miss with the punch, and he'd hit you with his bleedin' elbow! Whereas, Brian London hit you with his elbow on purpose. That was the difference. You knew the difference." I had heard a rumour that Richardson's manager, Wally Lesley, sent a friend into the dressing room especially to ensure that Jim Wicks did not attempt to slip a ringer into the ring by substituting Henry for George. George laughed, "Oh yeah, well he always said that. 'Ere, you aint' putting bleedin' Henry in with him are ya?' I don't know whether he ever did send anyone in or not, but that was always the joke. He always used to say that."

The following June, George avenged his earlier loss against Bob Gardner when he beat him on points over six rounds at Nottingham Ice Stadium. George conceded over a stone in weight and both boxers were bleeding before it was over. I wondered if it made George feel good to settle the score. "Oh yeah, it always did."

In September 1955 George fought Trevor Snell at White City. Once again, George's face paid the toll when he got cut in the second round, but he fought on with the injury and it was Trevor Snell who got stopped in the final seconds of the fight because of a horrible gash around one of his eyes. George laughed, "He was a Welshman as well, wasn't he?" I confirmed that, yes, he was; he was from Cardiff and I put it to George in the sternest manner that I could muster that he boxed quite a lot of Welshmen. "Yeah, well I'm forgetting, you know. I can't even remember who I've fought, whereas you've got all the record there. I haven't got a record of who I've boxed. We used to write in a book, and Henry's got that."

My good friend, Fred 'Nosher' Powell, who fought out of Walworth, boxed Basil Kew of Putney on the last fight on that show and the pair kept the crowds entertained with their clowning around. George grinned, "He's funny, Nosher. He was a comedian. Jack Solomons used to put him on last to keep all the crowd there 'till the end. I remember when he fought Basil Kew. After eight rounds they said Nosher had won the fight and he said, 'No. It's for the Southern Area. It goes ten.' So they went another two rounds and Basil Kew knocked him out! But there was always something funny with Nosher." Two months later, on the 15th November 1955, George fought Trevor Snell again and this time he beat him on points over eight rounds at Harringay.

George began 1956 with a January fight against notorious tough guy, Brian London. 'The Blackpool Rock' was undefeated when George fought him at Streatham Ice Rink. George out-boxed his Northern rival for the first few rounds. London seemed intent on landing one big haymaker to finish the fight and he was prepared to pay the price for it; and pay he did, when George dramatically knocked him down with a left hook to the body. From the floor, London indicated to the referee that the blow had been low. He got up at five and dropped back to the canvas again. After being cautioned by the referee to keep his shots up, George leapt in to finish the job. London held on and was back in the fight before the bell sounded to end the round. "They reckoned that was the longest count. They reckoned he was down for 21 seconds. He went down and the referee started counting, and then he started holding himself, making out I hit him low. After that, the referee talked to me and then he went back over and started counting again. 'Cos London got up and then he went down again, holding himself. I was the first one to put him down. Anyway, he got up and then he bleedin' nutted me. He used to blatantly nut you and he split my eye, bad. And that was the end of me. He stopped me."

It was a brutal night and London put George down five times before the fight was stopped. In the fourth round George stood and had a fight with him and London came surging forward to crack George on the chin. George stepped back and sort of crumpled to the canvas but he was up at the count of eight. Then London charged in again and knocked George off his feet. George was up at five. Then London hit George with a left hook and he went down again. George was up at seven. And then another left hook knocked George down again. This time, George was up at six and the crowd were shouting at the referee to stop the fight. The referee let it continue but, when a short right put George down again for the fifth time, it was stopped, although George was up and ready to have another go. "Well, I don't really remember a lot about it. I couldn't see. He cut my eye bad and I couldn't see, and he was hitting me all the time. He was hard to fight, Brian London."

Six weeks after losing to Brian London, George suffered another stoppage defeat. He retired in two rounds against Peter Bates of Shirebrook at the Albert Hall. George fought, as he often did, down the under-card which featured Henry at the top of the bill. For the record, Henry fought French Champion, Maurice Mols, and won it in four. Of George's fight with Bates, this was a case of straight back into the frying pan, having had such a tough one against London only six weeks before. "I boxed Peter Bates, who was one of the top fighters at the time. I got a cut eye; two rounds I think it was when he stopped me. It was a hard one, but I wanted to get back in the ring, quick."

It was nine months later before George was back in the ring. On the 26th November 1956 George was stopped on cuts in four bloody rounds against North Shields boxer, Manuel Burgo, at Granby Halls in Leicester. "Manuel Burgo. You're mentioning names now. I forgot about him. Anyway, after that, our manager, Jim, said, 'Look you can't be training and working. You've got to train during the day.' That's when we went full time professional."

In 1957 George fought twice. On the 19th May he was disqualified in the seventh round against Albert Finch at Stockholm, Sweden. Top of the bill was Henry versus Ingemar Johansson for the Swede's European Heavyweight Title. Johansson kept his unbeaten record when he knocked Henry out in the fifth, and George did not fare much better. "Well, it was unusual, because me and Albert Finch was both British, boxing each other abroad, and I was Henry's sparring partner and Albert Finch was chief sparring partner for Johansson, so we were the second top of the bill. I hit him a good punch up the belly and he went down, and then he started holding himself and the referee disqualified me. The only time I've ever been disqualified, that was. But you've just got to get on with it.

"While we were in Sweden we stayed in a lovely hotel. It was brand new. The Apolonia. It was all timber and pine and it was beautiful. Big firesides. One day, the headwaiter said to me and Henry, 'Can I come out and train with you?' Well, we thought, 'Cor, we don't want headwaiters training with us,' but we said, 'All right, you can come out in the morning with us.' He was only a tiny little skinny bloke and he was all dressed up in a dress suit. But, when he came out in the morning, he had all the gear. We was like, 'Blimey!' So he said, 'Ready?' We says, 'Yes, ready.' And he was off! He was only one of the top Swedish runners! His legs shot out and me and Henry was like, 'Woa, woa, woa! We just train, we just run for 45 minutes, we don't race.' He said, 'Oh, I'm sorry.' He was one of the top Swedish athletes of the time. We was like, 'God almighty!' So he used to come running with us, but he used to slow down; thank Gawd for that! But we used to run in big heavy boots. When we went training, we never wore trainers or anything like that. We used to wear big army boots so, when you boxed in boxing boots, they felt light."

The following September, George had a re-match with Manuel Burgo. The result was the same as the previous November. The referee intervened in the fourth round when George's left eye got badly cut, having already been down twice in that round. Shortly after that fight George was put down for the count by his own ill health. "After I'd been a professional for three years, I caught scarlet fever. I didn't train for a fortnight and the doctors said I could go back now. So I started going back, and I was skipping one day and me legs started to seize up. I came home and I said to my mum, 'Cor, my ankle aint' half stiff.' She said, 'Well, sit down.' I sat down and I couldn't move after an hour. I'd got rheumatic fever. They rushed me off to hospital. They had to fumigate the house. They said, 'You'll never box again.' They took me to the Fever Hospital at Hither Green. They was all isolated there, because it was a bad thing then. You could die of it. But, lucky enough, I had this old French doctor. He was the top man in the world for rheumatic fever and he said, 'If you lay still and don't move for a month you'll be all right. You'll go back boxing.' And that's what I did. I laid there on that bed for a month. I couldn't move. I couldn't listen to the radio. I couldn't listen to television. They wouldn't let me do that. I had me hair cut laying down in bed. I had to go to the toilet laying down in bed. They had to shave me. But they said I mustn't get up, and I didn't.

"Then I had plastic surgery to help with the cuts, because I kept getting cut. I went to [Queen Victoria] East Grinstead Hospital, where they specialised in plastic surgery, and I had the end of that bone in my eyebrow taken off." He indicated the bone on the inside corner of his left eyebrow. After that, that eye never cut again, but then all the other side and the underneath started cutting, so I still got stopped. But the left one never cut again. So I had another year out with that. After that I was perfect, and I had all my best fights."

In 1959 George returned to the ring to fight Sam Langford, namesake of the tiny black Canadian heavyweight who terrorised the boxing ranks for the first 26 years of the twentieth century. George fought the Liverpool based Nigerian version at the Corn Exchange at Kings Lynn on the 11th April. It was a top of the bill, televised affair and George was stopped in four rounds. "Oh, he was a bloomin' hard nut. Jim Wicks said, 'We'll try you against someone and see if you've still got it.' He was a bit too hard really for a first fight after such a long time out. I should have had someone a bit easier, I think." George had been doing so well, his boxing skills on top form that night, running rings around Lanford with speed and craft. Then the third round arrived and Langford saw his chance. He scored with a successful body attack and then followed through with a left hook and short right to the jaw. George sank to the canvas. He just made it up for nine but he was all over the place.

Langford came charging forward again to put George down once more before the bell. When they came out for the fourth George's face was a mess of blood. Langford put George down again twice before the referee, Pat Floyd, jumped in to stop it. Afterwards, Langford, elated by his victory, declared that he would be happy to give away weight to any British heavyweight, especially Joe Erskine and Henry Cooper.

After seven losses George was due a win, and it came later that year, on the 17th November, when he fought Alan Hands of Blackpool at the 18,000 seater Earls Court Exhibition Hall. It was the first time for George's hand to be raised in nearly four years. "I remember I fought a bloke called Alan Hands, a very big tall bloke, about six foot, five. Red headed. He weighed about 17 and a half stone. Well, in them days, anyone of that weight was considered dead slow. I knocked him out in two rounds. Today, if your not 15, 16, 17 stone, you're not classed as a heavyweight. Instead of boxing, it's all power today. It's like, you and him, and whoever's the strongest wins it. But, to me, boxing was boxing in our day. Even if I won a fight, if I didn't box well, I used to be disappointed with myself. It was a thing, you always wanted to box well, as well as win the fight. So anyway, he came charging out at me and I hit him, and he came right off his feet and went in the corner. I thought the ring was gonna' collapse, but it didn't."

1960 started badly for George. On the 26th January he was once again halted by facial lacerations. He was stopped in six rounds by Kitione Lave, a boxer who went under the name of, 'The Tongan Terror.' "He stopped me with cuts, didn't he? I was hitting him all over the place and then he just cut me, and that was it. That was at Olympia I think." The gash over George's right eye that stopped him in his tracks came straight from Lave's head of rock. The crowd expressed their disapproval darkly while the referee held Lave's hand aloft. But George Cooper was not a man for turning and, on the 26th April 1960, he was awarded another winning decision, an eight round points verdict over Nigerian, Alex Barrow, at the Wembley's Empire Pool. The Boxing News reported of this fight: *'One of the most pleasing performances of the night came from Jim Cooper.'* George laughed, "I never used to buy the Boxing News a lot for some reason. I don't know why. I should have bought it. They must have liked me. Alex Barrow, he was another hard nut, and he cut me as well." Keeping on the winning side, the following July George stopped Francis Magnetto in two rounds at Wembley. "I don't remember a lot about it, to tell you the truth. I knew he was the ex-French Champion. I know he came charging out at me and I caught him, and that was that."

Three months later, George went on the move. He travelled to Bolognia in Italy to fight former European Champion, Franco Cavicchi. It was a hard night's work and both boxers got their faces damaged that night. George put up a good show, but the Italian put him down twice during the fight. By the end of the seventh, George's left eye was badly gashed. The doctor examined the injury and called the fight off. In any event, losing abroad came as no surprise to George. "In them days you had *no* chance. You *knew*. I couldn't get fights over here, so Jim got me a couple of fights abroad. In Italy, if you knocked them out they disqualified you, so I knew how much I was gonna' win before I went. But I still went. It was work, and nobody wanted to fight me over here because they knew that, if they lost to me, they wouldn't get a chance with Henry."

1961 was a good year for George. He notched up three wins and a draw. On the 16th March he beat Jack Whittaker of Warwick on points over eight rounds at Brighton. "That was at the Ice Rink they had there at the time. I boxed quite well that night, if I remember rightly." The following May George boxed Whittaker again, this time in Glasgow. Again, George beat the Midlander on points, putting him down four times over eight rounds in a fight that was the main attraction at the Kelvin Hall Sports Arena.

In August that year, George returned to Kelvin Hall, this time to box Chic Calderwood of Craigneuk. The famous Glaswegian venue has been a home for boxing on and off for many years. Going there to challenge a Scotsman, particularly one with a record of 30 wins and 1 loss, you have to really want it. That night, George really wanted it. He was awarded a draw with Calderwood over ten rounds. It was a catch-weight contest; George outweighed the Scotsman by over a stone and Calderwood had come up in weight to take the fight. But, to balance the scales, Chick Calderwood was at that time Scottish, British and Empire Light-Heavyweight Champion. A year earlier, he had beaten Willie Pastrano at Glasgow over ten rounds on points. "Oh yes. He was number three light-heavyweight in the world at the time. He was a good fighter. I had Jock [Eugene] Henderson, the referee, and I was boxing the Scottish Champion of Britain. I won eight rounds out of ten and they've scored it a draw. Jim Wicks went mad; 'A bleedin' draw! They must be potty!'"

This fight was top of the bill and the arena was packed. Calderwood walked in to a tumultuous reception. George laughed as he looked back. "I must give them this, all the fans were cheering me at the end. They were all Scottish fans. They were all his fans and they were all cheering me in the end." Having said that, George was forced to walk through a baptism of fire before he could step into the ring. "Oh, yes. It was anti-me, anti-English. Especially at Kelvin Hall. But, as I say, at the end, no one booed me or nothing, so that was good."

George's last fight of 1961 came in October and he out-pointed Ray Shiel over ten rounds. Manchester's Free Trade Hall was full to capacity that night and the boxers had a television audience of millions. George and Shiel, a former St Helens Rugby League player, put up a performance worthy of any audience as they went at it for ten bloody rounds. George started bleeding in the fourth and, two rounds later, Shiel suddenly caught him with a right hand to the jaw. George went down and he only just beat the count. Jim Wicks, Danny Holland and Henry were going ballistic from the corner, and their frantic shouting eventually got through to George. He fought his way through the fog and staggered to his feet. He was out of it, but his instincts kicked in and he held on for the last few seconds before the bell saved him.

Two rounds after that, George floored Shiel twice. Both times the Scotsman struggled to make the count, but he managed to drag himself to his feet. Shiel looked a mess by now. Both of his eyes were closing and he had a horrible cut on his cheek, but he was a brave man and he fought on. Both boxers were battered and bleeding at the end of the fight and Shiel knew he had not won, a fact that he was prepared to acknowledge before George's hand was raised. "He was a right hard nut. He was a Rugby League player at one time from up North, and I boxed him a couple of times. The first time I boxed him, he hit me on the chin and I went down. Me foot crumpled under me and, as I went down, I hurt me ankle and I thought, 'Jesus, what have I done there.' Anyway, I got up, I boxed ten rounds and I won the fight on points. Took me boot off and it went whoosh, and I'd broke a bone in me ankle. Anyway, I had to go to Westminster Hospital then and they put me foot in plaster and that was that. Anything going, I got it." Four and a half months later George fought Ray Shiel again. Again they fought at Manchester, and again both boxers got cut up. This time, Shiel evened up the score. Jim wicks pulled George out at the end of the fourth round.

After a cheerless visit to Hamburg in May 1962, when George got stopped on cuts by former German Heavyweight Champion, Albert Westphal, the following November George came back with a win. He beat Peter Bates on points over eight rounds in a re-match from the Doncaster man's two round win over George back in February 1956. It was an ugly fight with a lot of holding and mauling. George's eye was cut in the opening seconds and, as much as Bates worked to make the injury worse, George's corner kept it under control. "After him stopping me at the Albert Hall, I boxed him again at the Bedford Sporting Club and I beat him on points. It was always good to get your own back on them." In December that year, George continued his winning streak against John Henry in Nottingham. Before the fight, a Board of Control official requested that the American shave off his beard but, because of his Moslem religion, he was excused. George, however, accepted no excuses and he stopped the tough black New Yorker in the seventh.

The memory of George's next ring battle still make his blue eyes sparkle. Johnny Prescott was made from that irresistible combination of devastating charisma and roughhouse toughness. In the boxing trade, he was known as a hot prospect and, by the time he fought George, he was boiling over. He was unbeaten in 22 fights, he had won the Midlands Area Heavyweight Title and the only way was up. And then he fought George Cooper. The collision happened on the 12th March 1963 and it was possibly the most outstanding performance of George's career. He stopped Johnny Prescott in two rounds in the Birmingham heartthrob's hometown, at the Embassy Sportsdrome. "I *loved* that, going up there to Birmingham to fight him." The stoppage came when George's big right cross connected mightily to Prescott's jaw. Prescott went down and his head cracked on the canvas. He bravely struggled to his feet and George tore straight back into him when referee, Mickey Fox, stepped in, as defenceless Prescott was on his way down for the second time. "When I knocked him out, I had that Mandy Rice-Davies, who was with Christine Keeler, she was crying, 'You 'orrible …' And there was someone else well known, a film-star, and she was crying, because Prescott was a bit of a ladies' man. He had them all there to watch because I was just a steppingstone. He had gone 22 without being beaten. I caught him well in the first round and he nearly went out then, so I pressured him again in the second and they had to stop it quick. All the girls were crying, 'I hate you, Cooper!' I couldn't help laughing, you know."

Six weeks after Prescott, George won a decisive ten round points decision over Italian, Federico Frisco, at the Midlands Sporting Club, Solihull. He followed this up with another points win six weeks later when he beat cagey Philadelphian, Don Warner, on points over eight rounds at Wembley Stadium. "I was the only one that won that night, when Henry boxed Clay at Wembley. It was Britain versus America. There was Henry versus Clay, me versus Don Warner, then there was Johnny Halafihi versus Jimmy Ellis and someone else versus someone else. I was the only one that won. Mind, I still got cut."

This was the night that will be hotly disputed by boxing fans forever more. Henry floored Muhammad Ali in the fourth round with his famous left hook but Ali got up off the floor and came back to stop Henry in the next round on grotesque cuts. I asked George if met Muhammad when he came over here to fight Henry in the sixties. The first time, in 1963, Ali was disrespectful to Henry, calling him 'A bum.' The second time, in 1966, he was much kinder, calling him 'An English gentleman and a worthy challenger for the World Title.' George grinned, "Yeah. It was a joke to me, and Henry used to treat it the same. People used to say, 'Don't you get annoyed?' But no, he's selling tickets all the time he's boasting. I knew Angelo Dundee two years before he came here with

Clay. He came here with Willie Pastrano, the light-heavyweight. I was the only one who used to spar with Willie Pastrano in the gym. He come over here two or three times, and each time he come over here I used to spar with him. So I knew Angelo Dundee years before he came here with Clay. He was a nice guy."

Time was marching on for George. By now, Henry now had a firm grip on the British and Commonwealth Titles and he was heading straight for a crack at the European. For every boxer, winning a title is the name of the game, and George felt that he had little to fight for. He could see no pot of gold at the end of the rainbow to keep him motivated. On the 22nd October 1963 George was stopped in seven rounds by part time Alabama cowboy, Jefferson Davis, at Wembley Pool. Over a year later, on the 9th November 1964, George Cooper travelled to Manchester to step through the ropes to fight as a professional boxer for the last time. In the other corner was tasty young American, Chip Johnson, whose first appearance in this country had seen him draw with Johnny Prescott. More of the blood and disappointment that had dogged George throughout his career was there at the end. He looked good at the start but by the end of the third it was all over. Johnson hammered George to defeat, putting him down five times and inflicting a massive cut on his left eyebrow in the process. George got up and was prepared to carry on but referee, Jack Lord, stopped the fight. George announced his retirement from the ring that night. "Well, it was getting very difficult to get fights. And, I mean, he wasn't that good, the American. Like I say, I used to always like to perform well and, when I knew I couldn't beat a bloke like him, I thought, 'Well, now's the time to pack up.' I made the decision that night."

So after a professional career of 31 fights, 16 wins and one draw, George 'Jim' Cooper stepped down from the ring for the last time as a professional boxer. I asked him to describe the highest and lowest points of his career. "The lowest was when I had to finish. That was the lowest point. The highs was when I beat Prescott and drew with Calderwood, especially as I fought them in their own backyards. When I went abroad I always thought I had no chance, I knew before I went. Going to Italy fighting Cavicchi, he was their idol, you know. I thought, 'Cor, I haven't got much chance here', but in this country I always thought I had a chance of winning. Nine times out of ten I was winning and then I'd get a cut eye. All the fights I lost on cuts, I was always boxing well and winning well, and then wallop! That's what was so disappointing about it.

"In my day, you had Erskine, Richardson, London, Snell, you had them all. They were all good fighters and hard nuts. You had to fight your heart out to beat them. I was number three heavyweight in Britain at one time but, all the time I was boxing, Henry was the Champion of Britain and the Empire and Europe, so I couldn't have boxed for any of them. Well, I could have done, but that's the way it goes, isn't it?"

"Oh, and the injuries, I had more bleedin' troubles - anything going, I got it. One fight, when I was still an amateur, I was only about 17 and a bit, and I fought this guy; he was about 30. I was thinking, 'He's a bit old. I'll be able to beat him all right.' He was a lot heavier than me and he swung a punch and it hit me round the back, and he's tore three of me ribs away from the cartilage. Cor, I couldn't breath, and then I lost that fight.

"When I was about 15, we were out on the green I was telling you about and I knelt down on a stone, and it went into me knee and I caught this really bad infection. I could have died with that, because it poisoned my system, because that was before antibiotics. I was in Lewisham Hospital for three weeks with that. And that was when all the doodlebugs come over. We used to stand on the balcony and watch 'em until they cut out and see where they was gonna' land. All the time you could hear them coming you didn't worry, and then when they cut out, we used to stand on the balcony at the end of the ward and watch.

"All these things always seemed to happen to me, and Henry went on and he never seemed to get anything. I copped for the lot for all of us. I even broke my leg playing golf not so long ago. I thought I was safe playing golf!"

When George retired as a boxer he became Henry's trainer. "Well, we always used to spar together, but when I finished I became his trainer. He defended all his titles while I was training him, and he only lost to

Bugner. We always trained at the Thomas A' Beckett in the Old Kent Road. Me and Henry both liked training. That's half the battle. If you get a fighter who doesn't like training, half the battle's lost. But, if you like training it's half won, and we liked training. If one of us was feeling a bit off, the other would say, 'Come on,' and that was it, whereas if you were on your own you might not have gone. So we always went. It was always the same, right from when we were nine years old until we were 30." When George finally walked away from boxing for good he turned his full attention on a thriving plastering business and, as he said at the beginning of this interview, he still does a bit today.

I had a lovely time with the Coopers at 'Fourwinds' bungalow but all good things come to an end, as they say, and my pal Jim Dawson arrived to collect me. He rang the doorbell and George and Barbara ushered him in the house. Before we left George gave us the promised tour of the Cinema that he has built in his loft to support his sons' theatrical aspirations. It truly is a mini-cinema, complete with folding rows of seats and a Mighty Compton organ, of which George informed us, "Yeah, it took about seven of us to get that up here." Barbara proudly explained that her friends from the local Women's Institute, where Barbara occupies a place on the committee, regularly visit for 'a night at the cinema.' George's face broke into a warm and rugged smile, "Yeah, I go up there in the interval. I'm the ice-cream boy."

CHAPTER TWO - CLINTON MCKENZIE

"If there's one boxer who I fought who taught me how to be a man, it was Clinton McKenzie. Clinton is a true warrior but he was too good for his time. He had a kind of bravery that was scary to watch. I would walk on bare feet to meet him." **(Sylvester Mittee)**

Introducing the famous McKenzie boys, they were brothers, the late Dudley (1961 to 1995) who was a brave and talented boxer and well respected as a fighter and as a man, Clinton, Duke, Winston, and their cousin Lee. Duke, a World Champion at three different weights, was the most successful of them all but, to my mind, the most exciting McKenzie, and possibly the most under-rated, was Clinton.

The crowd loves a boxer who comes to fight, and Clinton McKenzie always came to fight. He had a glittering amateur career, which culminated in him competing in the 1976 Montreal Olympics, where he reached the quarter-finals and lost a points decision to Sugar Ray Leonard. When he turned professional he won the British Light-Welterweight Title three times, along the way earning a Lonsdale belt to keep, and he also became European Champion. In his peak years Clinton's style was all passion and fire. He boxed from a southpaw stance, but he was naturally right handed, which made his right jab a devastating weapon. Towards the end of his career, he displayed the grace and wisdom of a master, out-boxing and outclassing much younger men and proving beyond doubt that you can't put a price on experience. He looked as fit for his last fights as he did for his first, and he was always dangerous. Therefore, when I was planning my 'hit list' for this book, Clinton McKenzie was a man in my mind for an interview.

It was a cold and wet winter evening and I was at Caesars Nightclub in Streatham to cover my friend David Wakefield's fight for the Surrey Comet. While the boxers weighed in, I was sauntering around the largely empty venue when I happened upon the stage, where there were several items laid out ready for auction. The prize that immediately caught my eye and drew me in was a big, framed photograph of Mike Tyson. He was sitting astride a monstrous motorbike sporting a beaten up black leather jacket and an easy smile. This picture was obviously taken during the blazing butterfly's sunnier days and, as I stood there gazing at it, my heart heavy with wistful memories, a man came and stood quietly by my side. He was black and he was wearing smart white training gear. Without looking properly at my new companion, I remarked, "That's a lovely picture, isn't it? He looks really happy there." The man in white gently replied, "Yes. That picture was taken a long time ago." I suddenly remembered my manners and, as I turned to face the man I was talking to, he politely introduced himself, "Hi. I'm Clinton McKenzie." I had him nailed down for an interview in five seconds flat, metaphorically speaking, of course.

We met a couple of months later in February 2004 at Clinton's gym above the Half Moon in London's Herne Hill. The pub stands on a street corner and two walls of the gym are lined with windows, which gives the place a bright and airy feel. Clinton has been working from there since 1994. Over the years, he has built up a successful operation, which accommodates boxers, along with men and women enjoying the benefits of Boxercise, a form of exercise that Clinton helped to pioneer.

When I arrived at the gym, I sat for a while and watched Clinton at work, diligently supervising, giving advice and pad work. When he was finished, he took me to a café bar around the corner and generously treated me to a delicious steak, a couple of pints of lager and a coffee, while we relaxed and did our interview to a backdrop of languid jazz music. Today, Clinton weighs in at 12 stone and he looks fit on it. He has an expressive face and a gentle voice. His is a captivating speaker, his eyes are deep brown and searching, and he has the most perfect teeth I have ever seen.

Clinton McKenzie was born in Clarendon, Jamaica on the 15th September 1955. He was to be the eldest of seven children and he came to England when he was six years old. "I remember, it was night time when I arrived so you couldn't really see a lot, but the next morning it was snowing, so I think it must have been about January time. It was the first time I saw snow in my life. Oh, I was *terrified.* I remember it to the day. I went under my bed and I hid there, and I wouldn't come out. I mean, in Jamaica it don't snow at all. So all of a sudden, there's this white stuff everywhere and I thought it was the end of the world." Clinton chuckled as he remembered. "My dad was trying to get me out from under the bed. He explained to me that it was snow, and eventually I went outside and picked some snow up and I realized that it was all right, but that was the most terrifying part for me when I was coming over."

Clinton started boxing at the age of 12. His trainer was boxing stalwart, Ray Chapman, who, along with his son, Tony, were the senior trainers at the Sir Phillip Game ABC in Croydon. The late Fred Rix was also very much a presence in the careers of the McKenzie boys and, during those early years, Clinton married Fred's daughter, Donna. Clinton has four children and three grand children. His son, Leon, is an extremely promising professional football player. He played for Crystal Palace and Peterborough before transferring to Norwich City in December 2003, where he scored two goals in his team-debut, one with his foot and one with his head. He remains at Norwich and he has become a true crowd pleaser. "Oh yeah, he's gonna be a big star. I can't wait until he plays for England. That's my dream. Can't *wait*! He's class."

Clinton's amateur triumphs include an NABC Title, a Junior ABA Title, and he was a European Quarter-Finalist. He boxed for England 12 times and in 1976 he won the Light-Welterweight ABA Championship. The general consensus has always been that the reigning ABA Champion should be selected for the current year's Olympic Games. Therefore, Clinton, who by now was 20 years old and working as a decorator, naturally assumed that he would be picked for the 1976 Montreal Olympics. However, because of a somewhat shady series of events, he nearly didn't get there.

It was reported at the time in the Boxing News that one of the Olympic Team Managers, John Davies, was making a case for his son, Chris, to box in Clinton's place. But Clinton had the support of the Boxing News, the National press and the Minister for Sport, not to mention some close and determined personal friends in his corner. "That was probably the most terrifying moment of my amateur career. There I was, ABA Champion. I've done everything that's been asked of me to support England. I've won titles, beaten everyone and I was the obvious choice to go to the Olympic Games. No doubt about it, I was the man. I mean, who else could they possibly put in front of me? And then this shocking news came up that I was not selected. I was absolutely gutted. So, straight away, my very good friend, Bruce Baker, rang me up and said, 'We've got to do something about this.' So the alarm bells start ringing and all of a sudden the newspapers start ringing me up, ITV rang me up, you know, we've got to start kicking up some noise."

Bruce Baker, who these days is deeply involved in professional boxing in a promotional and managerial capacity, was such a prominent figure in Clinton's fight for justice that I went to speak with him about it. He told me, "Well, in those days, I was Club Secretary for the Sir Phillip Game Boxing Club and I was responsible for the club. I was Clinton's 'amateur manager,' if you like. Clinton had won the ABAs at Wembley and he was in the England Squad. We all assumed that he would be going to the Olympics. He was the best Light-Welterweight in the country. What we didn't know was that a deal was done and the vote swayed for the son of John Davies, the Welsh ABA Team Manager, to take Clinton's place. It was all done behind closed doors."

Bruce continued, "The first we knew about it was when [National ABA Coach] Kevin Hickey phoned me up and said, 'Clinton has not been selected. What are you going to do about it?' I said, 'Well, I don't know. If he can't box for England, he might as well box for Jamaica.' Kevin said, 'Well, if it comes to that, I've got a sponsor and we can put some money into it.' Anyway, for a week all this was in the newspapers, and then the ABA came back and said that the fairest thing to do would be for the two boxers to have a box-off match to see who goes. I said, 'No, we're not doing that.' You know, you can get cut and there was only three weeks to go. I told them, 'It's a crazy idea and we're not doing it. We've got an opportunity to go to Jamaica and, if the ABA doesn't change its mind, we'll carry on talking to the Jamaicans.'

"So I took Clinton up to the Jamaican High Commission and we had a meeting there. After we came away we had News at Ten on the phone. Clinton and I wound up on ITN News at Ten. For a week it was in all the papers, because it was very controversial and it was unfolding every day.

There were a lot of accusations flying around. I mean, Clinton was the ABA Champion of Great Britain, Chris Davies was the ABA Champion of Wales, and the squad was a Great Britain squad.

"Anyway, in the final week, we're sitting in the office of the Jamaican High Commission and the bloody phone goes. The High Commissioner says, 'Oh, it's for you, Mr Baker.' It was my wife. She said, 'Bruce, Clinton's back in the team.' So, I had to backtrack it. I mean, the Jamaican High Commissioner was making all the arrangements and I had to say, 'Well, that's great, but can we come back to you?' Now Clinton's just *looking* at me! When we got outside I told him, 'You can either go for Jamaica, or you can go for England now. What do you want to do?' And, you know, Kevin Hickey fought really hard to get him back in. I think that had a bearing on it as well."

Clinton was also quick to endorse the staunch support of Kevin Hickey during that worrying time. "Yeah, Kevin Hickey was very supportive. He said that, if I didn't go to the Olympics, he would resign. That's how strongly he felt about it. I take my hat off to him, because he pulled out all the stops to see that justice was done, and obviously, at the end of the day, justice *was* done and I did go to the Olympic Games, and I got to the quarter-finals." So, in July 1976, Clinton was on the plane, along with team-mates: Colin Jones, Sylvester Mittee, Charlie Magri, Pat Cowdell, Robbie Davies and Dave Odwell, who was the Team Captain. "It was a great team. We loved it. I'll tell you what; it was a moment in my life that I'll never forget, a moment that you'll simply treasure for the rest of your life. The Olympic Games for me was the highlight of my amateur career."

Clinton was the first boxer of the British team to go on. His opponent was fellow southpaw, Daniele Zappaterra, of Italy. "Once that bell went I never thought about anything else. I just thought, 'This is it, I've got to get out there and win.' It was very nerve-wracking. I remember the fight. I was too classy for him." All five judges scored in Clinton's favour and he then went on to beat Puerto Rican, Ismael Martinez, on points. Clinton had reached the quarter-finals and his next Olympic opponent was Sugar Ray Leonard.

Despite the fact that Leonard won on a unanimous decision, it was a close fight. "I've got no comments really, because I thought Sugar Ray just won it. It was a very close fight, I must admit. I was walking up to the ring, and me and Sugar Ray came out at the same time. I remember looking over at him shadow boxing and I thought to myself, 'Bloody hell!' Those were my exact words. I shook my head and I remember getting in the arena and rising to the occasion. I thought, 'Yeah, all right, I'm going to go for it.' I must admit, I gave as good as I got. It was a great little fight, and I've boxed one of the greatest boxers who ever lived. Sugar Ray could do everything. He was superb. He was just amazing to watch." Leonard went on to win the Gold Medal against big banger, Andres Aldama, of Cuba.

At the age of 21, Clinton turned professional. "Without a shadow of a doubt, that's what I wanted to do. Boxing was my way of making something of myself in the world. I would have lived and died for boxing. Boxing was the *only* thing. It was my life. It still is." Clinton was managed by Mickey Duff and his trainer was the late George Francis, the legendary boxing mentor who did so much for boxers, particularly black boxers, during his exceptional career. George died in tragic circumstances in April 2001. "I had a very good relationship with George. I wouldn't say he was like a father to me because my dad was really close to me at the time, but George was like a very good friend as well as a trainer. He was very strict in his training. He knew how to get you fit and he was a very, very good corner man. George pulled me through a lot of fights. He just said the right things at the right time to get the best out of me. He always made me laugh. He always saw the funny side of things. I think that used to knock the edge off the training sometimes. He was a keep fit fanatic, George was. He used to run with us and I used to think, 'How can this old man keep up with me, running all these miles? What's going on?' But, he did. I couldn't believe it. When we went to Lagos to fight for the Commonwealth Title - 15 rounds - that was a war! He made me run five miles the next day! And I *did.* That's how mad I was! I think it was only because he wanted to go out for a run and he didn't want to get done by the natives."

On the 20th October 1976 Clinton made his professional debut against Jimmy King of Birmingham at York Hall, Bethnal Green. He won on points over eight rounds. "I didn't know then that York Hall was gonna become what it is now, and also where I would have some of my greatest fights in Britain. That place became very, very personal to me. It had a haunting effect. I had some marvellous fights there. My first professional fight, it felt very strange. I was half naked. Maybe that's why it felt different. You're bare. Shirts off. This is it now. This is the real thing. But, I must admit, I adjusted to it quite comfortably. Once I got the first round out of the way, I settled in all right."

Less than a month later Clinton scored another eight round points decision against one of the busiest boxers in the country, Barton McAllister of Clapham. "Yeah, he was an old campaigner, that McAllister, a journeyman. He'd been around a while. I wasn't considered a very big puncher and a lot of my earlier fights went the distance so, although I won quite comfortably, I don't think I was really box office stuff at that time. I must admit, as time went on, my style was exciting. I'd come to fight, you know, and although I was an aggressive fighter I didn't really take a lot of punches. I rode a lot of punches."

On the 1st February 1977 Clinton notched up another points victory, this time against George McGurk at the Albert Hall. The Jarrow man was another fighter who had been around the block more than once. He had shared a ring with the likes of Colin Power, Jimmie Revie, Dave 'Boy' Green and Cornelius Boza Edwards, but Clinton's first recollection was of the venue. "The Albert Hall was fantastic, and how many people can say they topped an Albert Hall bill?" Although this fight with McGurk was a show closer, Clinton went on to top the bill there. "Unbelievable. What a stage to be on. What an arena. Back then, I never really thought about it. I was just performing. But, as the years go by, you realize what an accomplishment it was. It's *unbelievable*!" As I sat there, munching my steak, listening to Clinton talk and watching his eyes gleam, I started to feel the thrill of it myself, if only by proxy. "I *loved* it. Yeah, and the thing about George McGurk was that he fought some top liners, some top people. Put it this way, they weren't too careful about who they put me in with, and I did come unstuck. But we're going to get to that, aren't we?" He laughed.

Clinton's 'coming unstuck' was to arrive later in his career in the form of disqualifications for low blows but, even as early as his third fight, the referee was warning him for a few wayward shots. "Okay, let me explain it to you. My style was based on combination punching, and I was a very good puncher to the belly. Now, most of the time, I'd get it right. I'd throw my combinations and hit to the body. But, now and again, one or two would go astray, accidentally, you know? It wasn't *deliberate,* it was just the speed of a punch, if you didn't time it right, it was just one of those things. But I want to quote here and now that it was never, ever intentional."

Two weeks later, Clinton scored a St Valentine's Day win, and it was his first inside the distance victory as a professional. In the other corner was shorter, stockier Harry Watson, who was thoroughly outgunned. As the exhausted Scotsman plonked himself down on his stool at the end of the third round, his nose bleeding freely, his manager made the compassionate decision to pull him out of the fight. "I think I gave away weight as well. I think he was about six pounds heavier than me, but I remember that as one of my most devastating performances. I went in there and I absolutely tore him apart. Nothing personal, it was just the way I felt at the time." Like Clinton, Watson was a southpaw. Boxers who have a left hand lead are thinner on the ground than orthodox boxers, so they don't get to box each other all that often. Therefore, when you get two southpaws in the ring, it can sometimes make for a pedestrian fight to watch. "Southpaws didn't worry me at all, because I found I could pick 'em off easier with my right jab than I could orthodox, so southpaws were *made* for me, because I was a *good* southpaw. But I always considered other southpaws to be very awkward. Although I was a southpaw, people used to say to me that I didn't *look* like a southpaw. They used to say I looked *good*, and I used to say, 'That's because I *am*!"

Amateur boxing is a sport and professional boxing is a business. Most of the time the boxers will tell you that it's nothing personal. However, between Clinton McKenzie and Paddington hard man, Colin Power, it was definitely personal. They boxed three times as amateurs, "And I beat him three times. Me and Colin Power, we go back a long way. I was the stronger lad, but he was a good boxer."

In 1975 Colin Power, who was of Irish descent, took the plunge into professional waters and, a year later, Clinton followed him. They would go on to have three fights for money and the first one happened on the 21st March 1977. They topped the bill on an Anglo-American Sporting Club show in Mayfair and the tall, lean Londoner turned the tables and stopped Clinton in two rounds. "Oh my God, yeah. I remember that to this day. He turned professional before I did. I think he had about 14 fights and I was having about my fifth fight as a pro. But, nevertheless, I thought, 'I beat him as an amateur and I'll beat him as a pro.' Another thing was, I had to lose weight as well. I was a light-welterweight and I had to come down to lightweight, so I took weight off. Then we realized how much he had improved and how good he was at the time. It was a personal thing anyway, between me and Colin. I heard rumours that he thought he could beat me as a pro, so I thought, 'Yeah all right, let's go for it.' So anyway, I've got down to the weight quite comfortably actually, and yeah, I took him on. Was it the first round he knocked me out? I can't remember." I confirmed it was the second. A right hook to the jaw sent Clinton face first to the canvass. He started to move in an effort to get up but referee, Sid Nathan, waved it off as Clinton climbed to his feet. "I remember the first round and he seemed so much *stronger* than me, and I thought, 'Hmm, maybe I'll warm up in the second round. Maybe I'll shake this up,' but I still didn't feel right. Then, I remember him hitting me with a right hand and down I went. Afterwards, I felt really sorry for myself." After the fight, Power was quoted in the Boxing News as declaring: *"I've never wanted to beat anybody so much. When I turned pro I told my manager, Vic Andreetti, that if McKenzie ever went pro he was the one I wanted to fight most of all."*

A month later Clinton was back in the ring to force Ormskirk southpaw, Al Stewart, to retire at the end of three rounds. "After a defeat by Colin Power, no one was going to beat me. I thought, 'I'm going to have to knock this bloke out.' I just wanted to get back into the ring that night and prove to everyone that I wasn't just a flash in the pan, that I *was* going to be Champion. I knew I was going to win that fight. I thought I had something to prove and, unfortunately, Mr Stewart was in the way. He took a tremendous amount of punishment and his corner done the right thing by pulling him out, because otherwise he would have got hurt, seriously."

In May 1977 Clinton travelled to Belgium to challenge a Belgian in the shape of former European Lightweight Champion, Fernand 'Freddie' Roelands. "I wasn't a very good fighter abroad. I seemed to be very nervous for some reason. Once I stepped into the ring the nerves didn't really bother me, but I never really seemed to perform at my best abroad. I just didn't flow the way I could normally. It wasn't until later on in my career, when I got used to travelling and I settled down, that my performances did get a little bit better." For all that, Clinton out-pointed Roelands and afterwards the Belgian announced his retirement. For the record, he did not retire. He boxed on for nearly four more years and had ten more fights.

Clinton returned to Belgium a few weeks later to score another eight round points win against Belgian based Algerian, Messaoud Bouachibi. But, the next time out, on 5th September 1977, Clinton experienced his first points loss, and it came against Johnny Pincham. They fought on an Anglo-American Sporting Club show in Mayfair and Pincham was the Southern Area Welterweight Champion at the time. Clinton knocked the Crawley man down in the second round and shook him a few times during the battle, but Pincham built up the points with his jab and his counter-punching to emerge the winner by one point. "I fought him as an amateur as well. I always beat him as an amateur. I remember the points loss was very, very close. I thought I won that actually. It was a very good fight and I thought I edged it. Johnny always boxed on the back foot. He had a good jab, fast, always moving. I had trouble pinning him down but, when I did catch up with him, I did sort of give it to him. But Johnny always made hard fights for me because of his style. He always gave me problems. And Johnny Pincham is a very nice guy. We've spoke a lot since then." After that fight, the boxers received a cascade of 'nobbins' (coins thrown into the ring by way of appreciation from the audience.) "Yes, I remember that. It did bring the house down, because it was a very exciting fight.

"I think the crowds quite liked me because I excited them. They loved to see a good fight and I always gave a good performance. But, I think to capture the general public's imagination I needed to be a bit more flamboyant. I was the quiet man in boxing. I'd get in the ring and do my business and look good, yeah. But, outside the ring, I didn't really say enough. I kept myself to myself and I never really exploited that side of it. That's just the way I am. I think *now* I would change things a bit."

A month after losing to Johnny Pincham, Clinton came back with a points win over Kevin Davies. Davies, another southpaw, was previously unbeaten in seven fights and they boxed on a National Sporting Club show in Piccadilly. Before they could don the gloves, these two had to set aside a strong bond of friendship, at least until their fight was over. "I remember Kevin. *Lovely* guy. We was in the Under 21s England Team together. He was a good little boxer and we got on like a house on fire. We were, like, best mates, you know, and when I heard I was fighting him, oh *mate*! I couldn't *believe* it. I've got to fight my best friend. How the hell was I going to do that? I remember he used to say, 'I'm boxing you,' and I used to say, 'No you're not,' and we used to have a laugh about it. But then we had to actually meet and I felt I could have stopped him, but I didn't. I remember fighting him. I looked into his eyes a few times when I hit him and I thought, 'I can take you out now,' but I didn't."

The following month Clinton travelled to Denmark to box Erkki Meronen. The Finnish fighter, who had a record of 37 fights with one loss, was forced to retire at the end of the fourth round and Clinton's victory caused a major upset. It is the way of the world that, when a boxer to travels away to fight somebody of Meronen's standing, the travelling fighter is usually the 'opponent.' However, Clinton did not see it that way. "No, not really. I expected it to be a fight where I could prove myself abroad. I just wanted to box really, and that was a fight that was offered to me. I always considered myself better than anyone else, never an opponent. I understand what you're saying. I was there to lose and he was there to win, but I put that right out of my mind. I always seemed to box better as an underdog anyway. The Boxing News wrote me a off a few times, but I earned their respect in the end."

Clinton began 1978 with a January points decision over Cardiff's Chris Davies. "This was a fight I *had* to win. He's the fella whose dad tried to get me out of the Olympic Games. There was no way he was gonna beat me. No *way*! I knew I was too good for him anyway. I *knew* that. So anyway, we had to fight in Nottingham and this is the final eliminator for the British Title. Now, you've got to remember that this is after I had lost to Colin Power. This was my big comeback trail. We both made the weight quite comfortable. The first round, we come out and I just picked him off. I think I won every round. Every round, I boxed his head off and I proved then that he was simply not in my class. That was a good feeling, because it was something that had to happen, and it did. That was a nice win. I did enjoy that."

The following March Clinton was on the move again, this time to Oslo. He won a ten round decision over roughhouse Philadelphian and former World Title challenger, Mike Everett. It was a barnstorming battle and Clinton won nearly every round. The last two rounds were rough, but Clinton stayed away from Everett's swinging punches and the two of them put on a thrilling finale. "Oh, Mike Everett! What an awesome fighter. I'd gone out to have something to eat and we bumped into each other in the lift. I looked at this awesome, stocky, black, bald headed boxer standing there and I thought, 'My *God*! Have I really got to fight *him*?' He looked twice the size of me and he looked like he could, you know, knock out *anyone*. And what a reputation! I thought to myself, 'This guy does look the business, and he can fight.' I must admit, I don't know what it was but I think that was probably one of my best overseas performances. I think that was the best win of my career. He couldn't get near me. I really enjoyed that performance."

Clinton's next fight was back on home territory. In May 1978 he won an eight round points decision against Chris Walker of Sheffield at the Michael Sobell Centre in Islington. "Chris Walker, good boxer, very tall, awkward. I couldn't really get nasty with him because he never really hurt me, so I just took that one on points." I asked, "Did you have get hurt then, before you could get nasty?" He thought for a moment and replied, "I think so, yeah, unless I was in that sort of mood. I'd box according to how I felt but, if I just felt like a workout, I'd just go through the motions. I was waiting for a shot at the British Title and I was playing things safe."

It was five months before Clinton boxed again. On the 11th October 1978 he challenged 'Rocky' Jim Montague for the vacant British Light-Welterweight Title and he stepped into the lion's den to do it. Montague, who was Irish Light-Welterweight Champion at the time, was powerfully built and pale skinned, with Irish black hair, beard and moustache. Clinton stopped him in ten rounds in front of the Antrim southpaw's home fans at the Maysfield Leisure Centre on this, Belfast's first British Title night since 1964. The hall was less than half full, but Montague's fans still made a lot of noise to get behind their man. "But I felt very confident. There I was in Belfast, and I felt I would win my title."

Jim Montague was five years the older man. He had lost more fights than he had won and he was one of those fighters who seemed to have been around forever. He had shared a ring with Kirkland Laing and had gone the eight round distance with a top form Dave 'Boy' Green at a few hours notice. To fight for the British Title was Montague's dream come true, but against Clinton that night, dreams were not enough. "I just *knew* that my time had come, and it was a very calculated and cool performance. I took my time, I boxed at ease and, yeah, I stopped him in the tenth round." This was Montague's last fight. He announced his retirement after it was over. "He was very brave, but I did give him a bit of a tanking." Montague had already been down three times when referee, Wally Thom, stopped the one sided demolition as the Irishman went down again. He sat in a dazed state for a couple of minutes before his corner helped him back to his stool, where he sat and wept tears of frustration and disappointment "But what a gentleman. I've spoken to him since on the phone. He had no picture of when he actually boxed and I sent him an article from the Boxing News about our performance."

So Clinton was now British Light-Welterweight Champion and he felt, "Fantastic! And the Belfast people were very kind. They really looked after me. They treated me like a king. I was aware of what was going on, but you wouldn't have thought so. I stayed in a little country village. Very, very nice." Before 1978 was over, Clinton slotted in a December eight round points win over Ghanaian, Tony Martey, and, at the age of 23, the best was yet to come from Clinton McKenzie. "Yes, I was starting to mature. Tony Martey was very brave and that was another good fight."

Clinton made his first defence of his British Title at Wembley Conference Centre in February 1979. In the other corner was his old foe, Colin Power. Power had won the European Title and lost it in his first defence to Fernando Sanchez in Spain five months earlier on a controversial twelfth round stoppage. He wanted the British Title back, seeing it as a steppingstone to a return with Sanchez and, after 15 fabulous rounds, the first time for both boxers to go that distance, he took Clinton's title away.

As Power walked to the ring, his fans raised the roof. When Clinton made his appearance, the crowd jeered. When I studied the tape, it seemed to me that Clinton looked uncharacteristically nervous, and Power stared hard at him throughout the preliminaries. "My first defence. Wow! What a fight. We went 15 rounds, toe to toe. I remember him coming out for the first round and I thought, 'Yeah, I'll get my time and I'll knock you out mate!' I thought I won the fight by about three rounds, but it went to Colin on a split decision. It was that close that the Board of Control wanted another return. The fight went backwards and forwards. I had Colin going, he had me going, and he won the fight. I couldn't believe it. I *loved* that Lonsdale belt. The first night I won it I slept with it under my pillow. Winning that belt was something I dreamed about as a kid. It meant that much to me at the time. It was a lovely feeling and to give it back on a fight where I thought I won was heartbreaking, but I *swore* I'd get it back. And yeah, well anyway, he beat me and that was it." As the final bell rang, Power slipped over in his own corner, jumped straight up and offered his glove to referee, Harry Gibbs, who had no hesitation in raising it. A deeply despondent Clinton returned to his dressing room where he flopped down onto a chair and sat silently, slumped forward, his head in his hands.

Two and a half weeks after losing his British Title, Clinton travelled to Las Vegas to challenge NABF Welterweight Champion, Bruce Curry. Clinton lost a ten round points decision to the American at Caesar's Palace, Las Vegas. Curry had shared a ring twice with Wilfred Benitez, both times going the distance with the outstanding Puerto Rican World Champion. "You've got to remember, Curry was no mug. Anyway, I went to Las Vegas and boxed ten rounds with him. I was jetlagged. I was tired. I had visa problems getting in there. Everything went wrong."

Because of the visa problems, Clinton and George Francis did not arrive in America until 12.30am on the day of the fight, and they had to be present for the weigh-in at 5.30 that same morning because of a stipulation from Victor Galindez, the Argentinian who was fighting WBA light-heavyweight Champion, Mike Rossman, on top of the bill, a fight that was actually called off minutes before the first bell was due to ring. "It was only three weeks after the British Title fight, and that was a hard 15 round fight, and then they shot me off to Las Vegas. I couldn't *believe* it! Anyway, I went to Las Vegas and I lost the fight. I remember I hit him with a body shot and then he hit me with a body shot, and it was the hardest body shot I've ever had to take in my whole life. My legs, everything, just went numb. The shock went right through me. I got through the round and I was on the back foot from that punch onwards. I just did not wanna go forward no more and, yeah, he won it on points." After boxing Clinton, Bruce Curry went on to win the WBC Light-Welterweight Title, which he defended three times.

Two months later, Clinton was back in action. This time he won a points decision over Bedford based Jamaican, Des Morrison, on a World Sporting Club show at Mayfair. This was a final eliminator for the British Light-Welterweight Title and it was open warfare. "Oh, the Des Morrison fight. The thing with me and Dessie was that, although I knew him, we just did not see eye to eye. I don't know what it was. He didn't like me, but *why* he didn't like me, I just don't know. I didn't *dis*like him, but he just had this thing. I don't know. Maybe it's just the way he was at the time. But anyway, I remember beating him quite easily. It was no big deal. He was quite an awkward customer, but I never found his style bothered me a lot." Referee, Sid Nathan, scored the fight to Clinton by half a point and declared afterwards that it was one of the easiest fights he had ever handled. Clinton scored the only knockdown in the sixth round. He was cut near the corner of his right eye in the ninth and, by the end of the tenth, he looked tired and wounded. "Well I accept all that, because he *did* give me a hard fight. But I felt that I *won* it."

Another man who felt that Clinton had won the fight was Colin Power. He was quoted in the Boxing News as saying: "*McKenzie well won it and I'll meet him any time. I'll beat him easier next time.*" I mischievously read those words out to Clinton at this point of the interview. He leaned forward across the table and his enthusiastic reply was delivered with enough gusto to attract the avid curiosity of several of the men who were in the café bar that day. "Great! *Great!* Let's get it *on*, Colin!"

Almost four months later, get it on they did. Colin Power was British Light-Welterweight Champion once more and on the 11th September 1979 Clinton challenged him for the throne. They boxed at Wembley and this time Clinton emerged victorious over 15 rounds. It was the first time for Clinton to beat his archrival as a professional and the last time the two would ever box each other. "This is our final meeting, yeah. Oh, do I want this title or *what*? I want this title so bad my bones are creaking. I want this title so bad I'm shaking with … Everything's on the line here: my *future*, my *pride*, everything you can *think* of. And I want my title back. Colin ain't getting away with it. He's not leaving that ring without giving me my title back. From start to finish, we fight toe to toe. We really get it on. The fight sweeps backwards and forwards. He had me going and I had him going. I think I threw more punches, more clusters, more combinations."

Clinton's mouth started bleeding in the eighth and, by the eleventh, his eye was badly swollen. "My eye was closing fast. He had this jab that I just could not get round. It was just in my left eye all the time. Anyway, I ignored all that. I just wanted my title back. I remember, at the end of the fourteenth round my eye was really closed, completely. The referee had a look at it and he said, 'Last round. I'll let it go. One more round, McKenzie, and it's all over.' I come back to my corner, and this is where George Francis comes into it, and I will never forget this. I came back to my corner at the end of the fourteenth round and George slaps me round the face and says, 'Do you want this title or don't you?' And I was feeling a bit sorry for myself now. It's the fourteenth round and I was shot, one eye closed, and I didn't answer him. So he leans over me and he says right in my ear-hole, 'Do you know what this bloke's been saying about you? You know he doesn't like black people, don't you?'" Clinton laughed raucously at the memory. "He was going to me, 'He thinks you're a stupid little black bastard.' Now, you've got to understand, you're in a 15 round title fight, you're brain is shot, you are totally knackered and anything like that is going to get you going, and I went, 'He *what*!' I remember looking at George and he looked so serious, and I thought, 'Okay! All right!' I actually remember getting of my stool and I thought, 'Right! I'm going to sort you out mate,' and that was it. I just went out there and did it. I went back out there and I give it to him. And I think that won the fight for me. George knew what to say just at the right moment. He knew me well." "So which was better," I asked, "beating Colin Power or winning the British Title back?" His answer came with a laugh, but I couldn't help feeling there was more than a shade of truth in it. "Beating Colin Power at the end of the day, because Colin always felt that he was my superior. Colin felt that I could not beat him and I proved, I *proved* that I could beat him. I had the last word, the last saying, and he was never the same afterwards. After that Sylvester Mittee knocked him out."

Not all boxing matches can be thrillers and in December 1979 Clinton took a rather routine eight round points decision over Midland Area Champion, Roger Guest. The Dudley man had stepped in as a last minute substitute to box Clinton at the Café Royal. "That was just a workout for me. Roger's a nice guy. He gave me a good work out." He also gave Clinton a cut in the fifth round that later needed four stitches. "Yeah, he did, yeah." Two months later Clinton fought Roger Guest again. Again, Clinton beat him over eight rounds on points. It was pretty much a repeat performance of their previous showing. Guest was brave; Clinton was class. "He was one of those fighters that I couldn't really get motivated for." As Clinton described these fights, the tone of his voice became flat, the energy and the vibrancy that came across when he was describing the Colin Power epics was gone.

Clinton's next fight was more of the same. On the 1st April 1980 he beat George Feeney on points over ten rounds at Wembley Conference Centre. The Hartlepool opponent was another brave man who was not in Clinton's league. "He was another awkward fighter. I boxed him twice. I couldn't knock him out. I think I showed my class in these fights, but they're fights I couldn't really get motivated for."

Later that month, Clinton did get motivated enough to stop Scottish Champion, George Peacock, on a National Sporting Club show at Piccadilly. Peacock was never knocked down, but at the end his face was cut up over the left eye and across the bridge of the nose. Peacock was indeed proud that night, but Clinton's stiff right jab and cruel body blows had the dinner show audience calling for the fight to be stopped in the third round, and referee Sid Nathan obliged.

During the next six months Clinton had three more fights, all of which he lost. In June 1980 he dropped a points decision to Hans-Henrik Palm in Denmark. "I never really got to grips with that fight for some reason or other. I couldn't really get to him." The following month, Clinton travelled to Lagos in Nigeria to challenge Obisia Nwankpa for the Commonwealth Light-Welterweight Title. Nwankpa was a tough customer who had won 18 out of 19 fights. They battled it out over 15 brutal rounds, at the end of which, Clinton failed to take the title from the Champion. "The Commonwealth Title is probably one of the hardest fights I ever had. Honest, from the first bell to the last, that was a *war*!" Clinton carried the fight to Nwankpa in every round except the sixth and seventh when the humidity got to him and he started to wilt. "Yeah, I think it did, but I got over it. But what a fight! It was a *great* fight! It was *so* hot and we really got it on. He was ranked about number four in the world at the time and we had a *right* ding-dong." While the scorecards were being correlated, an anxious hush descended over the 7,000 spectators at the packed National Stadium. "Yeah, it was very, very tense. Electric. And do you know what? I thought I *won* that fight. That's how I felt. It was very, very close.

"That was a bad time for me. It was just the wrong fights. They were fights that I didn't really need at the time. They just come up with a fight and I took it. I never turned any fights down." On the 27th August 1980 Clinton lost to Giuseppe Martinese in Italy. The fight was for the vacant European Light-Welterweight Title and Clinton took it at short notice. He had been doing well against the tall, awkward Italian but, by the sixth round, Clinton began to fade and he got cut, the blood running into his right eye throughout the rest of the fight. He was retired by his corner at the end of the tenth. He was never knocked down but he was taking a beating. "That was my first shot at the European Title. Now, this fight, I thought I was winning up until the tenth round. But I was jetlagged, I was tired, and it was one of those fights where I don't think I was a hundred percent fit. I definitely remember running out of steam. And people were saying, 'McKenzie can't go the distance. He's got stamina problems.'"

1981 arrived and on the 6th January Clinton defended his British Title. That night, Clinton turned his career back onto the winning road in the most emphatic way in brutal re-match with Des Morrison. He stopped Morrison in the fourteenth round at York Hall and he looked fantastic doing it. It was a magnificent fight between two of the bravest men you could ever find. It went first one way and the then other, like a devastating pendulum, and the fabulous victory earned Clinton a Lonsdale belt to keep. "Oh, what a war! 14 rounds, and he decided that was it. It must have been about the eighth round and Des Morrison was giving me the fight of my life. Now, Des always believed that he could beat me and this was the night he wanted to prove it. But he was *never* gonna beat me. I was *never* gonna let that happen. It was the fight of my life. I think that eighth round was one of the most exciting rounds ever seen in a boxing ring. My eye was bleeding and I just let him have it, and he let me have it, and I let him have it and, right before the bell rang, I let this terrific right hand go. Boom! Right on the chin, and he went down. That was right on the bell. That was drama! I remember thinking, 'He's not gonna come out for the next round. How could he?' His trainers jumped into the ring, pulling him back, brushing him down, trying to get the life back into his legs, trying to get him going, and he was slumped on his stool. And I'm there huffing and breathing heavily, because I've given it everything.

"Anyway, the old bastard only come out for the next bloody round, didn't he? Oh shit! Anyway, after that eighth round, I've made one more last attempt to put him away and I'm steaming in. I'm throwing punches from everywhere; upper cuts, left hooks, right hands, and he *still* wouldn't go. Then the cards turned and *he's* had *me* all over the place. I'm on the ropes and I'm covering up, trying to breath. The referee's looking, thinking should he stop it or not? And I'm thinking, 'My God, this is it,' and then the bell goes and I'm, like, 'Thank God for *that*!' I've held on to the rope, pulled myself back to me corner, sat down on the stool and I'm gone. I'm spent." Clinton was laughing as he looked back on it with me that day in the nonchalant way that boxers often do when they remember such moments in the ring. "I remember coming out for the tenth and, all of a sudden, life come back into me again. I started bobbing and weaving, jumping up and down, and then it was inevitable what was going to happen. We got to the fourteenth round and Des had really had it, you know. He'd shot his load. I just beat him to a pulp and that was it. I won my Lonsdale belt outright."

Clinton defended his British Title in March 1981 against one of his former Olympic team-mates, Sylvester Mittee. Sylvester is the man who speaks so eloquently at the beginning of this chapter and throughout this book. The performance put on by Clinton and Sylvester at Wembley Conference Centre that night had the crowd on their feet in rapture and, at the end of 15 rounds, it was Clinton's glove that was raised in victory.

Clinton and Sylvester were friends outside the ropes, but necessity dictated that they become adversaries for one night. "Sylvester was always, to me, the perfect puncher-boxer. He was the hardest puncher in the division. He could knock anyone out. They called him 'The Brown Bomber' of the light-welterweights. Now, I knew Sylvester. We went to the Olympics together, and his body was always well toned. He was always fit. I knew he trained hard. I knew everything about him, and he was *good.* Anyway, we didn't talk at the weigh-in. He looked at me and I looked at him. Boxing News said he was going to knock me out. They said he would be too strong for me, but I knew in my heart that no one was going to knock me out. No matter how hard he hit me, he wasn't going to knock me out.

"Anyway, we both weighed in and I think I might have been a pound over weight. So I took a pound off, which was a bit embarrassing because I've always made the weight, so I wasn't very pleased with that." This was a voluntary defence of the title and I asked Clinton why he chose to take on such a dangerous challenger at this stage. "Well, I'll be honest with you. I needed the money at the time and it was the best payday I had. I thought, 'I'm the Champion. Yeah, I'll defend my title.' Do you know, I've got to be one of the proudest British Champions going because I defended that title so many times that it became a personal thing to me.

"Anyway, the night of the fight I was nervous, but I wasn't *that* nervous. I wasn't any more nervous than I was for any other fight. It was natural fight nerves. So we're in the ring. In the first round we came out and, whoosh! Big bombs coming over. Woosh! Boom! 'Bloody Hell!' That's what I said. He could *hit*! These big bombs were coming at my head and he was hitting me hard, and I thought, 'No, I've got to hold this out.' Because Sylvester had it in his mind that one round and he would do me, and I took all he could throw at me. Second round, same thing, okay. Third round, same thing, okay. After the third round, now it's *my* turn, let's start turning the tables a bit. So I started to take the fight to him and I think from then on he realized he was in for a fight. So anyway, I remember it was the twelfth round and I was really getting into my stride now, really getting on top.

"We were standing toe to toe and we were punching, and I could sense that he didn't want to give any more. He was holding back. After the fourteenth round my trainer said to me, 'It's close. It's very close. You've got to go in there and win this round.' I was tired, but I always had this will to win or die, you know, so that's what I did. I went out there and I gave everything I had, and all the crowd were standing up and clapping. I was prepared to go that little bit further than him. I would have died that night, for that title. That's what separated us. That was the difference that made me the Champion that night and not him."

Sylvester Mittee had no problem with the decision at the time, and he once told me, "Clinton McKenzie, out of all the fighters that I boxed, was the one man who deserved to beat me. In my heart of hearts, I think I won the fight. But, when fighting a Champion, the challenger must dislocate the crown from the Champion's head and I did not do that. There was still an element of doubt, but it is a Champion's prerogative to maintain his title."

Clinton was flying high now. He was British Champion and the only way was up. On the 13th October 1981 he won the European Light-Welterweight Title at the Albert Hall against the muscular Antonio Guinaldo of Spain. The fight went the distance and Clinton looked exceptional as he took the decision over 12 rounds. The Spaniard spent much of the fight trying to catch Clinton with his right hand counter-punch. In reply, Clinton bobbed and weaved brilliantly, spearing Guinaldo with his right jabs. In the eighth there was a clash of heads and Guinaldo emerged with a cut across his right eyebrow, shaking his fist angrily at the end of the round, indicating that Clinton had butted him. In the ninth Guinaldo's other eyebrow came apart. The final round was a wild one, neither man prepared to back down. Guinaldo finished the fight bleeding heavily from his nose and with gashes over both eyes, and Clinton was declared the new European Champion. "That was a good performance. I boxed clever. I made him miss a lot and I made him pay. I tried to stop him in one of the rounds but it didn't come off. I went on and won the fight on points. Nothing was easy; I didn't take it easy, but I enjoyed it. I liked the competition. I thought, if I was the best, I was going to *prove* I was the best and I took every fight that was thrown at me at the time."

In February 1982 Clinton made another defence of his British Title and stopped Steve Early in four rounds at the Bloomsbury Centre. The tall, dark haired Coventry man won the right to fight Clinton by out-pointing the fine but faded former World Lightweight Champion, Ken Buchanan, 13 months earlier. Between Clinton and Early, it was very much a one-sided fight. Early had been bashed through the ropes, taken a count and looked to be there for the taking when Referee, James Brimmell, jumped in and stopped it. "I boxed Steve Early as an amateur, when I was about 16, and I remember he had the hardest right hand anybody had ever hit me with, so I was wary of it. But I was a seasoned professional and a class act. I knew that I was on the verge of fighting for a World Title, so

Steve Early wasn't gonna beat me. No way! So I just took that fight, put all my experience to it and simply outclassed him, at the end of the day. I've got a lot of respect for Steve. He's a very good and pleasant man. I've met him a few times and we've shook hands, had a chat and reminisced about the fight, and he's got no hard feelings. We were all good professionals."

On the first day of June 1982 Clinton took a fight that was meant to simply keep him simmering before he defended his European Title. But things did not go as planned and he was disqualified against American journeyman, Ernie Bing, in one round at the Albert Hall. Referee, Mike Jacobs, intervened after exactly one minute of the fight, citing that Clinton had landed a low blow. When the controversial punch was thrown, Bing fell to the canvas and writhed about in seeming distress. Clinton was initially bewildered and then indignant. As the realization dawned on the crowd what was happening, they became very angry. They booed and jeered and, as Bing slipped on his way down the ring steps, they cheered, but Clinton was not in the mood to see the funny side. "Oh! That was the down point of my career. That was the first of many low blows. I think one of the main reasons was because I tried to adapt my style slightly and it affected my punching ability. I think that's why those low punches occurred at that point in my career."

A second and far more devastating disqualification came four months later, on the 12th October 1982. Clinton was making his first defence of his European Title against fellow southpaw and French Champion, Robert Gambini. He was disqualified for a low blow in the second round at the Albert Hall, the scene of the previous disqualification. "Yeah, they say lightning doesn't strike in the same place, but it bloody does." As Clinton aimed for the body, a low and sweeping right hand caught Gambini right where he lived as he moved backwards. Gambini almost fell out of the ring and he was in obvious agony as he hit the floor. Clinton looked dazed while they waited an anxious two minutes for an announcement to be made, and the stern looks from his corner told their own story. Gambini's new European Championship status was bestowed on him as he lay on the floor being examined by Board of Control doctor.

There were no complaints from Clinton, then or now. "It was careless. But, like I said, I changed my style a bit and it changed the way I was throwing body shots at the time. I was on the verge of a World Title shot and those two disqualifications cost me dearly. In the dressing room afterwards, I wanted to blow my brains out. If you'd have given me a gun there and then, I'd have done it. I felt that bad about it. I just sat there all night gazing into space. I could not believe that this had happened to me. But, it happened, so I just had to deal with it."

My good pal, B.F. Williams (whose own chapter comes a little later in this book) remembers this time in Clinton's life well. "I sparred with him down the Thomas A' Beckett around that time. He probably wouldn't remember me for his life, but he hurt me. Nice guy, funny guy. I think he'd just been disqualified in a European Title fight for hitting low, because he had a pair of boxing shorts around the punch bag to keep his shots up." Clinton remembered the shorts, "Oh yes. That's right. It didn't help me a lot actually. I went out to America and did exactly the same thing, only I didn't get disqualified because they have different rules over there. Those two disqualifications really changed my career and I don't think I really recovered from the effect of them, on the international scene anyway."

Clinton went straight back into training and a month later he was back at the Albert Hall to halt Italian journeyman, Luciano Navarra, in five rounds. This was one of the easiest wins of Clinton's tough career. "Yeah, it was. I would agree with that." It was very noticeable that Clinton had become gun-shy with his body shots. "Yeah, that's right. I was a bit dubious. I thought, 'Well, I'm hitting low to the body now.' I was trying to adapt to my old style of boxing, throwing combinations, but I wouldn't go to the body very often because I was very aware of what was happening, and the referees were watching out for that as well."

Two weeks later Clinton was back in the ring to stop Guillermo Arreola in three rounds at Wembley. The Californian was of a stocky and powerful looking build, but Clinton was much the bigger man, and he was simply too strong and too clever. It was nearly five months before Clinton boxed again. In April 1983 he made a defence of his British Title against Alan Lamb of Lancaster. They fought at the Liverpool Stadium and the crowd really got behind the challenger. They went the distance and Clinton retained his title. "Yeah. I went to Liverpool for that one. That was an easy enough fight. I just won that fight on my pure ability." Clinton was beginning to drift back to his old style of body punching, the style that he felt comfortable with. In September 1983 his body assault stopped Tommy McCallum in four rounds at the Grosvenor House Hotel in Mayfair. The Scotsman had to take a few minutes to recover on his stool once it was over.

In January 1984 Clinton was offered another fight in America and he stopped New Yorker, Danny Young, in seven rounds at the Sands Casino Hotel in Atlantic City. "That was another good fight. Just one of my workouts really." Things could have got sticky when Clinton slammed in a low punch in the sixth. Young doubled up, but quickly resumed fighting. I remarked, "He was brave," to which Clinton laughingly replied, "Yeah, the referee said, 'Get up Danny, or I'll count you out.'"

In April 1984 a fiftieth birthday celebration night was held for Henry Cooper at the Grosvenor House Hotel. It was a boxing dinner show and Clinton fought 'Irish' Brett Lally in front of a packed house. The bell went, the boxers came out of their corners and every round was a banger before a backdrop of screaming punters and cigar smoke. When the final bell sounded, Clinton was awarded the closest of decisions from referee, Sid Nathan. Clinton smiled grimly as he explained, "Mickey Duff said, 'I've got a fight for you, just to keep you warm before I get you a World Title shot. This guy from America is coming over here and you'll win it easy.' Well, let me tell you about 'Irish' Brett Lally. That was one of the hardest bastards I've ever boxed, and when I say *hard*, they didn't call him 'Irish' Brett Lally for nothing. It was one of the hardest fights I've ever had in my whole life. He come out and put me down in the second round; left hand, over the top and, boomb! I was on my arse and I knew I was in for a bloody fight. Where did he come from? Somewhere in Texas, I don't know.

"And do you know why I remember that fight so well? Muhammad Ali was over here and he was actually at that fight. I think that might have had a bearing on my performance as well. I remember this big man as I was coming down to fight Brett Lally. Muhammad Ali was walking towards me and it was like it was in slow motion. I was speechless. He was my idol. This was the guy I saw on telly and he'd done all these great things, float like a butterfly, sting like a bee. I couldn't believe I was only that much away from him. My heart just stopped. It was a great fight I had with Irish Brett Lally, a fantastic fight, and I won, just about. How I won it, I don't know, because when he put me down it bloody hurt, and then I got up and all the crowd was cheering and it brought the house down. It was great. Whenever I remember that day I think to myself, 'Why didn't I go up to Ali and ask him what he thought of the fight?' If there's one moment in my life I regret, it's that. That was my moment. I could have said to him, 'What did you think?' And I didn't. I missed the opportunity. But at least he saw the fight."

On the 19th September 1984 Clinton marched out into the packed hall of the Britannia Leisure Centre in Shoreditch to defend his British Title. This was his fortieth fight in eight years of boxing as a professional. Waiting for him in the ring was former Royal Marine from Basildon, Terry Marsh. Clinton thrashed it out with 'The Fighting Fireman' over 12 fast and furious rounds and, at the end of it all, he lost his title. "I thought, 'He can't beat me. Look at him! He's skinny. He's got no muscle. He couldn't break an egg.' I thought to myself, 'I'll defend my title one more time against him, and then maybe I'll get a shot at the World Title.' Well it was a great fight. It went 12 rounds, a very, very, hard, gruelling 12 rounds. I remember hitting him with those body shots in the sixth round. I gave it everything. I could feel my gloves sinking into his belly and how I didn't break his ribs I don't know, but he took everything. I nearly punched myself out with him. Then I knew that I wasn't going to stop him. I knew then I had a fight on my hands. The last two rounds were like death."

The final six minutes of that fight was a bad place to be. Clinton looked exhausted as he trudged, bleeding, back to his corner at the end of the eleventh. Marsh looked like he was in a daze, like a ghost. "Yeah, he was just totally like ... I was panting heavy, but I came out for the twelfth round and, in my head, I was ready to do 15." The crowd rose to their feet as the gladiators got up from their stools and took their places in the ring centre, boots rooted to the canvas, throwing punches back and forth. Reg Gutteridge commentated from ringside, "You won't see a better finish to a championship fight than this one," and how right he was.

At the final bell the referee, Sid Nathan, saw Terry Marsh as the winner. The new British Champion had to be half carried from the ring, such was his state of exhaustion. "Yeah, he was totally shot, and if you ask Terry he'll tell you that was probably the hardest fight of his life." For the record, Terry Marsh's fight with Clinton was the one that truly launched Terry's career. He went on to win the IBF Light-Welterweight Title in 1987, which he defended once and was still undefeated in the ring when he was arrested and tried for the attempted murder of Frank Warren. He was acquitted of the charge, but he never boxed again.

Almost a year to the day after losing his British Title to Terry Marsh, Clinton returned to the foot of the mountain to embark on that toughest of journeys, back to the top. On the 7th September 1985 he fought Wolverhampton's Lloyd Christie in an eliminator for the British Title. Christie also came from a fighting family; his brother Errol was the middleweight hotshot. Clinton and Christie slugged it out over ten rounds at Douglas on the Isle of Man. Clinton, at 30, was the older man by seven years. "I remember that fight. It wasn't a very attractive fight. It was very untidy. I won it, of course, but it wasn't a fight that turned me on."

Three months later Clinton boxed Nottingham based Jamaican, Tony Laing, (younger brother of Kirkland) at the Albert Hall in yet another eliminator for the British Title. The winner would fight Terry Marsh, who still held the British Title at the time, and the winner on a points decision over ten rounds was Tony Laing. "That was a strange fight, because Tony Laing was really what I called my bogey man. He had an awkward, horrible style and I couldn't really get to grips with that fight. I couldn't really stamp my authority on him. Boxing News wrote me off, said it was all over."

Clinton was determined to find his way back to the top and on the 6th March 1986 he took the Southern Area Light-Welterweight Title from

Tony Adams, stopping the Brixton southpaw in seven rounds at the Free Trade Hall, Manchester. This was also an eliminator for the British Title. Adams had taken the Southern Area Title in his previous fight from Clinton's cousin, Lee McKenzie, so it was a case of keeping it in the family. Adams was seven years younger and a big puncher. The former ABA Champion had been doing well as a professional and was eager to prove himself, but Clinton's desire to prove that he still had what it took was etched far deeper and that night he put himself back in line to fight for the British Title once again. "That was one of my comeback fights. Tony Adams was a good amateur. He had quite a few good wins as a pro [16 in total]. They thought he was an up and coming star. They thought I would be a good win as someone on their block to get out of the way, but I turned the tables on that and showed that I was still in there, that I could still look after myself."

By this stage, Terry Marsh was European Champion. He had relinquished his British crown and he and Clinton were now stable mates. The British Title was vacant once more and, on the 7th May 1986, Clinton boxed his shaven headed bogey man, Tony Laing, for the Lonsdale Belt. As in their last fight, they boxed at the Albert Hall and Laing proved that he did indeed have the Indian sign over Clinton. Clinton started off in charge, but half way through the fight Laing turned things around and started to catch Clinton with painful regularity. At the end of the fight both men looked in a sorry state, tired, swollen and bleeding. Referee, John Coyle, declared Laing the new British Champion and the crowd booed loudly as Laing's fist was raised.

Tony Laing relinquished the British Title to go in search of the European. On the 20th September 1986 Clinton fought for the unoccupied belt again, this time against Leicester's Tony McKenzie, who incidentally was no relation. They boxed in a circus tent in Hemel Hempstead, and both men looked in great shape: sleek, black and muscular. Clinton was stopped in three rounds. "I'll tell you what. I'd just come off holiday with my family and I got a phone call for me to go and fight for the British Title. Now, you've got to remember, I was never much over my fighting weight. I was always pretty much near the mark. I hadn't been to the gym for about six weeks, but I was doing nothing anyway and it was a shot for the British Title again, so I thought, 'Why not? This kid ain't all that. Maybe I can just play about and sneak a decision.' Well how wrong I was. I wasn't fit and I tried to bluff it out. It was very hard work just getting through the first bloody round, and I just about scraped through. I got back to my corner and I felt terrible. My heart was racing away. I was shaking. No strength. I felt like shit. I came out for the second round and it was the same thing again. I managed to get through that round by the skin of my teeth. Then, in the third round, he caught me with a punch. I remember standing there and I was stuck to the canvass. I could see these punches coming, but I couldn't move. It was all in slow motion. And then this big punch come over and I went to the floor. I think I got up, just about. The referee looked in my eyes and that was it, and I didn't hesitate. I said, 'Yeah, all right.' But I knew what was wrong. I didn't give myself a chance." That night, Clinton announced his retirement, but a year and a half later he made a comeback.

I asked him, "So what made you decide to try again?" He took quite a few moments to compose his reply. "My marriage had broken up. I was skint. I was living in a one-bedroom flat and I was totally at my wits end. I had nothing. I'd lost everything. I lost my house. I lost my cars, my Rolls-Royces. I was back to living in a bloody bed-sit. I thought, 'Well, boxing's all I've got, so I'll make a come back.' I started training, clawing my way back. I used to use a gym down my way for a while, but then I went over to the 'Beckett and trained over there. See, when you retire like that, when you're off that stage and you decide to come back, you do look at yourself closer, more clinically. You also realize that you have to adapt your style to what you are now, and not what you was then, because what I could do then, I can't do now. You've got to find different things to put into your style to make you as effective, like you was before. What I realized was that I couldn't fight for three minutes of every round like I did before. I couldn't bounce up and down on my toes like I did then anymore. I had to be more subtle, more settled, more calmed down, more crafty. I learned all that."

Clinton won his first comeback fight in March 1988 against Southern Area Champion, Chris Blake. Both men hailed from Croydon and they fought on their home turf. Clinton was now 32 years old and he had indeed become a different boxer to the man who had been shattered 18 months earlier. Blake was 26 and this was his first fight since losing in one devastating round to Lloyd Christie in a British Title challenge four months earlier. Clinton won every round and looked graceful and stylish in the process. His right jabs, left crosses and left uppercuts found their target with relative ease and painful regularity. Blake tried over and over again to walk through Clinton's attacks, but his fine looking face began to show signs of reddening in the first minute of the fight. He remained on his feet to the last bell and he never gave up trying. "Chris Blake, he was the up and coming boy. We was both local, from Croydon. I knew this kid was very strong and I wasn't going in there to mix it with him. I knew that, with all my experience, I could make him look like a novice. I showed him that I was the teacher. I had all this experience and I gave him a boxing lesson. It was a great performance and I felt great after the fight. I had all the touches of an old master. It was all there. Beautiful. Slipping and sliding. He couldn't touch me."

Six weeks later Clinton continued on the comeback trail, winning an eight round points decision against Ensley Bingham at York Hall. This was Bingham's fifth fight and he was unbeaten before Clinton came along to steal his thunder. The tall, rangy Mancunian switch-hitter had the upper hand physically and was the younger man by seven and a half years. Referee, Larry O'Connell, scored it to Clinton by half a point and Bingham received a £50 bonus for the best performance of the night. It was an excellent fight and the crowd cheered throughout the final round as they witnessed the old Clinton McKenzie style of rolling and ducking, avoiding Bingham's shots and scoring time after time, confusing and frustrating, stepping in and out of range with the grace of a dancer. Clinton's voice was full of the enthusiasm as he declared, "Ah, yeah, well now Ensley Bingham, he had a good left hook on him. I was there as the opponent. He was gonna knock me out. But you see, again, it was experience. They hadn't done what I had done. These guys were young, they were fresh, they were strong, yeah, but they hadn't had my experience. I could see things coming that they couldn't. Oh man, those comebacks were classics, because I boxed tremendous. When I look back, I think they were superb performances, and I didn't get involved. It wasn't these wars any more. It was clinical, classy performances. Knowledge."

Clinton's next fight came in December 1988 and he won the vacant Southern Area Light-Welterweight Title against shaven headed Mike Durvan of Penge on points at Crystal Palace. This was the second time for Clinton to claim this title and it was a tough job. He looked in great shape but, there again, he always did. Durvan was primarily a counter-puncher, but he was also unafraid to stand and trade. Once again, Clinton put his experience to work and out-boxed the younger man, making Durvan miss and conserving his energy when necessary, before surging forward with hammering attacks to the body and head. When referee, Dave Parris, raised Clinton's hand to award him the title, Clinton smiled painfully though a cut mouth, his eyes swollen with purple bruises. "Another youngster. They all thought they could beat me and I showed them that experience conquers. That was what beat those lads. I wasn't stronger than them, by far, but I was classier. I all had all the ingredients that they hadn't achieved yet and, when you put all that together, it does the business. It clicks into place. I mean, it was getting harder, *definitely*, but I was so in love with boxing and I still wanted to achieve something. I had the desire; the hunger was still there. The roadwork was getting harder. I didn't want to get up in the mornings and run, and all that. I started to hate that. The alarm clock would go off and I'd knock it over. 'I'll run later.' You know, that sort of thing. But I still wanted the fame. I still wanted to be the Champion. Those things kept me going."

On the 24th January 1989 Clinton did what he set out to do. At the age of 33 he regained the British Title. In the other corner of the ring at Cocks Moors Woods Leisure Centre in Birmingham was the current Champion, Lloyd Christie. Clinton had out-pointed Christie three and a half years earlier, but the man from Wolverhampton had climbed his way to the top of the British Light-Welterweight tree and now Clinton was back to regain what he had always believed to be rightfully his, the Lonsdale Belt. "That was great. That was absolutely superb. Coming back to win the title again was probably one of the greatest moments of my life. The British Title. Something I had treasured all those years. I really loved that British Title. It was something that had become personal. I was passionate. It was something that had become my possession. I possessed it, and to win it back again was, like, 'Wow! I did it.' That was just so fantastic, and do you know what? After that, nothing else really mattered, I'll be honest with you. But I did go on for a little while longer after that."

Six months after regaining the British Title, on the 12th August 1989, Clinton McKenzie boxed for the very last time. He challenged European Champion, Efrem Calamati, for his title. The fight was in San Sepolcro in Italy and Clinton was stopped in the seventh round. The Italian was nine years the younger man and unbeaten in 24 fights. A big right hand flush into Clinton's face sent him to the canvas to be counted out. Afterwards, Clinton said that punch, which closed his left eye, was so fast that he simply hadn't seen it coming. "He felt as if he belonged to another time. I felt old. I felt sluggish. I couldn't get myself up. I had no power. It had all gone, and on that night it all came home to me. That was it. That was my last fight. I knew then that I wouldn't be in the ring no more. It was all over. It wasn't to be. It was a very emotional point, but that was the best thing that could have happened to me. It was a good way of going. I thought about it for a few days, spent a lot of money, done a lot of things." He laughed as he remembered.

Today, Clinton holds a professional trainer's licence and he continues to fly the flag for boxing at his gym above the Half Moon Pub. He told me he is currently nurturing a nice little stable of boxers there. This listed building has been part of the boxing world for over 50 years and holds so much boxing history. Years ago, the customers from the pub downstairs would often come up to do a bit of sparring after a few pints. During the past decade Clinton has developed his own form of Boxercise and he trains people of all different levels. "That's right. I'm a keep fit instructor. A boxing guru, that's what I want to be. My passion is professional boxing; that's where I want to be, but I also train the general public in Boxercise. They train like boxers but they don't get hit. That's what they enjoy, so I teach that as well.

"Eventually, I'd like to develop a champion in some weight category. That's my dream. I've got to be patient for that but I think it will happen one day. Boxing is my love affair, so I'll keep on searching until I find my champion. Every boxer looks promising, but in reality it's very hard when you actually get into the arena, step into the ring. Your dreams don't always come true.

"My dream today is to have a big boxing gym. I want to do this on a bigger scale because I want everyone to know about boxing training. I want it to be a workout that is recognized by everyone. It's the most natural workout that you can do and I think that it shouldn't be for the selected few people. More and more women are doing it now, because it's good for their self esteem, their figure, everything. And I think it should be back in schools as well, if not so much for the competitive side, then just for the training and the discipline side of it. It should definitely be back in schools, because it's such a natural thing to do.

"I've seen some great fighters but, for me, the best - and I fought the man - was Sugar Ray Leonard. I loved Muhammad Ali, but Ali couldn't fight on the inside. I'd have to tip Sugar, because he could do everything. He had speed, accuracy, balance. Big man. He was the complete boxer. For me that really sums it all up. You'll never see that again. And Wilfred Benitez was another great fighter. Benitez was probably one of the best defensive fighters I've ever seen. George Foreman is probably the most powerful heavyweight there was - such tremendous power. And another fighter I really liked was Donald Curry; defence, accuracy, beautiful. Some of my style, I based on him, the perfection of his hands and movement of his upper body. He was one of the sharpest fighters I've ever seen. Superb. And Mike Tyson, in his prime, awesome! He could destroy any heavyweight, I reckon.

"I don't go to church but I'm a God fearing man. My dad brought me up that way. My dad was my big influence on my boxing career because he encouraged me, not in a pushy way, but he saw the excitement of boxing. He followed us everywhere and he encouraged us. He's been such a big influence on my whole life. I mean, here was a man, he had seven children and he grew us all. We had a strict upbringing. He taught us discipline and respect. He worked every day of his life to see that we had the things that we wanted, and he's had it really hard. The way he used to dress, as well. He always kept himself smart. When you're a kid and you're growing up, you notice these things. It rubs off on you. I am what I am because of what I've learned from him. He's made me what I am today. He's about 75 now, but he don't look it.

"I'm with Rebecca now. She's my partner. Please give her a mention. She's been a great lady. She's really stood by me through my ups and my downs and my bad moods and my upsets. I'm very passionate about her because she just understands, you know? Because the thing is with fighters, we're very difficult at times. When we're fighting we go through our emotional points. It takes a special lady to be with a fighter, because he's not a normal human being. We're very fickle. Rebecca has always been there, someone to lean on when things have got really hard. What I admire about her is that she knew me at a time when I was right at rock bottom and she's stuck by me. She wasn't there for the glamour; she was there for *me*. At the end of the day, if I lived in a shoebox, she'd be there with me. I think that's what separates the real people from those who are phoney. We've been through hard times, our house got repossessed and things like that, and she's still there. Now things are looking up again, and it's great."

CHAPTER THREE - TEDDY LEWIS

***Though his name on a bill will help fill any hall, his family believe in letting young Lewis fight his way to the top the hard way, just like his father and grandfather did before him.* (Reg Gutteridge OBE)**

The most senior boxer in this book is Teddy Lewis. I have been a member of the London Ex Boxers Association (LEBA) for about ten years, and that is where I met this charming fellow. LEBA is the place where we all congregate on the first Sunday of every month and, for the hundreds of us who belong to this particular boxing family, attending LEBA is like going to church. Miracles happen there all the time. You will notice that the quote at the beginning of this chapter comes from Reg Gutteridge OBE, another LEBA member whom I love to see every month. Reg and Ted go back a long way and this quote was taken from an article that was written in the Boxing News in 1948. Ted informed me, "It was one of the first articles that Reg ever wrote. When I talk to him, he says, 'Oh, you make me feel old.'"

This interview took place on a Saturday afternoon in August 2005, a few weeks after the London bombings. Ted and I arranged to meet at Mile End tube station at two o'clock. For the record, the old out-door Mile End Arena (where Ted used to box regularly) was situated just behind where the Underground now stands. I arrived slightly early and, as I stood waiting for Ted to arrive, I took in the bustle of the vastly multicultural population that provided the backdrop to the regular security announcements that blared out from the entrance to the Underground, a harsh reminder of the troubled times in which we are currently living. At two o'clock precisely, I looked across the road and there was Teddy, waving and smiling. This is a man who knows all about war, but he is a symbol of peace. Ted comes from an era that favours that distinctive old-fashioned type of courtesy that is often lacking in today's society. His memories are vivid and his words are spoken with that special type of quiet wisdom that makes you sit up and listen avidly. He is smart and sprightly and, to this day, he weighs in at a few pounds over his fighting weight. His kind blue eyes twinkle when he remembers his days in the ring.

We stopped for a quick beer in one of Ted's local pubs to lubricate the vocal chords, and then he took me to his house where I met his wife, Betty. These two have been married for 50 years and Betty is also a fighter. A couple of weeks before I met her she had fallen in their back garden and broken her hip. However, she was up and about, moving around with the aid of a walking stick and, despite the obvious physical pain that she must have been feeling, she welcomed me warmly into her home and joined Ted and I for our talk. I could sense that she was getting very tired as the afternoon wore on, but she kept smiling right up to the end.

Ted was born on the 24th August 1929. He was christened, Edward Charles Lucioni, but his family changed their surname by Deed Poll in 1944. Lewis was the name they all boxed under and Ted told me, "Most people knew us by the name the family fought under. I was born in Bow, about 300 yards from here. It was in the late 30's and there was a slum clearance, so my family moved down to Beacontree in Dagenham. They had built the new estates there and Fords works had opened, so everybody was going down there and finding work in Fords, but my father still worked at Billingsgate. I was about six when we moved down there and then, when I was 25, I got married and moved back here to Bow."

Ted's father went by the name of Teddy Lewis and his mother was called Elizabeth. "I've got a younger brother, Billy, and a younger sister, Norma. I was the eldest of three." Ted was 10 years old when World War II was declared and I asked him what that news meant for such a young boy. "When war was declared we were hop picking down in Kent. It was a Sunday morning, a lovely sunny day, and I was carrying our dinner down to the local bakers to be baked for us when all the air raid sirens sounded that war had been declared. We stopped there for two or three weeks afterwards, still hop picking, and then we came back to London. When we got back, London was empty. Most of the children had already been evacuated. All the schools were closed. There was a blackout. You daren't leave a light showing through your curtains or someone banged on the window and said, 'Put that light out.' But, then it was like a false war. Nothing was happening really until the following June when the bombing started, and it also looked like we may be invaded. Anyway, mum decided we should be evacuated, so we went to the school and from there we were taken down into Devon.

"If you can imagine, there's three children, never been away from their parents really up to that time, and we get down to this little village called Uplowman. We were taken into the school hall and we stood in there with all these people around us, picking out the children they wanted. It was like a cattle market really, and they all talked foreign; 'Ar, you be' and 'Where be you from,' you know? I mean, we didn't even know if they were German or not. It was all a bit worrying.

"Well, my sister and her cousin were two pretty little girls, and they were the first two to be picked. It went on and on until there were only two children left, and that was me and my little brother. Nobody wanted us. You can imagine. We're standing there with our gas masks around our necks and our bags at our feet, and I was old enough to understand what was going on. Then one woman said, 'Mother said I shouldn't bring anybody home, but I'll take them home tonight as long as you promise you'll find somewhere else for them.' So this was what she did. She walked us down this country lane and it was dark. There were bats flying about. There were rooks making noises. My little brother's hanging onto my hand and we walked down to this farmhouse. We walked in and there was no electricity, naturally. There was just an oil lamp and on the right hand side there was one of those big Inglenook fireplaces with a log fire, and over the fire was a big black pot, like a cauldron. In the corner was an old lady all in black, with a black scarf on her head and a black dress. My little brother, he was only five at the time, and he thought she was a witch."

I wondered what must have been going through the minds of these two little Londoners, suddenly finding themselves so far away from home in such strange circumstances. "Well, first of all it was an adventure for us. I mean, we'd been on a steam train and all those sort of things, you know, but now we were beginning to worry. But you accepted things. You were told to do something by your parents and you did it, so we thought, 'Well, this is what we've got to do.' You behave yourself and you be as nice as you can.

"They gave us something to eat and they took us up to bed. We went in this bedroom and there were bare floorboards, because they hadn't been expecting anybody, and a single bed which they'd just made up. There was a little table on the side with a china bowl with cold water in for washing with. We climbed into bed, cuddled up to each other and went to sleep. The next morning the sun was shining and we could hear the farmer driving the cows into the cowshed. We jumped up and we looked out of the window. When we saw all this going on, it's all exciting, so we wash with this water and go downstairs as quick as we can. Then we met the people in the house and it was two single sisters and single brother. They must have been in their late 20s/early 30s, I supposed, and the mother, she was in her 60s, I think. Anyway, they looked after us. They were really nice to us. They decided that they wouldn't send us away and they kept us. We stayed there for about three years and we had a really good time.

"Being evacuated really changed my life because under the bed there was this big tin chest, and in the tin chest were all these books, children's classics and things. That was where I really first got interested in reading. I think I read all of them, and I read the Bible from beginning to end. We used to sit of a night with candles, reading, because there was nothing else to do of a night time. My little brother used to wander off down to the village cross and play with the other evacuees and children, but I never wanted to. I wanted to be on the farm and work on the farm, and do whatever I could on the farm, you know? I learned all sorts of things and I ended up talking like them.

"When I was 13, mum and dad decided I should come home and get a proper job to earn some money, so I came home and went to school for a couple of months. Then I left school and started work at the end of July. I was 14 in the August." Ted's first job was in a printing firm and one day he suffered a horrible accident. The two middle fingers of his left hand got caught up and mangled in a bookbinding machine. He recovered and returned to work, but he was unable to do his manual job because of the injury, so he ended up helping with the proof reading. "But it didn't suit me at all, because it was indoors and I'd been doing all this work on the farm. So I said to dad, 'I don't want to work there anymore. I want to come to work on the market,' and he said, 'No son of mine is going to work in Billingsgate.' So I ended up doing bomb damage repairs, but I didn't like that. I still wanted to go to the market. It was then that I started doing a bit of amateur boxing at the local youth club. I also met my wife, Betty, for the first time at the same youth club."

When Ted was 15, his father acquiesced to his request to work at the market. "There were no regular jobs then. I couldn't become a fish porter until I was 18. That was the age to do a man's work. It was hard work and you got a man's wages." The fish porters wore sturdy hats with flat tops so that they could carry the heavy crates of fish on their heads. This was the easiest way to carry heavy, bulky loads, and the hats had wide brims so that the smelly fish slush, which would drain out of the boxes, would not run down the carrier's cheeks.

"Billingsgate is in a valley. All the roads that lead out of Billingsgate go uphill, so when fish porters are delivering fish they load it onto a barrow and then they push it to the different vans all around the market. But, when they were going up the hill, if they had several boxes on there, they couldn't pull them up, so there was always people about, usually it was tramps and people like that, who would stand on the corners waiting. The porters would shout, 'Up the hill,' and someone would run behind and push. When they got to the top of the hill the porter would give them tuppence or thrippence, or something. The firm dad was working at, I used to go with the porters and I used to push the barrows and help lift the boxes onto their heads. Anyway, when I was 17, I put my age up and I applied for a porter's licence, and I started portering then. By the way, I'd just turned professional [in boxing] then."

But, before we moved onto his days as a professional fighter, I wanted to know about Ted's amateur boxing career. "I started off at the Campbell School Youth Club. It was during the war and it was hard to get fights, so I joined several other clubs. I joined West Ham for a while. I boxed for Buxton ABC in Walthamstow, and I also boxed for the Navel Cadets. I wasn't a Naval Cadet, but I joined their boxing team so I could get fights. I had several fights during the war. The air raid sirens used to go and they used to say, 'If anyone wants to leave, leave now,' and then we used to carry on boxing.

"I quite enjoyed it as amateur, but I wasn't suited to the amateurs, I don't think. After about three fights, they entered me for the Junior Amateur Championships and the ABA Championships. In 1945, I was in Class A of the Juniors and I reached the semi-finals. I was boxing someone from Wales, someone named White. It was the same year that Randolph Turpin was boxing. He was boxing in the Class As. He was 16 then and he looked fantastic. I mean, we watched him and he was out of this world. We said 'He's gonna be World Champion.' That's how good he looked.

"As an amateur, I won most of my fights. But I did a lot of body punching, which I'd been used to from sparring with my father. All the time I was boxing, the referee would be saying, 'Keep your punches up.' Anyway, I entered the Senior Novices competition, and I had to have four fights in one night. That was at Mile End Baths. I won all four. I knocked three out and I won the fourth on points, and I got a silver rose bowl. It was worth about £5, and I thought, 'This is ridiculous. I've had four fights for £5.' That was when I decided to turn professional.

"My father was managing boxers then, but he wouldn't manage me. His friend who had managed him when he was boxing, George Morris, he became my manager. The first professional fight I had was at Romford Drill Hall. I was just 18 and very baby faced. I seemed to stay 18 for years, because no one seemed to think I was getting any older. I looked so young. They said I had a complexion like a dairymaid, but I didn't *punch* like a dairymaid. Anyway, the first fellow I boxed, he was shorter than me, right stocky, and he must have been about 33. He had about three days growth on his chin and I'd never fought a man like that before, but I knocked him out in four rounds, I think it was. And professional boxing suited me. When they bandaged and taped my hands, when I closed my fists, I felt like I had knuckledusters on. Boxing at Mile End Arena, most of them were old gloves that you just broke up, sort of thing, so your knuckles were more or less showing through. It was great. I was just knocking people out. Most of the fights were just going one or two rounds, and I'd suddenly found something that I could do.

"Because up to then, I'd always felt a little bit inferior. I hadn't had enough education and I didn't like confronting people and things. I was a bit unsure of myself, but when I was in the ring that seemed to change entirely. I mean, outside with my suit on, I'd be quiet and wouldn't say much. Put me in a pair of shorts and put me in the ring and I felt I could do anything. This is where I felt I was in charge. I never believed anyone was stronger than me. I never believed anyone was better than me."

During the summer months, professional boxing has always taken an unofficial end of season holiday. "During that time, unless you had a manager that was in with one of the big promoters like Jack Solomons, you couldn't get on a bill. So they said that where I *would* get experience was in the boxing booths. There was a chap that used to come down from Scotland every year who had this boxing booth, Tommy Woods. He came down and I went to see him. I said I could box on the booth for him. We would stand on the front and we would, what they called, 'take on all comers.' I mean, you didn't actually take on all comers. I was nine stone, and I would fight anybody up to ten stone, seven. Most of the fights were fixed. If no one came up to challenge you, you couldn't shut down for the night because you wouldn't earn any money. So you always had two or three in the crowd that would say, 'I'll fight him.' And we had some good fighters.

"In fact, some of the gee fights that I had were better than the real fights, because half the real challengers that came up were kidded by their mates and they didn't know anything about fighting. They might be able to have a fight in the street, but you put a pair of gloves on them and gave them the rules and they didn't know where they were. They used to pay me £2 a fight and it wasn't bad, because I could have several fights in a night. You'd have two fights on for each show and people used to pay a shilling to come in. We wore gloves and they were old gloves. Usually, if the opponent was someone you didn't know, you gave the opponent the good gloves and you had the old gloves that you could break up so your knuckles would come through. After the fight we used to go round with the hat in the crowd collecting money. Sometimes I used to get more doing that than the £2 that I was getting for the fight. We had some marvellous experiences and, of course, you had to be an actor too.

"I boxed at Tottenham once and nobody came up to challenge. So anyway, one of our own came up and we had this gee fight. Every time we got into a clinch I would say to him, 'Hit me up the belly,' and every time he's hit me up the belly I've gone on the floor, haven't I? And then I've got up and, in the corner where I am, I can here this group of youngsters; well, not youngsters, but anyway, I could hear them saying to one, 'Go on, you could have him. He can't take it up the belly.' So anyway, at the end of the fight, this chap's jumped up. 'I'll fight him,' he said. So I walk out for the first round and I lift me arms up and he hits me in the belly, and I didn't move. You've never seen a fella's face change so much!"

Having joined the professional boxing ranks, Ted had a lot to live up to. His father, Ted Lewis, boxed out of Bethnal Green in the 1930s and had over 200 fights as a professional. "My father often used to box for sixpence and a bun when he first started. Because different managers would be there to see if they could pick up anybody, so they boxed for nothing." Ted's uncle, 'Young' Bill Lewis, won the Southern Area Bantamweight Title. Ted's grandfather, Bill Lewis, was probably the most famous of them all. He boxed the likes of Peerless Jim Driscoll. "My grandfather had about 286 fights, but he was killed in action in France during the First World War [1916]. I never saw him."

In 1947, the British Boxing Board of Control outlawed all boxing booth fighters from their ranks. I asked Ted how he felt about that. "Well, I didn't like it but, you see, I never used to box under my own name." During his career under the Marquis of Queensbury Rules, Ted boxed at featherweight and lightweight and he had 38 fights. He won 29 of those (21 inside the distance.) He had 1 draw and 8 losses. His fighting style was all guns blazing, and he could punch with both hands. "They say punchers are born and you can't make a puncher. I just don't know how true that is. But I was lucky then - I was born as a puncher. I still believe there's a technique to it and that can be passed on, but timing is something that maybe that you have to be born with."

Ted's fighting philosophy was that, while you were stopping punches, you could not be delivering punches. Therefore, he always tried to slip punches while, at the same time, punching himself. I asked him how much attention he used to pay to defence and he hesitated before answering. "Enough, by slipping punches. You have to use defence for aggression as well. If you're defending something, you've got to try and use it." Ted's manager, George Morris, worked closely with Ted's father. Together, they gradually built up the distances for Ted's fights and the level of his opposition. "For the first fights I had, I got £5 a fight. That was the pay then. That was for four three-minute rounds. When I went up to six-threes I was getting £12.50. I had a few of those and then I went up to eight-threes, and I think it was about £35 that I was getting. If I topped the bill, I could get £50 or £60. A lot depended on how many tickets you could sell. And, I mean, when I was portering, I could earn £20 a week."

Ted boxed at least once a month, sometimes two or three times. "My favourite fight that I had, it wasn't even a big fight, but we were going to Manor Place Baths for me to box there one night. As we've crossed the road, a chap's come up to me and Betty. He's all dressed up, he had this gabardine raincoat on, and he said, 'I've fixed it up. We're on third. I want to get away early.' And that's the first I knew that he was my opponent." Betty explained to me, "He had just me with him; nobody else was with us." Ted continued, "Yeah, it was just me and Betty, crossing the road, and how he knew me, I don't know. Anyhow, we got in the ring and I stopped him in the fourth round, and I went over to his corner and I said, 'Was that early enough for you?' And that was a thing that gave me pleasure, because he *was* flash. But, the thing was, he was right flash doing that, but the next morning he came to the market to find me, 'cos he had to come and shake my hand.

"The first time I ever got put on the floor sticks in me memory, and I can't even think of his name. Somerville, or something, I seem to remember his name was. But at the end of the first round he caught me, and I didn't stay down. I jumped up straight away, because I'd never been on the floor before and I didn't know. Anyhow, I came out for the next round and knocked him out at the beginning of the second round. It upset me a bit, because I didn't think that anyone could ever do that to me. Because it's ego all the time, isn't it? I think, as fighters, this is what we live on.

"I loved training. Working in Billingsgate I used to finish early, so I could go straight to the gym. I used to train almost every day. I used to go to Jack Solomons' gym because it was the nearest to the market. The only day I did roadwork was on a Sunday morning, because every other day of the week I used to get up at 3.30 in the morning to go to work. I used to be on my legs and running about all the time while I was working. But on Sunday mornings, I used to get up and we used to run for quite a while. I could run 12 miles on a Sunday, and I always wore heavy army boots. I always run backwards up hills, and I used to stop and do shadow boxing and things like this, you know?"

One of the most vital elements of boxing training is sparring and, in his time, Ted sparred with the best of them, including former British and European Lightweight Champion, Billy Thompson. "I sparred with a lot of people, but Billy Thompson was the only one who really hurt me. He hit me with a left hook up the belly and I felt as if he'd left his glove there. I just couldn't breathe, so I'm dancing round then with a silly grin on me face, you know, like you do. 'He's not hurt me.' And I can't get me breath back. Eventually it came back again, but that was the first time that I really felt hurt. I mean, I boxed with these people because I was learning off them. They were the Champions, so they weren't there to learn off *me*. But I was fast and this is what they was using me for, and I punched hard.

"Another one I sparred with was Tony Lombard, who came over from South Africa. He lost the fingers on one of his hands; his left, I think. He was, to me, a typical South African; arrogant. We used to get in the ring and he used to try and take liberties, you know, and it used to end up like a real fight between us. But I always found that, when I was getting on top and hurting him, he would go, 'Oh, my hand's playing up.' One time we ended up on the floor, you know? We wrestled each other to the floor, and I'm getting paid £1 a round for this fight.

"When we finished training, we would go and have our showers and I always used to rinse my face with surgical spirit. It was like an aftershave. It would get all the stiffness out of your face and it used to sting, but it was always good for hardening the skin up. So anyway, one day I'd poured this on me hand and I was rubbing it on my face and Tony Lombard said, 'What's that?' So I said, 'It's surgical spirit. It's good for your skin.' So he said, 'Could I have some?' So I said, 'Yeah,' and I give it to him, but I didn't tell him how much it stung! So he put it on his face and he screamed. He said, 'You bastard! You're trying to blind me!'"

These days, a lot of the boxers have almost as many products in their bags as I have in my bathroom. They have gel for their hair, cream to put here, spray to use there. I asked Ted what he thought about this modern day image awareness, which made him laugh and shake his head. "Oh, we had nothing like that in my day. We just used to wash with soap and that was it. We always used Vaseline before our fights, and we used to use the cheap Whitehorse oils; lubrication oils, they were, and my dad used to make up his own oils. He used to use oil of eucalyptus and surgical spirit.

"I used to train down in Bill Kline's gym, in Fitzroy Square. It had a stone floor ring in the middle. The wrestlers used to use it a lot for rehearsing down there. There was a little room built into the gym that Bill Kline used to sleep in with his dogs. He had some Great Dane dogs and they used to mess on the floor sometimes. One had pups and you had the pups running about. You had a little changing room with a shower in there and, if you got under the shower and you was having a lovely hot shower, suddenly it would go stone cold and Bill Kline would say, 'You've had enough hot water!'"

Ted's mother hated him boxing. Perhaps she had seen enough of it over the years, what with her husband and her father having turned to the ring for a living. I wondered how Betty used to feel about it. She told me, "I quite enjoyed it at first." Ted interjected, "Because I was winning."

Betty continued, "But, when he got his eyes cut, I wasn't all that happy then. And his uncles used to come and, if anybody was shouting out for the other one, they'd turn round and shout back. 'What's the matter with you, ref?' you know, and all that." I asked Betty if she ever felt like shouting herself. "Not really, no. I just used to sit there quietly but, if I saw him getting hurt, I didn't like that very much."

Ted retired from professional boxing in 1951. There was one particular fight in that year that he wanted to tell me about, which incidentally was his first fight out of London. "I went up to Preston to box someone called Ronnie Grebb. I went there straight from work. I got up there for the weigh-in and then went out to look for a cheese sandwich, and I think Preston was closed! Anyhow, when I got in the ring, this Ronnie Grebb comes in. He was shorter than me, with long arms and two big cauliflower ears, and the referee only had one eye. So we walk out for the first round and the first thing this Ronnie Grebb does is he hit's me low. I mean, if you're wearing a cup it's not supposed to hurt. But if you knock it sideways, it *does* hurt, and it went boyynnnggg! So I've gone down on the floor and the referee started counting me out; never warned him or anything." Ted was chuckling as he remembered. "Anyway, we've got in a clinch and the referee's holding both my arms, pulling me back, saying, 'break,' while the other fella's still hitting me. This went on and I thought, 'Well, what's happening here?'

After three rounds I thought, 'Now I've gotten on top,' and I'm catching him with good left hands and right hands, and then suddenly he's dived straight out, came straight at me with his head. He's hit me on the forehead and split my head right open, and the referee stopped the fight straight away and gave it to him. Anyway, they've took me back into the dressing room to stitch me head up, and I'm sure there was more people in the dressing room watching him stitch me up than there was outside watching the fights. So I was all plastered up and I got back to London to go back to work at four o'clock the next morning. I couldn't wear my leather hat because of the plaster, so I had to wear a cap and carry boxes of fish on me head with that."

Ted's final professional fight came on the 28th October 1951. "I was boxing Johnny Lewis. Johnny Lewis, I've seen him since, and he said he didn't want to fight me 'cos he was frightened of how hard I punched. I was on top in the fight. I was winning the fight, and I walked back to the corner at the end of the third round and I was feeling a bit funny. Things were a bit blurry. I just shook me head, and they say that before I got to the corner I just collapsed. They tended me there and I was semi-conscious when they got me up. They took me to St Mary's Hospital and gave me a lumber puncture, and there was blood in the fluid that they drained from my spine. Anyway, they gave me another lumber puncture and that one came out clear."

That was it for Ted. He decided his days of performing in the ring were over and he retired from the sport that had made him feel so special. "It did affect me at first, because you feel like you've lost a lot. But there were still so many people about who *knew* what I'd done and *respected* what I'd done. I still got a lot of respect off people. I left the market for a while and went to work at the docks for two years. I had started writing poetry and reading Dickens and things. I had been doing that for a long time and, I mean, dockers don't *do* those sorts of things. But nobody ever said anything or thought I was different, because they knew that I could fight so, therefore, I *must* be all right. Anyway, I have dreams sometimes of making a comeback now, but would they let me come back at 76?"

We got onto the boxers of today and Ted told me that he likes Ricky Hatton. "Yes, I like him because he reminds me of how fighters used to be. But I think it's entirely different now. I think boxers today don't know as much as we did. They don't get the experience. They don't *learn* as much as we did, because they don't get the competition and they don't have the fights. I mean, I talk to people who were boxing at the same time as me and most of them say we had the best of the times. The way fighters are now, I reckon Amir Khan is a prospect, but he's got so much to learn. I feel sorry for him. I like him. I like the way he fights and I like his enthusiasm, but I feel sorry for him because so much is expected of him.

"If you want to see a real boxer, watch Joe Louis. Watch him shuffle. He was never out of distance and he didn't miss with punches. I mean, Muhammad Ali was fantastic, but he was one on his own. His footwork and his speed and all that sort of thing was great, but the only problem is that all the fighters since then have tried to copy him. And you can't punch if you're feet aren't on the ground. I mean, I could watch Muhammad Ali and I could see so many mistakes he was making, but he was so good that he could get away with it."

This is probably going to come as no big surprise, but Ted is a staunch advocator of bringing boxing back to schools. "It encourages discipline. I mean, I turned professional at 18, but I never had a fight on the street. Well, I mean, I did when I was about seven or eight in school. Because having a name like Lucioni, people used to call me Lucy for short and that's not a boy's name, is it? Also, I had a terrible singing voice and some of the kids used to take the rise out of me about that. But, when I started boxing, I never fought on the street. I mean, all this aggression, what they do now, kicking and things.

I'm not all that old, but when I was growing up if you kicked someone you was a coward. You didn't use your feet and you didn't use knives and things like that. If it was a fight, you had a fight and that was it. People have got no respect for themselves, and no respect for other people and other people's property. These days, the kids are only being told what they're entitled to, but not what they're supposed to do to be entitled *to* it. How teachers cope with a classroom full of kids today, I just don't know."

These days, Ted spends much of his spare time at the Ragged School Museum in Bethnal Green, a place devoted to making the history of the East End of London accessible to everyone. "Since I retired, I started going to this Ragged School Museum. I talk to classes of primary school children about what life was like when I was growing up, and the kids seem to gel with me. They talk to me. They ask me questions. They're *interested* about how things were. It doesn't matter what religion they are, or who they are. They're all listening. They're all interested and, I mean, I love talking to 'em.

"One time, it was really touching. This one little girl come up to me. I don't know; I think she come from Kosovo or somewhere, but she must have been here for quite a while because she talked good English. She come up to me, all quiet, and she held my hand and looked up at me, and she said, 'Was *you* treated bad when *you* was a boy?' I said, 'No, I've been very lucky.' She was only about eight. Then, another little girl, a little Muslim girl, she come up to me and she said, 'You're just like my granddad.'

"I used to get loads of letters from the children. There was one little boy, I don't know how old he was. The thing is, sometimes when I sit, my knees tremble. It's like you're on a nerve, you know? So I've sat down to talk to the children and me knee's trembling a bit. So this little boy wrote to me and he said how much he had enjoyed it, and he said, 'You seemed very nervous at the beginning, but you was really good at the end.'"

CHAPTER FOUR - BOB 'B.F.' WILLIAMS

B.F. was the most honest fighter you could ever meet, without a doubt. He was a delight to work with, and to think that while he was boxing he had a whole other life as a fireman. Lovely kid. (Johnny Winter)

Books last forever and boxing is a short career. One of the many things that keeps me passionately driven as a boxing writer is the knowledge that, by writing books about boxers, I feel that I am in some way immortalizing my subjects. If that sounds egotistical, I apologize, but that is simply the way it is and it is a wonderful job. However, at the same time, writing books would be a fruitless task if nobody were to read them. No matter how diligent the labour of love, the end product needs to be commercially viable. Books must sell and that is why, when you visit the sports section of a bookshop and seek out the boxing books, they will invariably be about the big names that everybody knows, because those are the tomes that are likely to the attract the attention of the public. It is for that reason that the 'middlemen,' for want of a better expression, often have to take a back seat when it comes to the written word.

Bob Williams was a professional boxer. He fought under the ring name of B.F. Williams. He boxed at light-welterweight and had 33 paid fights, of which he won 20. In his own words, "I was one up from a journeyman and one down from a Champion." The first time I ever met Bob was at a London Ex Boxers Association (LEBA) meeting. I cannot remember exactly when that was, but it was a fair while ago now. I was still writing *'Sweet Fighting Man'* at the time and the interviews for that first book were already lined up but, as I got to know Bob, I recognized what a lovely chapter his story would make.

By the next time Bob came to LEBA, '*Sweet Fighting Man'* had been published and I was setting about work on this volume. I tentatively broached the subject of interviewing him for Volume II and I will never forget the look on his face when I put the idea to him for the first time. It was a mixture of stunned surprise, and perhaps a little concern that I had mistakenly approached the wrong chap. "Okay, I'd love you to come over to Watford and interview me, but are you sure you've got the right guy? I'm not Cleveland Williams, you know, or Danny Williams, or

Robbie Williams!" I explained to him that it was indeed B.F. Williams that I wanted to talk to. He laughed happily, suddenly seeming far more comfortable with the idea, and cheerfully replied, "Okay. We can sit down and have a chat. I've got some great stories, but I'm by no means a Robinson, Cantwell, Cook, Dunne, Walker, Winstone, Minter or Oliver [reeling off a list of names from *'Sweet Fighting Man'*]. I mean, ask Crawford Ashley about B.F. Williams. He'll say, 'B.F. who?' But I had a great time and met some wonderful characters and sparred with some great fighters down the Thomas A' Beckett, even as a boy. I never won a title or made a million, but I've got some brilliant memories, and a flat nose and a cauliflower bum. Listen to me. I'm off already!"

I went to Watford to meet Bob and his family in May 2003. Spookily enough, this interview took place 17 years to the day since his professional debut. In those days Bob weighed nine stone, eight pounds. Today he still radiates fitness, for that is part of his job as a fireman. As he drove me from Watford Junction train station to his house, he told me, "I weigh 11 stone, 13 ¾ pounds. I'm not in bad shape. I'm carrying it okay. I'm five foot, 11." We arrived at Bob's house and he made me a cup of tea. While he riffled through the kitchen cupboards he pulled out a tiny bottle, "Look, I still carry adrenaline even now, just in case my missus cuts me!" There is no chance of that. His lovely wife Shlomit (Shlo for short) arrived a couple of hours later with their delightful son, Dean, who was at that time 16 months old, and I didn't see one punch being thrown. Dean is a lovely, laid-back little boy. No tantrums or screaming, just a little peach. Bob has his son's name tattooed down the back of his right leg. "It's really scary. Everything I do is involved around boxing, and if you mention the word 'boxing' he bangs his bloody hands together now. My missus is terrified.

"Shlo's from Israel. I went out to Las Vegas about five years ago for the boxing and the gambling, and the women. We met at a nightclub. I invited her back to England a couple of months later and we enjoyed it, and then I invited her back again. I can't get rid of her now! We've been married for two years. We went back out to Vegas to get married. We had about 20 or 30 friends come out and we had the reception in the Stratosphere Hotel. It was fantastic. You couldn't afford that in England.

Everyone had a Limo and, because we all stayed at the Stratosphere, they gave us the reception room free. We spent three weeks out there. We had a brilliant time. And Vegas is brilliant for the boxing, as well. I try and get out there every year. I met Wayne McCullough out there. We hung about together, me and Wayne. He took me round his house and everything, had a great time. He lives for the sport."

Bob has blue eyes and bright smile. His sense of humour is naturally spontaneous. Apart from being a full-time fireman, he has his own boxing equipment company and deals in boxing memorabilia. He is a born salesman and, when you see him out and about at the amateur shows selling his gear, Bob's genuine interest in the lads and his gift of the gab is highly evident. At the time that I interviewed Bob I was deeply involved in the amateurs myself. I remember watching him in action once and thinking to myself, 'He could sell a pair of boxing gloves to a man with no arms.' When I told him that, he replied, "If I was a natural salesman, I'd be a millionaire by now. I just love being out and about around the amateur shows, still being involved. I always tell it like it is."

Robert Frank Williams was born at Park Royal, London on the 14th December 1965. "Where did my boxing career start? Probably, like everyone's boxing career starts. The old man messing around with his son. My dad's still alive. He's in his late 60s now. I was 13 years old and it was the time when you had Mark Kaylor and Charlie Magri. Magri was one of my favourites because he was exciting. Muhammad Ali was just coming to the end of his career. Me and my dad used to wrap tea towels around our hands and just go for it, and my mum used to scream and shout. There was a local boxing club around the corner from me at Bushey. My dad fell upon it by accident while he was doing some electrical work over there and I said, 'Take me down there, dad. Take me down there,' like you do. He took me down there and it was in a big old Nissan hut. This particular night, they had a boxing show on there, an open show, and I just fell in love with it. I was playing football, like every other kid, but this was intense. This was one-on-one. You didn't need to rely on anyone else. Met the trainer, John Scott, who stayed with me throughout my career and a little bit after. In my opinion, John was the best schoolboy trainer ever for teaching a kid how to box. He wasn't great on fitness and strength, but on technique he was the best. And onwards with my amateur career."

Bob's first amateur boxing match was on the 8th November 1980 against P. Symons of Old Actonians. "I had my first amateur bout. It was at the Bushey club. It was an open show. I lost a disputed points decision, and it just rolled on and on and on. I've got me card here." In preparation for my visit, Bob had dug out his amateur boxing card, along with all his local write-ups, and an array of photographs and videos of several of his fights. He told me that his extensive collection was down to his mum. "These are just some of the things that my mum kept. My mum used to love doing it. My mum was so proud of me. She was great." His voice became tender. "My mum passed away a few years ago now. Her name was Mavis. My dad's name is Bob. They weren't mad for the boxing. They didn't push me too much, which was probably good." As I studied Bob's card I was amazed at how often he fought as an amateur. "Oh yeah, sometimes I boxed three times in a week. I smudged out some of the dates so the officials would let me box three times in a week. Everyone did it.

"Oh, I've got something fantastic to tell you. I'd been boxing probably about a year now, and it was obviously in my blood. Anyway, one day my dad's sitting there and my dad's *so* laid-back. He said, 'Oh, your great-granddad used to box. We've got his Championship belt upstairs.' And I said, 'What title did he win?' Well, he won the English Bantamweight Title and I'm gonna show you the belt now. It's fantastic!" Bob knelt on the carpet and, from a drawer at the bottom of the unit beside us, he carefully retrieved the belt. It was securely wrapped up in tissue paper and, as Bob reverently uncovered it, he told me, "His name was Jim Williams and he boxed out of Marylebone. In them days they hadn't invented gloves. And that's where I got it from. It *must* be."

For the record, Jim Williams was born in 1876 and he died in 1946. He boxed from 1891 to 1909, during which time he had 127 fights, in another time and another world. As Bob pointed out to me, "Those were hard times." Bob let me remove the last of the wrapping and, as it dawned on me that this belt was over a hundred years old, I felt the hair stand up on the back of my neck. I was holding a real piece of boxing history in my hands. The belt was for the National Sporting Club Championship of England. Bob's great-granddad won it at six stone, ten pounds and he took the title from Pedlar Palmer. "1902. That was before the Lonsdale Belt come in. Pedlar Palmer was like Mike Tyson. He used to challenge anyone in the country for a £100. £100 then was like five years wages! My great-granddad came in for that fight eight pounds overweight; that's pounds, not bloody ounces. I hope they don't want the belt back!" The belt is deep turquoise velvet with gold braid and bears two silver shields with boxers on them. Bob was quick to cut in, "For insurance purposes, it's diamond studded!" Bob laughed about his father's laid-back attitude regarding the belt. "It's not like he thrust it in me hands as soon as I wrapped a tea towel around my fist! He waits until a few years later and says, 'Oh, by the way, son …' That's what I wanted, was to show my great-grandson, there's a belt around my waist. I would have really liked it, but it didn't happen. I nearly got there, but it's better to be a 'has been' than a 'never was.'"

We began to sift through the pile of memories on the coffee table before us and I could sense that Bob was emotionally travelling back in time. "I remember I was training for the ABAs, the first time [November 1984], and we had a fire at our gym. It was only a small fire but the smoke damage was terrible. We just had the clock and the one bag, and I trained in the smoke. The quality in those days, to win your area, you had to be something else. Every fight was just a battle. I *loved* the amateur game and I'll tell you why; because that's your apprenticeship." He reached out and picked up his card. "It's not the best in the world. I've seen some *great* cards of boys, some England boys. But towards the end of my amateur career I was representing the County in every fight. The best I got was to the NABC semi-finals, Class C. That year, the final in the weight above me involved Georgie Collins, who got beat by Gary Stretch, and they televised it. I wanted it *so* much, and I got beat on a majority decision by a guy called Gary Andrews from Fitrzroy Lodge. I cried my eyes out after."

Bob picked out a newspaper clipping from the coffee table. "This was an awards ceremony for Herts and Beds; best stylist, best boxer … Oh blimey, who have we got here? Good looking Bob Williams, Paul Tynon, Danny Porter … Danny Porter, what a fighter! Monty Wright, British Champion. Billy Schwer! Billy you look like a baby there, and you're ugly now! Sean Murphy, British Champion. What a team! It was like one big party. And there's my trainer, John Scott. That's Terry Dearlove. He was my club mate. He made it to be a professional. He had two pro fights. Lovely guy, and so dangerous in the gym because, if you weren't on your toes, he would bash ya'. I was about 16 or 17 there. In those days we used to spend Sundays down the old Thomas A' Beckett. We used to get good quality sparring. One day, we went down there and they wouldn't let us in. There was a fighter called Eleoncio Mercedes, who was then World Flyweight Champion, and he'd come over to defend his title against Charlie Magri, who was my hero.

"So anyway, John Scott mooched his way in and we got some sparring with the World Flyweight Champion. I was only 16 or 17 and I was a bantamweight then. I was a tall, lanky boy with a long jab. I did three rounds with him. I did three *good* rounds with him. I caught him with a good left jab." A dreamy smile lit up Bob's face as he remembered. "And into the gym walked Vic Andreetti and Frank Warren. I was a cocky little bugger and Vic Andreetti shouted out, 'Throw one up the middle!' so I went bump, threw the shot up, and I *caught* him." It was obviously a left, because Bob threw it as he got caught up in the memory of it all. "And Vic Andreetti and Frank Warren were told by the gym manager, Danny Holland, to stop coaching! Anyway, they were so impressed with the sparring that they invited me back, and I got paid a tenner for every round I sparred. It was brilliant! So I did another three rounds with him and they wanted me back again, but I had a fight coming up so I couldn't do it. So they give me some tickets for the fight.

"It was about six or seven years later, I remember coming home. I think it was Christmas Eve and I was drunk, tired, and my dad was there with my uncle. My uncle had cut out from the paper that Eleoncio Mercedes had got shot in an argument over a car parking space. Yeah, he got killed. He gave me a little speedball as a present. Couldn't speak a word of English but, like they say in boxing, it's universal, isn't it?" Together, Bob and I studied a black and white photograph of Bob sparring with

Mercedes. Bob was as thin as a reed and he looked so young. For the benefit of the tape, Bob declared, "He's not catching me. I've just parried it!

"And Cornelius Boza Edwards, he was another one who I sparred with at the Wellington Gym. What a gym *that* was. I did okay against Cornie. What a talented boxer. I was about 18 then. I mean, you see some of Boza Edwards' World Title fights. What battles! Epic battles."

Bob selected another newspaper cutting. "This is the fight against Paul Harris. I'd just started with Rolls-Royce. I did six years there; a four year apprenticeship, two years on the shop floor, and I had a great following. It was wonderful. I was cocky, I had all the badges on the shorts and I could do no wrong. Anyway, I was about 17. Paul Harris was tipped to beat me. He was a swinging puncher. All my mates came down. I've got the tape of the fight here." We watched the video together and young Harris' cockiness made me smile. Bob pointed out that those were the days before head-guards and, as the fight went on, Bob bobbed and weaved with the punches as he sat on the sofa beside me. Bob won the fight in the second round, and the young man with the badges on his shorts leapt up and down ecstatically on the screen before us.

"Around this time I won our 'Boxer of the Year' for Bushey, and what John Scott did was take us to America. He took me and Dave Fallon, who went on to box as a professional, and it wasn't a holiday; it was a tour around all the gymnasiums. We went to Manhattan, New Jersey, The Bronx, and Joe Frazier's gym in Philadelphia. We met Joe. He told me off! I was a cocky kid, and John never used to like us wearing head-guards because they land you into a false sense of security. You can't slip a shot and they fall over your eyes, and it's just no good. I was sparring with this big, big pro, who was a welterweight, which was big for me, and all of a sudden Joe Frazier's voice came booming out, 'Hey, the kid gotta wear a head-guard.' I wasn't having none of it, so down came Joe Frazier; Stetson, cowboy boots, and he told me off. I wore a head-guard then!

"I went to Gleason's, sparred with a very famous fighter called Saoul Mamby. I had a move around with him. We went to Trenton, New Jersey. What a shit-hole. As we were driving in, all the cars were burnt out by the side of the road and the taxi driver said, 'Where're you going? Don't go there! You'll get shot. You'll get raped. You'll get murdered.' We walked in the gym and I was the only white kid there, and that was your apprenticeship. It was a fantastic time. That's what got me good enough to be a pro.

"I went to Germany many times with the Home Counties Squad. I boxed 11 Germans and beat ten of them; lost against the last one. I had three fights in four days and had three first round knockouts, and I was on the front page of the local paper. I wasn't a puncher. I just threw my punches correctly. We used to wear horsehair gloves when we was in Germany, and you had to hit them before they hit you because there was no padding in the old horsehair gloves. And I'll tell you, what a great laugh. You're 17, you're away, you get spending money. Danny Porter took all me money off me at cards, the bugger! We spent a lot of time in Bavaria; beautiful countryside.

"I had about 75 amateur fights altogether, with about 50 wins. I boxed the top three Norwegians, and I beat their number two and three when they come over. Per Carlenius, he was a top boy from Norway and I wobbled him with a left hook, right in the last round. He got the decision. And then I boxed the number two and number three Norwegians, and I beat them both." For the record, the Norwegians who Bob is talking about were Harald Torgersen and Kjell Fossen, and Bob beat them both on points.

"The whole thing, the whole team factor, you don't get that in the pros. The pros is a lonely game, I don't care what you say. You're looking at money and, with all due respect, it was 17 years ago today since my pro debut and I thought I'd be British Champion. If you'd asked me 17 years ago when I signed up with Frank Maloney, I'd have said, 'I'll have everything. I'll be in a book. I'll do TV interviews. Film contract.' And you should have seen my first fight. And it went downhill from there!

"The majority of my boxing relied purely on skill. But you also needed that inner-strength, man-strength, and I didn't have it until I reached the age of about 26. Maybe I should have held off from turning professional for a couple more years. My last amateur fight was Anthony Carolan of Hitchin Boxing Club." This was on the 15th February 1986. "It was for the Home Counties Championship and I got beat. A coach load came down and I got knocked down in the first round badly. I can't remember the next two rounds, but everyone said I walked it. That grates on me a bit still, bad decisions, but you get 'em, and I'll tell you, it does make you stronger.

"Recently, at the Junior ABAs, I was talking to this kid. He'd just been stopped and he was in tears. I said to him, 'Listen son, in about five or ten years time, when you are professional, you might be boxing for the European Title, and you'll look back at today and you'll laugh.' The kid smiled, and I said, 'No, I'm not a silly old bastard. I've *done* it.'

"I was one of Frank Maloney's first fighters. I was a bit sick of the amateur decisions and I said to John Scott, 'I'm going to go over now.' He said, 'Well, I'll arrange a meet. There's a new guy called Frank Maloney just started up.' So Frank came round. He was sat on my sofa and he had the gift of the gab; and generally a nice guy. Wanted to make a few quid, like everyone. He sat down and talked to my mum and dad about a professional career. In hindsight, which is a wonderful thing, I could have probably waited another two years, got my England vest, which was near but not quite."

I asked, "So where did the 'B.F.' come from?" Bob grinned, "Well I used to say it stood for 'Bloody Fast', but it didn't! There was another professional called Bobby Williams from Southampton. He was black as the ace of spades and he was a light-middleweight, but they said Bob Williams was too much like Bobby Williams. We had the 'F' because my middle name is Frank."

Bob made his professional debut on the 28th May 1986 against Ken Watson at Lewisham. Bob won by stoppage in the fifth round. He showed me a photo and I could not believe his curly perm, bushy on the top and long down the back, straight out of the '80s. "Look at that hair!" He laughed raucously. "They all come across from the pub one day. Someone walked past the hairdressers and saw me with the curlers in. It was my local pub, The Tudor Arms. Cor, I got some stick over that. I had a good following from there.

"I felt a bit apprehensive going in as a pro for the first time, but Ken, I think, had had about 20 or 30 bouts. He was a journeyman, but he was no fall-over. I was still a skinny kid of 21. I was working for Rolls-Royce and a big coach load came down. It was great. I fought Watson and he was, like, a fully matured strong man. I'm in the first round, and I'm messing around and listening to the crowd and boom! I get knocked down. It wasn't because I was chinny. I just wasn't focused, and I did get caught a few times. I can't remember what round it was; it was either the first or second, and I broke my hand a round after. So after two rounds of professional boxing, I've hit the canvas and I've broke my bloody hand! I'd sold about £800 worth of tickets, which wasn't bad. But the hair used to bounce about so it looked like I got caught, but I was missing a lot of the shots." As we watched the tape, a left hook to the chin put Bob down in the first round. "But look, I stayed down, I know where I am. I'm thinking, 'Fucking hell, this wasn't meant to happen.' But I don't give up. That's one thing I never did. I never gave up. Don't ever give up. Be positive. Always be positive. And again, that was experience."

In Bob's next fight, in October 1986, it was he that was halted by Andrew Prescod at Lewisham. "Strong, strong black boy. Andy Prescod was a different kettle of fish. Which round did he stop me?" I confirmed that it was the fourth. "Well, I'm surprised it lasted that long. He was such a strong guy. He was a full welterweight. It was only my boxing ability that kept me in there that long." We put the tape of the fight in the video-player. "Look at the arms and shoulders on him. Didn't have a lot of skill, Prescod, but *Christ* he could dig. I've got a pair of football shorts on there. Don't know why. They make me look even bloody thinner, don't they?

"I mean, here I am thinking about TV interviews and everything, and I fucking go down like a sack of shit! My mates are big piss takers and I love it. I wouldn't have it any other way. I'd had a few knockdowns in my amateur career, and then what happens? They start running a fucking sweep at Rolls-Royce, what round I'd get knocked down in!" The bell rang to end the fourth round as referee, Larry O'Connell, waved the fight off. Larry is a good friend of mine, and I jokingly told Bob that the next time I saw him I was going to tell him off for not stopping the fight earlier. "You know what he'll say, don't you? He'll say, 'B.F. Who?'"

Bob's next fight was in January 1987 and he lost on points on against Jess Rundan in Plymouth. "I went down to Plymouth and a car load of my mates drove all the way down there, and they got so drunk that they couldn't drive back. So I ended up driving them all the way back from Plymouth with about a hundred and eighty quid I'd earned, and I'm thinking, 'Hang on a minute! Where's the TV cameras?' I'll never forget it. I had the hump anyway; bruised hands again and I was, like, 'Thanks guys?' But that is the reality of it and Joe public don't see that. But, that's life. I wouldn't have done it if I hadn't had the support that I did. I swear, I never lost a round against Jess Rundan, and I had people writing me letters about it. But he was the house fighter, and you knock him out and you get a draw. I think I lost the fight by half a point. At the end, both his eyes were shut and there's me, like, still as ugly as ever, but it was diabolical! I *paid* him with my jab.

"I tried to get a return with him years later at Watford Town Hall. But that sort of set the trend, you know. I got a tough introduction to the pro game. Knocked down in me first fight, broke my hand; got stopped in my second fight and in my third fight I got robbed. I thought, 'Where am I going from here?'" I asked Bob what gave him the drive to carry on. He pondered for a few seconds, and then, "I knew I had the ability to win a championship. I *knew* I was good enough." Then came a wistful silence.

Bob was back in the ring three weeks later and he knocked out Dave Nash in three rounds at the London West Hotel in Fulham. It was the Lymington boxer's professional debut. "We were sponsored by the local brewery called Benskins, and they got me all my gear. I knew one of the managers and he said, 'Just go out to Lonsdale. Get all you want.' It was great, yeah. This was more like the sort of bout I needed at the start of my pro career, not men like Andy Prescod, to be honest. I think I knocked him down a couple of times. I remember once I knocked him down. We both ended up on the canvas and he was on top of me, and I remember thinking, 'I thought *I* hit *him*!' He was sparko on top of me, and I've sort of got away from him and he sort of got back up, but it was really weird. I don't know whether he boxed after this fight." Nash went on to have two more fights that year, both of which he lost inside the distance. After that, he retired. "I was really throwing my punches correctly. I think I caught him with a textbook left hook and he went down, and Larry O'Connell stopped it. We can all look good when we're on top. I had Frank Maloney and Johnny Winter in my corner.

"He's a nice guy, Johnny Winter. He's a scouser. We had such characters in the gym. We had a guy called Tim O'Keefe, and Tim was a drinker and a smoker and a party animal. Frank Maloney said that Johnny Winter refused to train anyone who could drink or smoke more than him. It was hilarious."

The following month B.F. was back in action, this time against Les Remikie at York Hall. "I won a points decision, and it was probably one of the few fights when *I* hadn't gone down, or *they* hadn't gone down or something silly hadn't happened." Bob lost on points over six rounds to John Mullen a month later. "Oh fucking hell! I'll tell you what. He hit me in the first round and I don't really remember much of the fight after that. He really hurt me, but I got up and held on for six rounds. He was a late substitute. He come from Scotland, Glasgow way, and I remember someone saying, 'Your opponent's just got out of the taxi,' and he had his hands taped up ready. He never got on the scales. I don't know what weight he was; 11 stone maybe. It was at Lewisham Theatre. I got knocked down so many times at Lewisham Theatre." He put the video in the machine and Mullen indeed looked very big. I had to ask Bob if he felt like running back to the dressing room when he looked across the ring and saw the size of Mullen, standing there. "Yeah, but you've sold a lot of tickets. You want to fight. My defence was good. I was a good counter-puncher. It's just that I got caught now and again." He laughed.

"The pro game's hard." On the screen, a right cross caught Bob and he went down. He got up and he sort of skimmed back down on the canvas again, on his knees. "And you wonder why they called me 'Canvas Arse!' My mate won 50 quid on the sweep at work! And the rest is history. Another fight when I hit the deck, but I got up."

Six weeks later Bob was back in the ring to win a six round points decision against Paul Kennedy, and it was five months later before he boxed again. In September 1987 he went to Swindon to mix it with blond, tattooed Mike Russell. Both of them had shaggy perms, a far cry from today when so many fighters shave their heads. "Oh, the Plymouth Gunboat! That was murder again. Eight-twos. Top of the bill. Lovely jubbly. He lost a lot more than he won, Mike Russell, but he was *strong*! He used to bring his punches up, very much like Prescod, and he caught me with his head. Johnny Winter had this iron. You keep it in the ice and you smooth the swelling away, and that hurt more than Mike Russell's punches! But it kept the eye open. The last round I'm out on my feet and my eye's shut, mainly due to the iron, and I won a half point decision. I was in the toilet afterwards having a pee, and the referee come up to me and he said, 'All right, son?' I said, 'Yeah, thanks ref.' And he said, 'I had to give it to you.' Like, he *had* to give it to me, and I won the fight *easy* really. He knocked me down in the last. He went bosh, and I'm down there again! I went down to Swindon, which was his neck of the woods. That eye was shut for about three weeks after that fight, and he messed up my perm. Fucking hell! Sod this! What a way to make a living. It was tough. And all my mates got pissed again and I had to drive them home from Swindon."

After a points win in November 1987 against Ian Hosten at Wandsworth, Bob drew with Chubby Martin the following month over eight rounds at the Borough Hall in Greenwich. "They bought in bookmakers to take bets at the show. It was a very, very close fight. I was the house fighter and I thought I might have nicked it; I don't know."

Bob kicked off 1988 with a February points win over eight rounds against Neil Haddock at York Hall. "Yeah, he was a good boy. It was a good fight. I was coming into my own strength really. It was one of my last fights when I was still at Rolls-Royce." Bob started the video tape rolling. "It was on the under-card of Tim Witherspoon versus Mauricio Villegas. I boxed well behind my jab. Neil Haddock was a journeyman. Strong boy. He went on to win the British Super-Featherweight Title. It was a comfortable points win, but just being on the under-card at York Hall was nice. Without a doubt, York Hall was my favourite place to box. Mind you, saying that, crowd-wise Watford Town Hall was something else. Because it was built for music, the sound of the crowd used to echo round there when we sold it out, but I went down a few too many times at Watford Town Hall. I won all my fights at York Hall, but I didn't always get the rub of the green at Watford Town Hall." As the tape came to an end, Bob pointed out that the perm was on its way out, the curls remaining on the top only.

In September 1988 Bob was stopped in the seventh round by Cardiff's Tony Borg at Edmonton. Bob played the tape for me. Borg was the first one to hit the canvas. Bob caught him with a perfect left hand counter-punch in the first round. In the seventh Bob was floored by a right hand. As he went down he tried to hold onto Borg's legs to stay up, but it was not to be. Borg shook him off and Bob stayed down for the count of nine. Bob got back up, brave, bleeding and ready for a fight, but Borg came piling back in and referee, Jack Snipe, jumped in to stop the fight. As we watched the last few seconds of the fight, the commentator declared, *"He's caught. He's going. Down he goes. That's the beginning of the end for B.F. Williams."* Bob snorted in disgust. "Beginning of the end. Cheeky bastard! I had about another 20 fights after that! I was winning the fight, but after seven rounds I went down like a sack of shit and he sliced me. I had to have four stitches and they didn't even take the gloves off. I remember the doctor came in and just sort of grabbed hold of me, laid me on the chair and stitched me up, and that was it.

"I'd just joined the fire service. When I was at Rolls-Royce, all I used to do was walk around talking about boxing, and someone said, 'Why don't you join the fire service? You get lots of time off to train.' They kept pushing this advert for the fire service at me, so I went along and had a go. Got the interview. Did all the tests. After my 16 weeks training, I joined Watford Fire Station. I joined Green Watch, Watford. I had a good following there. Got lots of stick. It was good, but the nature of the fire service is that there's always a lot of stick flying around, and I got a *lot* of stick. I used to get called 'Brain Damage' and 'Rembrandt', because I was on the canvas so many times. But I loved it. It was good fun. It was good natured, and I had plenty of time to train as well. So the Tony Borg fight was the firemen's introduction to my professional career, and I was on me arse again! Tony Borg was a very good boy. He's involved in an amateur club down in Wales now." As Bob ejected the video from the machine, I pointed out that the curly perm was no more. "I'd joined the fire service. You weren't allowed to have none of that there, girl! And then I went back on duty with my stitches."

At this point Shlo and Dean entered the house. Dean toddled over to us and Bob said "Box, box", which made Dean automatically bang his hands together. Bob said, "Show us your jab," and he did. Bob said, "One day …", and Shlo smoothly countered, "One day he's going to be a pop star!" Shlo offered me some lunch, which I gratefully accepted and, as she headed for the kitchen, I asked her if she was into boxing. "Yeah. I wasn't exposed to boxing before I met Bob. Yeah, I'm all right with that, a good fight." Bob chipped in, "She *loves* a fight."

Bob continued with his story and we had now reached November 1988 on his record. "Then I lost a points decision to Jim Lawler in Birmingham. I used to do a lot of training up the 'Beckett in them days. I was up there about five days a week. I had decided to go my own way. I worked with several other promoters and I managed myself. I'm sure Lawler dropped me in the first round and I lost a half point decision. Again, I was boxing a local boy in a local town, losing a half point decision. Hey, that's professional boxing."

Bob began 1989 with a bang when he knocked out Danny Ellis in six rounds on the 31st January at York Hall. "Again, I'm boxing a West Ham boy at York Hall. I'm working with Jimmy Evans now and I've come back to train at my local amateur club. I was really sharp. I think I got about £300, which wasn't bad money in those days. And they said, 'Right, we'll have a £25 weight forfeit if you don't make the weight.' I was about half a pound over so I went in the sauna, which boxers should never do. But I just had a little sweat and a shower, and I'll tell you what, I felt like a million dollars and a different fighter came out that night. I was really sharp, really focused and I really did a job on Danny Ellis. Poor lad had only had a few fights." From the coffee table, Bob could even produce the weight forfeit card from that fight. "Here you are, £275 I got paid for that."

As Bob played the tape of the fight, his individual fashion sense was once more highly evident. This time he was wearing cycle shorts under his boxing shorts, and I asked him why. "I don't know, to be honest. I was just trying to do something different. It was a good fight. I'm getting a bit stronger now, because I'm doing a more manual job. But there's a hell of a lot more ups and downs to come, unfortunately. There's a hell of a lot more rolling around on the canvas to do, I'll tell you. But, being self-managed, it was nice because I could choose my own fights, and I could always go to Jim Evans or John Scott for advice. Jim's as honest as the day is long. I used to box amateur with Jim and his boy Justin, who was a good fighter, a good southpaw."

In March 1989 Bob won a six round points decision against Paul Charters at York Hall. The crowd booed the decision and Bob was philosophical about it. "He went on to be a European Title contender. I nicked the fight by half a point, and I didn't get knocked on my arse in this one. I'm starting to knock a few people on their arses now."

A month later, the pendulum swung the other way and Bob was stopped in six by Seamus O'Sullivan at Battersea. Five months later, in September 1989, Bob was back on the winning side, with a points decision over six rounds against Tony Gibbs of Barking. This fight was the show opener at High Wycombe Town Hall. "He was quite a flashy boy, tassels on his shorts. This is a good fight. I'm buzzing now. I won the points decision and I'm starting to punch a bit harder. I thought I won it on my jab, and the bandwagon rolls on." I asked him what sort of reaction he received at the fire station when he won a fight. "They still gave me stick. Bastards! But it was natural. I mean, the fire fighters followed me, but it was more or less the local crowd, the ones who had been there from the start who were still coming to see me, from my local pub and from Rolls-Royce. Still had the nicknames; 'Canvas Arse', 'One Rounder', 'Brain Damage.'"

Richard Joyce was undefeated in six fights and he was being brought along nicely until, on the 25th October 1989, B.F. Williams came along and spoilt his perfect record. Bob stopped the Burton southpaw in four rounds. The fight was the main event at a European Sporting Club show in Stoke. His fashion sense as individual as ever, Bob marched to the ring adorned in running shorts with a pair of cycle shorts underneath. "So I'm going up to Stoke. I'm self-managed. I knew he was a counter-puncher and he was a southpaw. I didn't mind boxing southpaws. No problem, just lead with a right hand. I knew I weren't going up there to win; you just know, you know? But, I don't give up.

"We drove up to Stoke. There was me, John Scott and my mate, 'Squid', who was the best man at my wedding. Good guy. Big boxing fan. His real name is Wayne. We were apprentices at Rolls-Royce together and he followed me everywhere, from my first fight to my last fight. What a piss taker. He always used to win the sweepstake for me getting knocked down. I remember John Coyle refereed it and, after about four rounds, he called us together in the middle of the ring before the start of the round and he said, 'I want to see more action, especially from you, Williams.' Because I weren't giving him the lead. I wouldn't throw a shot at him, and I don't know if it was because of his inexperience but he tore right into me, and I hit him with some peachy shots, right hand, left hook, and he went down. He got up and I caught him again and he went down again, and I remember the referee helping him up. Helping him *up*! Obviously, he's a ticket seller and he's on his own show. He went down again and they stopped it, and I was so chuffed. I don't know how many contests he had after me but he was a champion in the making, and it was about time that *I* knocked someone on *their* arse. Who's next?"

Next was a second round stoppage of Steve Taggart at Brentford in December 1989. As we watched the tapes, I was starting to notice that Bob was looking more mature with every fight, and this time he was sartorially elegant in a pair of knee-length rainbow coloured shorts. "This was on Jimmy Evans' show. I worked with Jimmy Evans, Billy Ball, and

Dave Davies, who was the house second, and he was always telling jokes in the corner at York Hall. We all did little bits and pieces. I think Taggart went down twice and the referee stopped it. I *loved* those shorts."

The good times rolled on and in January 1990 Bob won a points decision against former amateur international, Pembroke's Mike Morrison, at the Star Leisure Centre in Splott. "Frank Turner phoned me, who was a matchmaker for Barry Hearn. He said, 'B.F., I've got a job for you. Nice little easy number. Mike Morrison.' Mike Morrison was as tough as nails. They were definitely doing a job on me, boost him up a bit down in Wales. It was something like 500 quid I was being paid for six two-minute rounds, which was good money then. I said, 'Okay Frank, no problem. I've got to take a day off work, which will cost you another 25 quid.' He was a strong boy and I did win every round clearly. Outrageous shorts as well." He was wearing the rainbow ones. "Well I knew it was going to be on Eurosport, so I went down, got my hair cut.

"Anyway, I got in the ring and they announced it was a contest over six-*three* minute rounds! I'm like 'Hold on, hold on.' This was on Eurosport." We watched the tape and listened to Jim McDonnell commentating, *"I don't know what the problem is? He must be not happy with something."* "The problem was that I weren't being paid enough to box six-threes, and I went storming off, started arguing with them. 'No, I'm not having that,' and I started getting out of the ring. I was my own bloody manager. They tried to have me over. They had already done the programme for six-threes! Dave Davies [Board of Control] was on the scene then. He started to help me. I wouldn't have minded if they'd said, 'We'll give you £1,000.' I walked the fight on my jab and he hits me with a shot in the last round, and he must have caught my diaphragm or something because I said, 'John, I've got to get out of the ring because I'm going to collapse.' I didn't want to collapse in the ring in front of the TV cameras. I've got in the changing room and I've just gone down. I can't breath. I was in agony. A big black mark come out a couple of days after. I'll never forget it. When I was getting out of the ring it was like I'd been stabbed. He was a big strong boy, Mike Morrison. Didn't get many decisions, but he was tough. I *like* them shorts."

The following month Bob boxed Michael Driscoll at the Latchmere Leisure Centre in Battersea. Bob was stopped in the second round and it was a messy ending to a tough fight. Bob was sort of half punched and half pushed through the ropes and he fell right out of the ring, taking a turbulent tumble backwards. Under a rule that had just been instated by the Board of Control, the referee was supposed to count to 20 if a boxer fell out of the ring completely. Bob managed to climb back up onto the ring apron but referee, Roy Francis, called it off, having only counted to ten. "I sparred with Mickey Driscoll at the Thomas A' Beckett and dropped him, but that was a bad decision by myself to box him. He was a tough guy from Portsmouth. I hit him with some shots and I broke both my hands in the first round. I fancied the job because I did okay sparring with him. He took Ross Hale to 'Fight of the Year' once. Tough man. Nice guy. Don't know what's happened to him now. Roy Francis got it wrong because you were allowed 20 seconds to get back into the ring. They'd brought a new rule in and Roy counted me out after ten, but I wasn't that bothered. I tried to get back in, but I'd broke both me hands and I think I'd already been down once. I did have trouble with my hands, but it's every fighter's problem. He was relentless, Driscoll, a real pressure fighter. Fair play, he done a job on me. To be honest, I probably wouldn't have gone another round. I reckon Roy Francis did me a right favour there!"

It was eight months before Bob had another fight. In October 1990 he lost a points decision to Southampton's Danny Cooper at Battersea. "He's back in professional boxing now. He had 14 years out and he's back. I see him now and again. He's very, very fit Danny and he's boxing out of Southampton. He sells a lot of tickets. And I'll tell you what, he could well get there." For the record, Danny Cooper had his last fight in October 2003, five months after this interview.

Self-managed boxers often take fights that are heavily loaded in favour of the other corner. The price of managerial freedom is the lack of managerial protection. Three weeks after his last fight, Bob was back on the move, this time to Sheffield to box the hometown boxer, Nigel Bradley, at the City Hall. Bob was knocked unconscious in the second round. "Pretty uneventful. I had some time off. My station manager said, 'Come back when you've had your fight, Bob.' And I think I earned quite good money, about 500 quid for that fight. I had a pretty decent first round. I held my own, and Bradley just came out and took it out on me basically, and knocked me spark out. My mum never saw this video because she'd have had a heart attack. I hit the canvas and I lay there. I was out, sparko." Bob slipped the video in the machine and at the same time, he called out to Shlo, "Do you want to see this, babe?" Shlo replied, "Yes, okay," but she didn't sound too sure. Bob asked her, "Why, does it upset you?" Shlo gestured to little Dean and declared gently but adamantly, "He will never box." Bob pressed <play> and the room filled with the sound of the crowd chanting Nigel Bradley's name.

"I drove up to Sheffield with my trainer, Johnny Scott, and I drove halfway back because John was really tired. Then I went into work that nightshift at about four o'clock in the morning with about 500 quid in my back pocket and they all went, 'How did you get on?' I said, 'I got knocked spark out,' and someone called me a tosser. I went to bed and I woke up with a sore chin the next day." Bob, Shlo and I watched the knockout. It happened so fast. I asked if that was a left hook that did the damage. "I dunno, but I landed on me head. Good shot." Bob was unconscious before he hit the floor. "Now, I get up and I'm thinking the referee stopped it early, and he could have counted to 99! I'm out like a light. Look at me. I'm arguing that I want to carry on. What a sucker. Again, I went to Sheffield, fighting him in his back yard. Some fighters, that would have finished their careers. The next fight, I got bashed as well, and then I took a break."

The man who "bashed" Bob the next time out was Ricky Bushell, who fought out of Herne Bay. They fought in February 1991 and Bob was stopped in two rounds. To add insult to injury, this was Bob's first fight in his hometown of Watford. "Yeah and I had some *terrible* defeats in Watford, which *everybody* remembers! Ricky Bushell did me. That hurt. It forced me to have a bit of a layoff afterwards. Ricky Bushell was a good fight for me after that knockout defeat. I had all the press cuttings and I sold loads of tickets. He come out in the second round and he caught me with shots, put me over, and that was it. I'll always remember it was my first fight at Watford Town Hall, and it was snowing that night.

It was a bloody nightmare. He did a proper job on me. So I took a year out, but I felt almost immediately that I would be back. But only when I was right, because mentally and physically it does take it out of you.

"The thing is, it's impossible to burn the candle at both ends in the fight game. I was always in training. Even after I boxed, I was in the gym a few days later. I never had two or three weeks out, but what I used to do was, when I was fit and running and everything, I did used to have a drink and go out regular. But I was burning it up through training, because I was always on the road. Then, two weeks before a fight, that was it. I would knock everything on the head and just focus on that six rounds or that eight rounds.

"So anyway, I had a wonderful year of partying. Oh yeah, I partied hard, but I was always planning on making a comeback. You'll see now that in all my next fights I tucked my chin into my shoulder, like Mark Kaylor did. I just knew that I couldn't go on like that. I took a pasting against Bradley, and then what hurt was I took a hiding from Bushell in front of my own fans. They don't forget that and that really fuckin' hurts."

My heart went out to this brave and sensitive man, and I asked if people were kind to him afterwards. "They were immediately afterwards. Anyway, I used to see Steve Holdsworth on a regular basis and it was time to come back, so we decided to become Firefighter Promotions. We only did four or five shows at Watford, but with Steve's help I positioned myself into a title shot. I couldn't have done it without Steve. I owe him a lot and I owe John Scott a lot. So I had four or five more fights, good wins against solid opponents."

Before Bob had those comeback fights he made a ring appearance that will never appear on his record. "Yeah, it was a hell of a party during that time, but I stayed on the road and I'd been back in the gym a few weeks and things were just taking shape for my return. Billy Schwer had won an ABA National Title and he had just turned over. He was to top the bill at Watford Town Hall, my bloody town, and he's from Luton! It was a Mickey Duff promotion. I knew Billy and his father well from the Amateurs, although he was younger than me. He was a good, classy boxer as an amateur, there's no doubt about that. Anyway, I had finished my gym session and decided to go straight up the Town Hall to watch the show. I sat down to watch the fights, and I'd only been there for ten minutes when Steve Holdsworth came up to me and said, 'Hello Bob. Do you want to earn yourself £1,000?' I immediately thought that what he had in mind was illegal!

"What had happened was that Billy's proposed opponent had arrived at the venue and failed his pre-fight medical from the doctor. Billy had a great following and he'd sold out the Town Hall, so they needed to get someone to fight him. I must be honest. The money was nice and I could have probably held out and got another £500 out of Mickey Duff and taken the fight, but Billy was a good boy and I was just back in training for my comeback, which was more important to me. This was about *my* career, no one else's, and if Billy had stopped me, that would have put the final nail in the career coffin. Anyway, I said, 'No' to Steve almost immediately and Steve never really pushed the case, as he knew how serious I was about *my* career. He said, 'Okay then, how about an exhibition bout of three rounds for £100?' Come to think about it, I could have held out for £150! I said, 'Yes' and we moved around for three rounds, threw a few shots at each other and I actually never visited Mr Canvas once. £100, thanks very much. Can you imagine if I had taken the fight and beat him? I was heavier and much more experienced as a pro. But, to be honest, I just couldn't risk another loss at this stage and don't think for a minute that Mickey Duff or, in fact, Billy, would have taken it easy because I was on home turf. As my record proves, I went on to string a nice few wins together and actually stay off my canvas arse for the best part of two years. So, if anybody ever asks the question, 'Who was the first boxer to share a professional boxing ring with Billy Schwer?' it was me. And Billy? He only went on to win titles at British, Commonwealth and World level.

"My comeback was against Cliff Churchward." This was the 12th February 1992 and Churchward came from Bournemouth. "Steve Holdsworth was the unofficial matchmaker and we had some great shows all around Watford. This was like my second career. It was basically shit or bust. I beat Cliff over six rounds and I never lost a round. He was a big guy, but I wasn't bothered. I knew if I got on my boxing I'd hold it together." After another six round points win in April 1992 against Erwin Edwards at a Southend nightclub, Bob scored another six round points win against Scunthorpe southpaw, Trevor Meikle, three weeks later at Watford. "Trevor Meikle was a journeyman, but he was a tough boy. I said in the local paper that, if he'd had a glove on his head, he would have beat me on points. My God, I got caught so many times with the head. Good class boy. No problem. Who was next?"

Next came James Campbell on the 17th September 1992. It was another fight in Watford and another six round points win for Bob. "A Nobby Nobbs fighter, but a Nobby Nobbs fighter who had just come off a first round win. He was a strong bloke, Campbell. What happened in this fight, I remember someone turned the lights out half way through. I think it was probably Nobby, and you can tell him I said that! I boxed really well. I was really coming into my own. I was putting my shots together, tucking my shoulder in, sitting on my shots. Dave Davies took the forefront there. He helped me a lot. John Scott was still there for the skill, and Dave took me on floor exercises and weights. I was just maturing at the right time and I was winning back in Watford. No one in Watford remembers these fights. They only remember when I got knocked on my arse, which does hurt a little bit.

"The publicity was second to none. Me and Steve were promoting. I was like a different fighter. I knew that, if I was going to come back, I'd have to come back like this, because I couldn't come back as a skinny kid rolling around on the canvas. That's how it ended up, but most careers end up like that. I had great support.

"Again, I was partying. My local pub then was the Fishery Inn in Elstree." Bob slotted the tape into the machine and it has to be said that the shorts had become a lot more conservative now. I pointed out, "They're a sort of claret colour with a very discreet gold stripe. Classy shorts!" Bob was quick to respond, "Not *my* claret! I was selling thousands of pounds worth of tickets in Watford. Campbell was similar to Nigel Bradley, strong as a lion. I used to be led into the ring by the fire crew, and the paramedics used to carry me out! That was the standing joke. I've not hit the canvas for two years now, but that's what happens with confidence. Fighters have an unbeaten run and it does help. There's nothing like experience, but experience includes losing. You don't pack in because you lose a fight. You don't give in. You *never* give in."

On the 17th April 1993 Bob fought abroad for the only time as a professional. He lost an eight round points decision to Jean Chiarelli in Gaillard, France. "This was a money earning fight. I think we was offered about £1,200 or something. I'd never boxed abroad as a professional and this was an opportunity. Met him at the weigh-in, which was at a pub. I'm sure we had the weigh-in in Switzerland. I think the WBO, who had just come in then, had him rated as number ten. We was down for six-threes. He was a little guy, strong as an ox. I had bad hands and I put foam under one of my bandages, and they didn't care. Then they wanted eight-threes and I thought, 'Fucking hell, here we go. I'm gonna have another argument here. I'm not boxing eight-threes.' But I was building up for a title fight and I thought I'd get the experience. They said, 'Do eight-threes. He won't try and kill you. It'll go the distance and we'll give you another 250 quid.' That's what they say in the pro game, 'He won't hurt you,' but I got on my bike anyway.

"On my way down to the ring, I held my hands up and I start shaking hands with everybody. Dave Davies was pulling his hair out, but they all got behind me, all shaking my hand and everything. I got in there and I was waving to the crowd because I thought, 'I've got nothing to lose.' Then they gloved us up in the ring. Anyway, I got behind my jab. I nicked him in a couple of places, cut him, and eight-threes is, like, forever. I kept moving, and every now and again I'd run behind the referee to hide, messing around. I chased after the ring card girl in between rounds and the crowd were whooping it up. And I lost. I don't even know what the points were. I don't even know if I won a round, but I boxed well. We stayed out there three or four days after that, and they took us out to dinner in this restaurant overlooking the Swiss Alps and we got introduced to the chef. Dave Davies ate a basket of bread before we'd had our food and we just had a great time. The money was good and it ain't no good boxing for nothing. You've just got to weigh up the pros and cons. We had our flight tickets paid for, everything in, and I was like a superstar out there. It was wonderful."

Nine weeks later Bob stopped Michael Dick in three rounds. "Yeah, Mickey Dick from Aylesbury. Nice guy. Didn't realize he cut so easily until I hit him. I boxed him twice. The first one was at Watford Leisure Centre promoted by Steve Holdsworth and myself. We were top of the bill. Eight-twos I think. I stopped him at the end of the third. Great night at the Leisure Centre. Michael Dick was strong but, again, you'll see me tucking my chin behind my shoulder. I sliced his eye open. I don't think Michael Dick won a professional fight."

In October 1993 Bob boxed Michael Dick again. This time Bob stopped him in 52 seconds after inflicting a nasty cut on the Aylesbury man's left eyebrow. For the record this was Michael Dick's last professional fight. Incidentally, Michael Dick was not the original opponent in Bob's sights for that night. "There was another fighter in Watford who was coming up at the time called Ojay Abrahams. Now I'm all right, I'm pretty laid-back. I'm not up my own arse. I'm confident, but I like to think that I'm not too arrogant, because there's a fine line between confidence and arrogance. People who haven't got confidence will call a confident guy 'arrogant.' There's a lot of people like that in boxing, and there's a lot of people like that out of boxing. A lot of the mugs out there, they'll stab a boxer in the back, call him punchy, nasty little bits and pieces, but they won't say it to your face because they're scared you'll bang them out. I've had to bite my tongue a few times. Ojay Abrahams was on the scene then and we didn't get on. We *really* didn't get on. He would badmouth me and I don't like that. I show respect to everyone. But *now*, I've got a lot of respect for Ojay. He's been in with some of the world's best. These days, we're always amicable to each other when we see each other, because normally I've got a shirt and tie on for the Board of Control and he's got his boxing shorts on.

"Anyway, basically we've promoted another show in Watford Leisure Centre and I'm going to box Ojay, and he pulled out with a bad hand, so they've got me Michael Dick again. Banged him out, no problem. After we booked the venue the date sounded familiar, and what have they got on? The England versus Holland world cup qualifier on that same bloody day! Steve had booked the fights and financially we were going to lose out big time. So we booked a big screen to show the game, and that's even better because now we've got the football fans paying to come in, we've got my fans paying to come in and it was a sell out. It went really well.

"However, we couldn't afford to pay all the fighters and book the video screen. So what we did, Steve knows Brendan Ingle very well and Brendan had a novice called Naseem Hamed, so he boxed on the under-card for 50 quid. Everyone knew that Naz was going to make it. He was a good strong boy. I was telling everyone to watch this boy who was boxing an exhibition before me in leopard skin shorts because he's going to be really good. Half my mates didn't know what they were watching because they were so drunk. It was such a buzz. We used to come out to Queen, *'We Will Rock You.'* It was fantastic. I was wearing a 'Where's Ojay?' tee-shirt and I could have got knocked on my arse. I would have *never* lived that down! I was out on duty the night before, out on fire calls and all sorts."

In December 1993 Bob was boxing back at Watford Town Hall. In the other corner was Herne Bay journeyman, David Lake. Bob, resplendent in a turquoise satin jacket, had a look of strong self-belief about him now. Lake, whose balding head made him look much older than his 29 years, caught Bob with a big right hand punch and knocked him down at the end of the first round. Referee, Kenny Curtis, counted to seven and Bob was back on his feet, complete with a sliced right eyebrow. The end came in the fourth round when Bob let loose with a bunch of six punches and put Lake down on one knee. He stayed down for the count of eight and, when he got up, he tried bravely to get back into the fight, but referee Curtis rescued him before he got badly hurt. "David Lake is with the amateurs now. I met him on Saturday and it had taken him 11 hours to get from Herne Bay to Bridlington because his car broke down. He had a boy in the finals. Nice guy. He's doing well for himself. I knew, if I could do well against him, I would get the fight for the Southern Area Title, and that's what I wanted. I boxed well but he knocked me right on my arse in the first round. Got back on my boxing and I hurt him at the end of the first round. I won't give up. Brilliant night, and what a party we had afterwards. We all went back to my house. I lived about five minutes from the Town Hall and it was brilliant."

And finally, on the 10th March 1994, B.F. Williams had his final fight in the ring. It was indeed fitting that this proud and brave man's last appearance in the ring should be for a title. It was the Southern Area Title, it was at Watford, and the man in the other corner was Jon Thaxton. Jonathan Thaxton was from Norwich and fought out of Brendan Ingle's Sheffield gym. This former kickboxing Champion was previously undefeated in five fights under the Marquis of Queensbury rules. Bob was by now 28 years old. Thaxton was 19 and he was dominant and confident, having stopped Dean Hollington in three rounds in his previous bout, a result few had foretold. "We discussed it. Steve felt he could get belts for me. The thing was, Thaxton had beaten a guy called Dean Hollington. Hollington was a brilliant boy. He works as an area rep now. What a fighter. Dean Hollington would have torn me apart, to be honest. He was much too strong for me, but I fancied Thaxton. Thaxton scored what was a shock win over Dean Hollington, so it was me and Thaxton for the Southern Area Title, which was vacant at the time. I had pictures of Thaxton stuck up on the wall for three months while I was training for the fight. Like I said, in the past I had enjoyed life a bit when I was boxing, but when it came to the Thaxton fight I did three solid months of training. I still remember the date of the fight; 10th March1994. Because that was the time I was gonna win and I was going to get my belt. That *was* my World Title.

"Leading up to the fight I had to be re-medicalled and I'd burst my eardrum previously. About two weeks before the fight, the doctor had to check my eardrum and he syringed it with cold water. He burst it again and I was in fucking agony, but obviously you're not going to tell the doctor what's happening because you don't want it to wreck your medical. Even on the day of the fight I was thinking, 'The doctor's going to call the fight off,' but that's no excuse. Again, we got it hammed up in the press. We signed the contracts at the New Harlequin Centre. We sold the place out. The tactic was to go four rounds with Thaxton, because we knew his stamina wasn't good, and after the fourth round start upping the pace. I hadn't been put down for a few years and Steve Holdsworth was right behind me. We were aiming for that goal. A Championship belt."

Fight night arrived and Thaxton was simply too strong to lose. Bob was thrown to the floor in the second. He started to have some success in the third, but not enough. In the fourth round Thaxton connected with a blow that sent Bob crashing down, collapsing in a defeated pile. Bob managed to get to his knees and climbed to his feet by the time Dave Parris had counted to eight, but the referee didn't need to see any more. It was all over. "Jon Thaxton come out like a fuckin' whirlwind. He caught me a couple of times but I was moving away from a lot of the shots I got caught with. I got caught with a bad shot in the fourth and I landed on my head." The memory of this fight is still very painful for Bob. He made no move to show me the video and his next words were quiet, deflated. "I got on my knee and I took the eight count, as I have done throughout my career. I think Dave Parris looked at my corner and my corner said pull it off, but my head was clear. I would have rather gone out on my back, to be honest. He caught me in the throat. He caught me on my Adam's apple and I couldn't speak. He really, really hurt me. And that was the end of it really.

"I mooched around town, had a couple of drinks with a few friends, and that was the end of my career. If I'd won that fight, there might have been a British Title fight. There might have been a couple of defences. The Thaxton fight was my best payday. I got two and a half grand for that fight. It still grinds a bit that it was stopped when it was stopped. I've only seen the video once, and that was too much. But that's life. And fair play to him, he's gone on to bigger and better things."

Jon Thaxton went on to issue two brave challenges for the British Light-Welterweight Title, the first against Jason Rowland and the second against Ricky Hatton. Thaxton went the distance with 'The Hitman' and gave the popular Mancunian a tough fight, becoming the first man ever to take him the 12 round distance. He also challenged Eamonn Magee for the Commonwealth crown. In 2002 Jon was the victim of a car crash. The injuries that he sustained seemed destined to mark the end of his boxing career, but two years later he defied all the odds to step back into the professional boxing ring. In 2005, Jon won the WBF & IBF Lightweight Titles. He is still boxing today.

And, as for B.F. Williams? "Should I have stayed on? I probably could have. Keith Marner beat Thaxton in his next fight. Keith Marner was stronger than me; he was a good boy. But everything happens for a reason and it's all experience in life. I'd rather have gone out when I did than hang on for another three or four fights, tempted by the money. I trained so hard for the Thaxton fight that I might have retired if I'd won the title anyway."

Bob is now a Board of Control Inspector. "I wanted to be a referee for about seven years. I rang up Simon Block, who was then Area Secretary, and he said there were no spaces yet and to write a letter. Then I rang up two years later and by that time Robert Smith was Southern Area Secretary, and he suggested that I become an inspector. You get expenses for it, but that's as far as it goes. You have to weigh the boxers in, and check the tape and their hands. You have to make sure the seconds don't over-coach between rounds and you have to make sure that the gloves are the right gloves. To be honest, I want a more active role and my aim is to be a referee.

"Professional boxing is not easy. It really isn't, because if it was that easy I'd be coming back today. I do run four or five days a week. That's part of my fireman training, to keep physically fit. But there's physically fit, and then there's fighting fit. Don't worry about the 20 minutes in the ring; it's the sparring, the roadwork, the exercises, the dieting, everything that goes into it. Your body can't take it all the time. These top fighters, they're sparring ten hard rounds in a training session to box a 12 round fight. All I ever wanted was to win a title. I was sparring with Champions; but sparring is one thing, competition is another. But that's where I wanted to be. I wanted to pay people to spar with *me*, you know?

"My favourite boxer of all time has got to be Ali. Ali was everyone's idol. And when I was at school Johnny Owen was my hero. When he died against Lupe Pintor in Mexico City ..." Bob's voice became so quiet that it was suddenly difficult to pick out his words on the tape. "I was about 13 or 14 and I'd fallen in love with boxing, and he was 'The Matchstick Man,' just like me. Boxing is such an unforgiving game. When I think about him being carried out of the ring and the way they treated him. Johnny Owen was one of the greats."

Our day together came to an end and, as I packed up my tape-recorder and papers, I thanked Bob for the guided tour into the life and times of B.F. Williams. I thanked him for the film show and we had a laugh about the fact that, every time he had been knocked down, it seemed that I had been looking away from the screen. "You must have spent half the day bloody looking away. I got knocked down so many times, Slumberland wanted to sponsor me! Anyway, I've really enjoyed this interview. In fact, I want to make a fucking comeback!"

* * *

As this book is about to go to print, I would like to add this footnote. I am pleased to report that B.F. has now achieved his ambition to become a referee. As in his boxing days, his favourite venue to officiate is York Hall and he recently told me, "Yes, and it doesn't hurt as much!" One day, Bob would love to referee a fight in Las Vegas. He now runs a sports memorabilia company and he MC's and auctions memorabilia at amateur shows all over the country. He and Steve Holdsworth have been a major force behind the newly formed Home Counties Ex Boxers Association, of which Bob is the Chairman. Bob and Shlo now have a little daughter called Jodie. Dean is four and a half, and Bob reliably informs me, "He's still jabbing!!"

CHAPTER FIVE - MICHAEL SPROTT

"I've been involved in boxing all my life, and when Michael retires, I'll retire. That'll be it for me. But I'll see it through to the end with Michael first." **(Johnny Bloomfield)**

This is a story of determination. This is a story of a staunch and solid campaigner who has featured in some of the most exciting and controversial British heavyweight fights of recent years. This is the story of Michael Sprott. I first got to know Michael at Jim Evans' cosy boxing gym, which is nestled snugly at the bottom of Jim's garden. You will find the gym, fondly christened 'Jim's Gym,' by walking past the side of Jim's house on the Windsor Road, and when you reach the bottom of the garden path you won't find any fairies down there, just some of the hardest working men in the business, the boxing business that is, and Michael Sprott is nothing if not a grafter.

Michael and my good pal, Tommy Eastwood, who is a professional cruiserweight, have been sparring partners for many a fight. These sessions have always taken place down at Jim's Gym and presiding over fistic proceedings was a great man called Johnny Bloomfield, who was Michael's trainer for many years. Michael and Tommy have always worked beautifully together. Despite the weight difference of about three and a half stone, Michael is no liberty taker. He once shook his head in wonder as he told me, "Johnny Bloomfield calls him, 'Tiger Tom' but I call him, 'Tommy the Lion Heart', because sometimes I really have to hit him in there and he's still there, still in my face!" At many of these gatherings you would also find Tommy's uncle, a man who goes by the name of Champ, a moniker that suits him down to the ground. Johnny Bloomfield used to train Champ when they were both much younger and, when Tommy started training at Jim's Gym, the bond between Johnny and Champ became rekindled. It was like one big, happy family and I felt very proud to be a part of it.

Johnny Bloomfield and Michael were exceptionally close and this interview was originally planned to include Michael and Johnny as a team. Tragically, that was not to be. Johnny died before we got the chance. Later in this chapter, when we get to the sad part, Michael will speak about Johnny in depth and with love.

In the gym Michael uses this black, shiny tape over his hand wraps. The first time I ever witnessed the spectacle of him shadowboxing in the mirror, giant fists all taped up in black, wide eyes focused and alert, I thought he looked positively gladiatorial. On the other hand, Michael is a such kind man who is ready to treat everybody the same. He is softly spoken and he's quite shy really. During our interview he told me that he wishes he could talk like Nigel Benn or Chris Eubank. "They just come right out with whatever they have to say," he said, "whereas, with me, it all just comes out in a rush." He has the brightest smile and big, heavy lidded eyes that are full of soul. His laugh is deep and warm and it fills the room, and he's got a sweet sense of humour. One of the more contemporary training aids are strange contraptions that look like a tall, bulbous version of the old fashioned crash helmets; I believe they are called macro balls and I don't think they ever really caught on. I once saw Michael pick one up, plonk it on his head and start wobbling about, pretending to be a Martian. Johnny Bloomfield was there at the time and he gave me a look that said, 'What can you do with this boy?' And Johnny was right. There is nothing that you *can* do with Michael. That is the way he is, always ready to have a joke and he doesn't care if it is at his own expense.

I arranged to meet Michael for this interview in his hometown of Reading in April 2005. He collected me from the train station and we headed for a local coffee bar. Having got to know Michael over the years in the relaxed atmosphere of Jim's Gym, I could not help wondering how a taped conversation would work out. Michael is rather a private man and I was a little concerned that the intrusion of the tape-recorder might make him feel uncomfortable. I need not have worried. He submitted himself readily to my stringent questioning and his answers were honest, funny and sometimes moving. There were plenty of big smiles across the table that afternoon.

Michael was born at the Royal Berks Hospital on the 16th January 1975 and has lived in Reading all his life. He is six foot, two inches tall and these days he fights at about 17 and a half stone. "Mum and dad are still alive and well, and I've got three sisters. The youngest is 17, followed by the middle one who is 33, and the oldest is 36." He laughed, "They didn't used to beat me up, but they used to tease me when I was younger, not the young one obviously, but the older two." Michael also has a son named Darnell. His face glows with pride at the mention of Darnell's name. "Yeah, he's three and a half now [at the time of the interview]. I was there when he was born. It was funny. Angela's mum had come from Barbados and we got the call so we went round to the hospital and she had a Caesarean. When I saw the long needle down her back it made me feel a bit tingly, and as they brought the baby out I was sick! I think it was the smell of the gas." Michael managed to recover quickly enough to be the first person to hold his newborn son. "It made me feel happy and proud, and I'm still happy today, because he *is* a good boy.

"When I was about six or seven, my dad used to watch boxing and I used to jump around, shadow boxing. We used to watch Muhammad Ali, and then obviously you had young Mike Tyson coming up. And that's what made me do it. My dad wanted me to start boxing when I was younger but my mum said, 'No', so I waited until I was 13. My dad took me to Reading Boxing Club first, but I think he took me on the wrong day because it was all Thai boxing and kickboxing. I did that for a few months, but I didn't like it. So then my friend, Simon Tituis, said he knew a gym in Woodley. It was Bulmershe Boxing Club, in Bulmershe School. So me and him and some other guys, we all went down there, and that's where I started. I was the only one that carried on going. The rest of them all gave up. I think they all wanted to go out clubbing and partying, and I was so determined to do well. At one point I was the only member. Whereas everyone drifted in and out, I was the only one person who kept the club going. They were going to close it down but, because I was so determined, they kept it going, and then they all started coming back again."

It was at Bulmershe Boxing Club that Michael met a man called Ricky Maslin. "I've been with Ricky from the start. I trained with George Costin as a junior and as a senior as well. Then, when I became a senior,

Ricky started training me. Ricky turned professional with me and George still comes to see me train now. He trains other boxers from Bulmershe."

Michael was 13 when he had his first amateur match. "It was very hard for me to get fights because I was quite big for my age. I didn't enter the Schoolboys or the Novices. I had to wait until I was 16 to get into the ABAs. At one stage, I didn't box for two years. They just had to keep me training." In 1996 Michael was ABA Super-Heavyweight finalist. He lost to Danny Watts of Peckham. A swollen left eye cost Michael the fight and the title. He also boxed for England. "That's right, against USA, in London. I was a super-heavyweight, and I had to lose so much weight in a week to get down to fight this guy that I had no energy. The first round I was all right, but after that I ran out of steam and I thought, 'I'll never do that again.'"

The same year, in an effort to qualify for the Atlanta Olympics, Michael switched allegiance to his parents' homeland of the Caribbean island of St Vincent. "I felt I should have been picked for the Olympics that year, and the Olympic Committee overlooked me. Me and Ricky wasn't happy, so Rick said, 'I'm going to ring up St Vincent boxing committee and see if we can get you boxing for them instead,' and he got a letter back saying, 'Yes', they'd have it. So we flew out to Canada to clarify it." Incidentally, this was to compete in the North American Qualifiers.

"There were supposed to be a load of them from St Vincent meeting me and Rick in Canada and, when we got there, there was only one boxer who turned up. When Ricky rang them they said, 'Oh, they're not coming now.' So there was me and this guy from Orlando, just the two of us." Michael laughed heartily at the memory. "But we still had a good time and we done well. I beat the Mexican Champion, stopped him in the first round. Then I fought the Canadian Champion and you had Canadian judges, a Canadian referee and everyone there thought I won, but they gave it to him. Anyway, I came back home with a bronze. Then I had another chance at the Liverpool Multi-nations and I came back home with a bronze again. I fought the German heavyweight [Erik Fuhrmann] and I was doing well, but the referee disqualified me in the third round. He said I was ducking too low, which everyone thought was crazy because I wasn't, but the same referee stopped me when I fought Danny Watts. Only a minute to go and I would have been ABA Champion. So I always thought that referee had something against me; I don't know."

Later that year Michael made the decision to turn professional. "From an early age I've always wanted to be a World Champion, and that's what I'm still intending to do." Michael was one of the last boxers to sign with the legendary trainer and manager, Terry Lawless. "Yeah, me and young Blue Stevens were his last signings. Terry said in the paper, if there was a boxer who boxed like Muhammad Ali and punched like Mike Tyson, that's the only way he would come back. But he never did."

Michael made his professional debut at Wembley on the 20th November 1996. He stopped Geoff Hunter. Hunter looked out of shape and Michael looked fast and sharp, and he did what he had to do. He put the Mancunian down twice and stopped him in 58 seconds. "I was very nervous and I felt naked without the head-guard and the vest on. I was just shaking really. There was ages to go, but I was still sort of nervous. It felt strange." I asked if he still suffers from nerves a lot. "Not as bad as I did when I was amateur and when I first started as a pro, but I think being nervous is good really. I think in *any* sport, being nervous is a good thing."

Michael's next fight was in February 1997 at Acton Town Hall. He stopped Swansea's Johnny Davidson at the end of the second round with a left hook to the ribs. A month later Michael stopped Doncaster's Alvin 'Slick' Miller in one round. It was a no contest really as Miller, who had come in as a late substitute, was basically a cruiserweight at the time and a seasoned journeyman who went in with anybody they put in front of him. Michael walked right through him, putting him down twice with body shots. "You see, Terry Lawless, he loved his fighters and he made sure their career was protected. Every fighter was a different level but not too much. They was all learning fights, he was giving me. Journeymen are very good to learn from. They're slick and they're all kind of things really."

A month later Michael continued his bulldozing start to a promising professional boxing career and halted Tim Redman in two rounds at York Hall. Redman was another Welshman. "He was a good boxer. He was a good fight. I caught him with a body shot. My success was my body shots. I've neglected that a bit. My first three or four fights were all body shots, and then for some reason I just stopped it. I don't know why."

Michael went the distance for the first time against brave and resilient Pole, Waldek Franas, over six rounds in May 1997 at the Lee Valley Leisure Centre at Picketts Lock. "Oh, I hit him with everything! I thought, 'What have I got to do?' I could hammer him and he'd still be there! He was a tough character. He kept coming forward, trying to catch me with these big haymakers. At the end of the fight he looked like he'd been in a car crash. He was tough. And I haven't heard of him since." Franas never actually boxed again.

The following September Michael fought Gary Williams at the Elephant and Castle. Michael knocked the hard Nottingham man to the canvas in the first round, but Williams saw the fight through and Michael won on points. A month later it was another points win over Darren Fearn at the Elephant and Castle. Fearn was another Welshman, from Carmarthen. He was a big man, almost two stone heavier than Michael. "He was a fireman. I didn't know who he was and, when I came in, Ricky said, 'That's your opponent there,' and he was like a big, muscular bodybuilder. He looked really mean. I thought, 'Oh, right!' I was training at Pinewood Starr then, with Georgie Smith and Les Stevens, and they all come and supported me. It was a good fight. I thought I could have stopped him, probably in about the seventh or eighth, but he survived. I had to keep leaning because he had such big arms. He was such a big puncher, I didn't want to be caught by one of them. A strong guy from Wales, yeah."

Michael finished 1997 in fine style with a December one round stoppage against Nicky Howard at Wembley. Michael knocked Howard down twice in the first round. The second time Howard rolled over onto his back and remained prostrate while referee, Mark Green, stopped the fight. Howard was another Welshman, from Hengoed, and in January 1998,

Michael stopped John Davidson in two rounds, in a re-match with the Swansea man at York Hall. As I often do when I'm talking to a fighter that beat up so many of my countrymen, I teasingly berated him about it. Michael's effortless defence was a disarming blush. "I'll tell you, it's amazing you're saying that. Until now I didn't realize how many Welsh ones I fought." I sternly warned him not to start picking a fight with me! He chuckled, "The Welsh, they like a fight, don't they?"

The following month Michael scored a St Valentine's Day one round knockout against Dubliner, Ray Kane, at the Elephant and Castle. This was Michael's seventh stoppage win in ten fights. "I felt like I could go with anyone and not worry. But I needed journeymen. I needed learning fights. I knew it was going to get tougher sooner or later, and then people would see if I've got what it takes to box at higher class."

Michael Murray of Manchester was one such journeyman, the type of boxer that Michael was cutting his teeth on. Michael boxed him in March 1998 and won on points at York Hall. Murray managed to get through Michael's guard on quite a few occasions and the fight became messy and rough. Michael chuckled as he explained, "I fought him when I had the flu. I've never told no one this. I was in the changing room and they were saying, 'Are you all right? And I was saying, 'Yeah.' Because always, if I've had the flu or an injury, I'll still go and fight. I've never been one to pull out because I've got a bad hand or something."

Then came Michael's first loss as a professional boxer. He fought Charlton's Harry Senior at York Hall on the 12th September 1998 for the vacant Southern Area Heavyweight Title. At that time Senior had won four and lost four. He had a shaved head, apart from a pile of dreadlocks on the top tied in a ponytail. He was slightly the taller man at 6' 3 and it had been pretty much an even fight, when Senior caught Michael with a devastating body shot in the sixth round. "I was training up Pinewood Starr with Ricky and Georgie Smith, and I was sparring in London with Danny Watts and Julius Francis, and one of them caught me with a body shot and damaged my rib. So I couldn't spar for about three weeks before the fight. Anyway, Ricky said, 'I think you should pull out,' but I took it and I fought Harry and, as I threw a big haymaker, he threw a shot straight where I'd been injured, and that was me finished. I went down and I got back up, and he caught me in the same place again, and that ended the fight. Afterwards, I was so angry because I knew it! But it's a learning thing, you know? He won the fight and that's it. After the fight I was down and upset about it, and people thought I wouldn't come back. But I'll always come back. I won't let defeat upset me or stop me."

This turned out to be Michael's last fight for Terry Lawless. "Yeah, because Terry wanted me to be brought along just right. I think they wanted to push me up and Terry said, 'No', and I think they had a bit of a fall-out. That's when Terry gave up, and that's when Dean [Powell] came along."

Michael had two fights in 1999, a January points win in a re-match with Gary Williams and a four round stoppage over Chris Wollas. He started the following year with a six round points win over Hull journeyman, Tony Booth (who has his very own chapter in this book.) Michael and Tony boxed in January at Mansfield Leisure Centre. It was a mauling, spoiling fight, after which the Boxing News called Michael: *"One-time heavyweight prospect."*

Michael didn't box again until the following October and things did not go to plan. He was knocked out in the third round by Beckenham southpaw, Wayne Llewellyn, at Wembley Conference Centre. Llewellyn was not a journeyman. Far from it. He had won 20 fights and lost three by the time he fought Michael and, for the record, he is still boxing today. "I got a phone call from Dean saying did I want to fight Wayne Llewellyn, and for some strange reason I took it. I only had two weeks to prepare for it and I was doing well. He even said that I shocked him. I was *winning* the fight, and then what happened was, at the end of the third round I forgot he was a southpaw. I threw a double jab and a right hand and he stepped back, and I forgot all about his left hand and he caught me right on the chin. I went down and I got up at five or six, and I was just seeing, like, purples and blues all over the place, and the referee said, 'Box.' I carried on, but as I went to throw a punch I couldn't throw nothing, and he was coming on in leaps and bounds, so the referee jumped in and stopped it. I was out on my feet. He caught me with a good shot. I feel a lot more confident about fighting southpaws now, whereas before I wasn't really used to it because a southpaw is, like, once in a while and sometimes you can always forget about their left hand."

Michael had now had 16 professional fights, two of which he had lost, both times when he had stepped up in class. After losing to Llewellyn, people started to write him off as not being good enough to make the grade. I asked him if this made him feel sad. "A little bit. I mean, people were saying, 'He's turned into a journeyman,' and things like that, but it never stopped me from achieving what I wanted to achieve. I thought, 'Give me a chance. I'm still young.' Anyway, it's good then, because then I've got to prove them wrong, regardless."

In February 2001 Michael did indeed prove them wrong. He fought giant German, Timo Hoffmann, and won on points over eight rounds at York Hall. The previous November, Hoffmann had suffered his only defeat in 22 fights when he challenged and went 12 rounds with Vitali Klitschko for the vacant European Heavyweight Title. "Yeah, he was six foot, eight. He was a huge man, but I'd sparred with him a couple of times beforehand in Cologne. I'd sparred with some other heavyweights and I see this American guy called Jade Scott sparring with Timo. Timo was really going hard on him, you know, really determined to try and bash him up, and I thought, 'No!' I get so excited when I watch things like that, because I really don't like bullies.

"So I came back to England and then they called me back over for some more sparring, and they said, 'Will you spar with Timo?' So I sparred with him and I gave him a really good run for his money, and the German camp were happy. Then, I was supposed to be fighting Michael Holden and Timo was supposed to be fighting someone else at York Hall on the same night. Both fighters pulled out, so they thought A meets B; Michael Sprott versus Timo Hoffmann. I said, 'Yeah, I'm happy with that,' because I knew what I'd done in Germany, but I don't think his camp knew that it was *me* that he was fighting. So when I went to the Lennox Lewis College for the weigh-in, there was Timo and some other guys there. Timo jumped on and they called, 'Michael Sprott,' and I jumped on, and their faces were, like, in shock. And they just changed after that.

On the night, he looked a bit nervous to me. Anyway, I beat him by one point, but I *knew* I could beat him"

Michael has travelled to many places as a hired sparring partner. "Yeah, I've been to Germany, America, Denmark and all round Europe really. When they're looking for good sparring, Dean's the matchmaker and he calls me and asks if I want to go to Germany to spar with this, or Denmark to spar with that. It's okay. They put you in a good hotel and they really look after you. The best place I've been looked after is Germany, in Cologne. They're very good and everything's so *organized* out there. I know all the staff there, because we've been out there three or four times. They're so *nice* and everything runs on time. It's such a nice, *clean* country."

A month after his victory over Hoffmann, Michael fought the colossal German again, this time in Germany. Michael lost a points decision over eight rounds. "Well, I won, but yeah, I lost!" During the fight, Michael actually knocked Hoffmann's gum-shield out twice, and his corner went berserk when water was given to Hoffmann while the errant article was being washed out. Hoffmann went down in the seventh and again in the eighth, but the referee, Walfried Rollert, considered that he had not been hit on either occasion. "He didn't count it. It was just, 'Get back up, wipe the gloves and carry on boxing.'" When the decision was announced the 8,000 strong German crowd were not happy. "Yeah, he was booed back to the changing room. Recently, he fought the Australian heavyweight, Bob Mirovic, and everyone thought Mirovic won. But they gave it to Timo and he got booed back to the changing rooms again."

In November 2001 Michael was on the move again. This time he travelled to Carnival City to box South African southpaw, Corrie Sanders. Sanders was former WBU and South African Heavyweight Champion at the time. Two fights after Michael, Sanders caused an upset by knocking out Wladimir Klitschko in two rounds for the WBO Heavyweight Title, but failed in his next fight to do the same to the Ukrainian's brother, Vitali, for the WBC version. Michael obviously knew what fight was coming up next and he actually started laughing before we got on to this one. "Corrie Sanders, yeah!" He said the name as if it were the punch line of a joke. "We went to South Africa to train for a month, me and Rick. Every morning we were doing our runs out there. When we went to Johannesburg, the town centre, that was when I started to realize how rough it was out there. It was just ghetto to ghetto.

"Anyway, the first day we went in the gym there was guys coming in, taking out their guns, unloading them and putting them on the table before they started changing. I was like, 'What!' But I think it was a rule. Before you start training you've got to unload your guns and put them to one side. I was like, 'Oh no!' I was really nervous. They call the gym 'The Sweatbox' because it gets really hot in the sun. It's got big windows and they close everything up, and it's *really* hot in there. I nearly ended up fainting because of the heat. It was really, really hard training and I was in there for the next month. The first few days were all right, but on the fifth day, that's when I was sparring and I was getting beaten up every day. The altitude was so high, there was no oxygen and I couldn't cope. It took me about two and a half weeks before I got used to it.

"Every day we did our runs, and I didn't like it because these houses, every house has got, like, five dogs and sometimes the gates were open. So every day when I was running I used to get nervous that I would get chased by a dog or something. One time, we had gone out for a run and Rick said to me, 'This end to this end. I want you to run up there fast, and then turn around and come back slowly.' So Rick carried on cycling normally and I ran up the hill fast, like he said, and then he saw me come running back down the hill, *very* fast! I had been chased by about five Rottweilers, all at the same time. Rick said, 'What's wrong?' because I was out of breath. I said, 'I've just been chased!' And you know, they don't mess about. If you are near the house or whatever, they'll just attack you. So I asked if I could bring a running machine into the gym and run on that every day, but they said, 'No.'

"I didn't get to know Corrie Sanders at all, but he was talking in the press conference like he'd already won our fight. It was like, 'After Michael, we'll be going on to Lennox Lewis,' and all that. When I fought him I thought, 'How does this man have such *power*?' He has this amazing strength. But then, I've always thought with South Africans, it doesn't matter what colour they are, they're always strong. When Lewis retired I always fancied Sanders to be the next World Champion, which he could have been, but apparently he doesn't train. He just plays golf all day and they've got to get him off the golf course to get him in the gym. But, when I saw him I thought, 'No, this is rubbish. Of *course* he's trained.' That was the best shape I've ever seen him. Usually he's chubby, but he was like a racehorse and I thought, 'This is just a rumour. This guy *has* trained for this fight.'"

Corrie Sanders stopped Michael in the first round and, looking back at it with me that day, Michael explained that he felt that the referee, Thabo Spampool, acted far too hastily in stopping the fight when he did. "That was definitely premature. I got up at eight and I was fine. I mean, he caught me with a good shot, it took the air out of me and he heard me go, 'Ohhhh.' I went down and I got up at eight, and the referee didn't even look at me. He just waved it off and people in the crowd were booing. I pushed the referee. I said, 'What are you *doing*? Just give me a *chance*. I've only been down *once*. I've been training out here the whole *month*.' And then the referee does that. There again, I guess he done it because he probably knows what Corrie Sanders is like. He's quick and he's a dangerous finisher, so he probably thought enough is enough really, but I still think he could have given me another chance."

I was interested to learn if Michael felt much racial tension during his stay in South Africa. "Kind of. You can still see things. The staff at the hotel were saying it's not as bad as what it used to be, but there's still a lot of it going about. When we were coming back in a taxi from Carnival City, we went past two schools and it was, like, all white kids in that school and all black kids in that school. And you get the big Afrikaner with his big moustache, and they're like pigs. You can see there's still quite a lot of friction there. It's quite sad really."

In December 2001, six weeks after the Corrie Sanders fight, Michael travelled to Holland to box New Yorker, Jermell Lamar Barnes, at the Topsportcentrum in Rotterdam. Michael won on points over eight rounds. "They were trying to bring boxing back to Holland and they got some fighters from everywhere. They were all fighters from different

Sylvester Mittee - Master Blaster

The Inseparable Twins Henry & George

As Children

Back home for Mums cooking

Sparring together

Off to the Army

Marching in the same squad

George Cooper and the author

Clinton McKenzie - Moody and Magnificent!

Clinton McKenzie - British Light-Welterweight Champion

Clinton McKenzie

Teddy Lewis in his fighting days

Teddy Lewis with George Morris and Teddy Lewis senior - Morris managed father and son

Teddy Lewis and the author

Clinton McKenzie, Charlie Magri & Sylvester Mittee - The A Team!

Signing for a fight - BF Williams & Jon Thaxton putting pen to paper for the Southern Area Title

BF Williams - Fire Fighter

BF Williams - It's a fair cop ref!

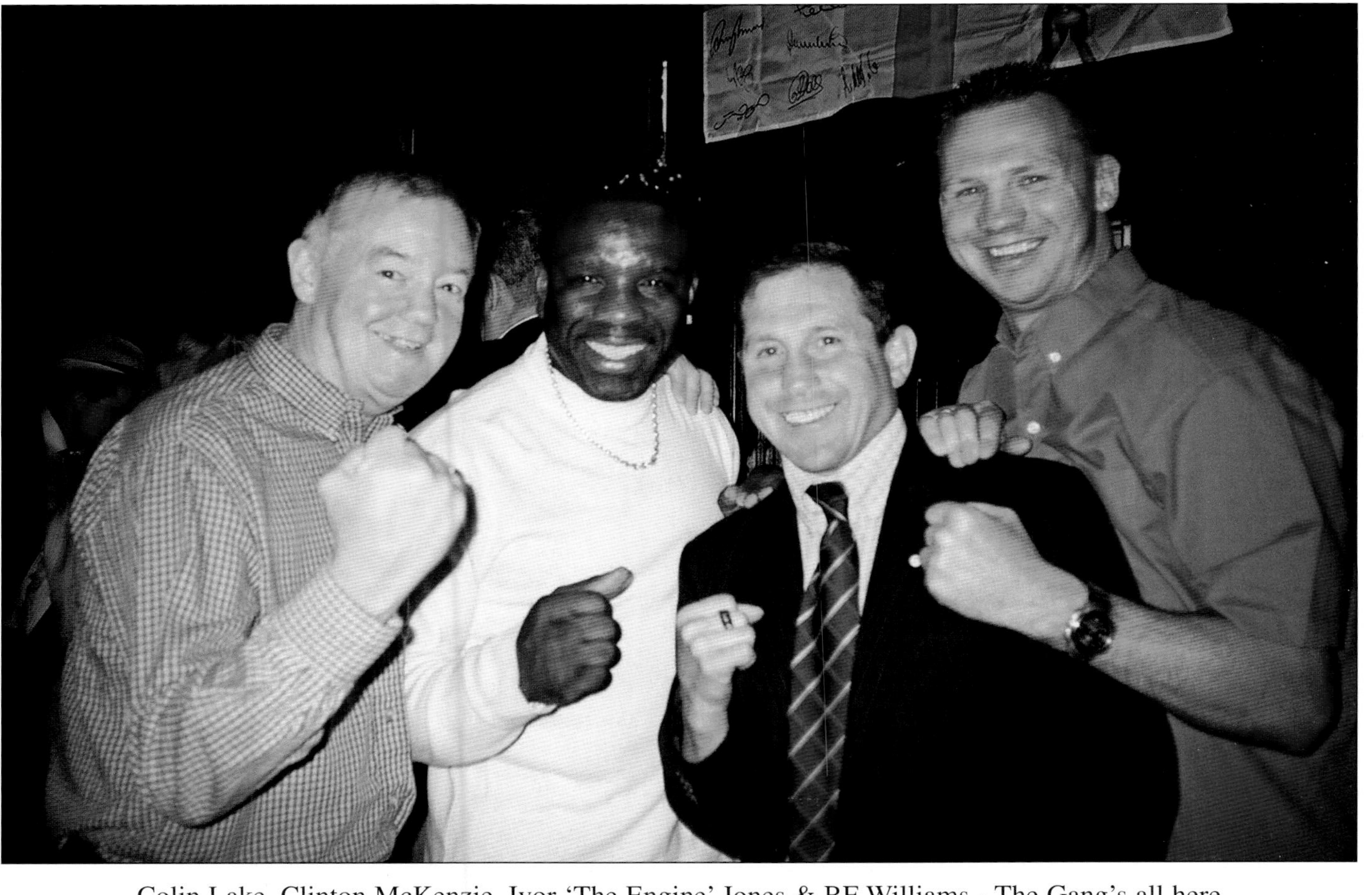

Colin Lake, Clinton McKenzie, Ivor 'The Engine' Jones & BF Williams - The Gang's all here

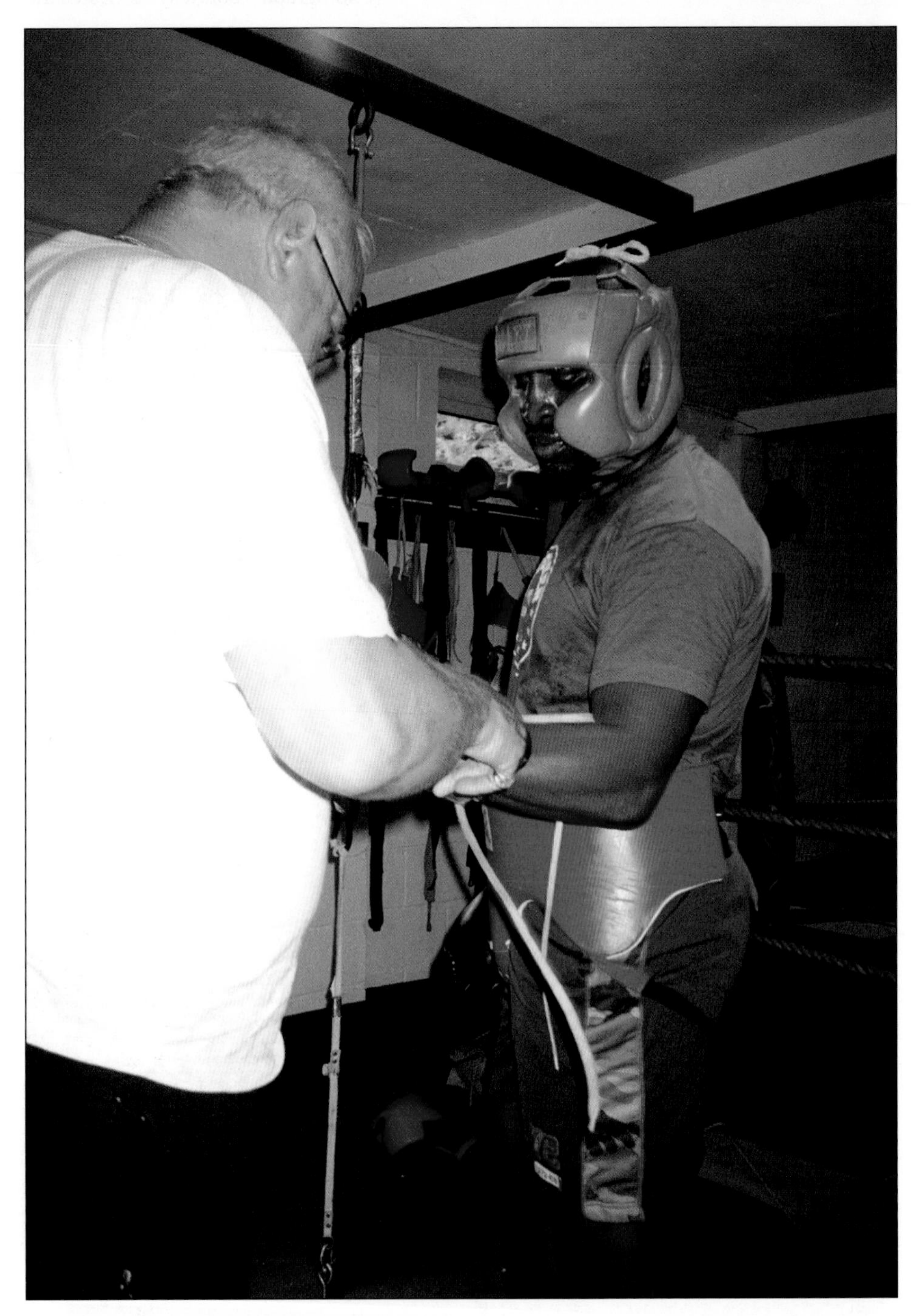

Michael Sprott & Johnny Bloomfield

(Photograph - courtesy of Les Clark)

Michael Sprott - European Union and English Heavyweight Champion

Michael Sprott - Smiler!

places. They got me against Jermell Barnes and this American trainer, he brought all these American boxers over there. There was this really famous boxer in Holland [lightweight veteran, Regilio Tuur] and he boxed an American [Shawn Simmons] on top of the bill, and they done it with a fashion show. So they'd have a bit of boxing, and then they'd stop and have the fashion show. It was really, really good. There was all these women everywhere, all wearing their fashion clothes, and when the boxers came in, they had to wear the fashion and go out on the fashion walk into the ring." Michael laughed fondly at the memory. "Anyway, it was a good show and an eight round fight, and I think I won it by about two points." This was Michael's third fight abroad in a row and the first time he came home a winner. "Yeah, this was the first one I won away. Mind you, I know it was a loss with Timo Hoffmann, but in my eyes I won. But, on my record, it will say that I didn't."

Michael and Brixton's Danny Williams have had three fights. On the 12th February 2002 they met in the ring for the first time. On the line were Danny's British and Commonwealth Heavyweight Titles. They boxed at York Hall and Michael lasted seven rounds before Danny stopped him. "What happened was, I had been on holiday in Barbados for three weeks and when we got indoors I got a phone call from Dean saying, 'Do you want to go to Blackpool and spar with Matthew Ellis for a week?' So I flew down there and did that, and I was in the hotel when I got the call saying Keith Long had pulled out of his fight with Danny Williams and did I want to take the fight? I wasn't too sure at first. I was asking Matthew Ellis and his dad, and everyone, 'What do you reckon?' Matthew said, 'I'd go for it. For the money you're getting, I'd probably risk it.' But I was thinking that I hadn't prepared and, if you haven't prepared, then prepare to fail. I can't be having that loss on my record. I don't *want* that loss on my record. In the end I thought, 'If the money's right, I'll risk it,' and the money was right."

Michael was straight into the fight, but as early as the second round Danny's jab began to find it's target with painful regularity. Michael slipped over half way through the round and it got a bit messy when a wrestling thing started going on, earning Michael a telling off from referee, Richie Davies. When the bell went to end the second round trainer, Jimmy Tibbs, launched straight into a lecture before Michael's bottom hit the stool. They got through to the fourth and Michael came out with a flurry of shots in the opening seconds but, as the round progressed, Danny got on top, and in the final minute he knocked Michael down. Michael was straight back up and Danny rocked him again at the end of the round, this time almost lifting him off his feet with a right, left combination to the face.

The fifth round arrived and Danny's punches were piling on the pressure. Michael began to look devastatingly tired. Suddenly, Danny let go with a ramrod right hand lead punch, which lifted Michael off his feet and sent him back towards the ropes. At the end of the round Michael sat exhausted on his stool, brave and bleeding. "Yeah, I was knackered and they were saying, 'Step it up! You've *won* this round,' and I was like, 'Yeah, but I've got nothing in the tank.' I'd been going out drinking and partying, just having a good time. I'd put all this weight on and I thought, 'I can't go 12 rounds.'" The bell rang to begin the next round and the power ratio between the two boxers was growing. Michael kept chipping away and Danny's bombs were becoming more explosive. At this point, Richie Woodall, who was commentating for the BBC that night, praised Michael for his bravery. In the seventh and final round Danny piled straight in and trapped Michael in a corner, clubbing away with both hands. As he punched Michael across the ring, Jimmy Tibbs leapt up onto the ring apron and started frantically waving the towel. At that moment, Richie Davies jumped in and stopped the fight. Seconds later the two boxers were hugging each other and, as they parted, Michael flashed Danny a resigned smile. "Jimmy threw in the towel in the seventh round. I was knackered. I thought I done well though, considering I hadn't been in training. I was well overweight and a lot of them had me down to lose in one or two rounds. Danny knew I was getting tired. That's why he stepped up a gear."

If proof were needed that you can't keep a good man down, three months later Michael stopped Pele Reid in seven rounds in a real upper and downer at the Equinox Nightclub in London's Leicester Square. For the record, this was Michael's first fight with Johnny Bloomfield in his corner. "Well, from the Pele Reid fight I was with Johnny Bloomfield, and from then on all my successes were with John. He changed my career. I used to throw punches and John used to say, 'Michael, I don't know how you've managed to get where you are from what you've being doing,' and he really changed my career. Everyone noticed that. I really miss the guy. It's never been the same since he died. It was so much one-to-one. He was always telling me to twist. That's all I remember, 'Twist! Twist!' And he weren't just a trainer, he was a good friend. He always gave me positive and good advice in all aspects of my life. And he was good with Tommy [Eastwood] as well. I know he used to ring up Tom a lot. He was always there, John.

"I first met John a couple of years earlier, when I first turned pro. I met him at Hayes. When I first saw him, I thought he was some kind of gangster, you know? He was such a big guy and, with his dark glasses, I thought, 'Jesus! He's a *big* guy.' I was sparring with some of the guys down there and he said 'Hello' to me, but I didn't really know him yet. Then, when Jim Evans opened his gym at Maidenhead in his back garden, it was a bit hard for me because Ricky was running his own business and he didn't really have time to train me. I was sort of stuck, so I thought I'd go down Jim's and see what was happening down there, and Jim introduced me to John. John come up to me and said, 'Do you want to go on the pads, Michael?' And that's how it all started. He took me on the pads and, when I was punching and doing different things, John was saying, 'No, it's all *wrong.*' I threw a left hook and he said, '*That's* wrong.' It was like I had to learn boxing all over again. When he started teaching me how to punch properly, that's when I started stopping all these guys, and he helped me a lot with my defence. He was great, John. He knew what he was talking about."

Pele Reid was a flamboyant performer, an ex-kick boxer from Birmingham who was always in the most supreme physical condition. The fight was for the vacant WBF European Heavyweight Title. I asked Michael if winning this belt changed his life in any way. "Not really, no. But it did feel good, obviously, them putting a belt around my waist. It doesn't matter what the title is. A title's a title at the end of the day but, deep inside, it didn't really mean anything to me."

The fight was a war with its fair share of drama. Reid threw Michael to the canvas WWF style in the third, earning them both a stern warning from referee, Marcus McDonnell. Michael shook Reid up at the end of the forth with a big right hand right on Reid's jaw and the Birmingham man was rescued by the bell. Michael stormed out for the finish in the fifth but he walked straight onto Reid's left hook and lost control of his senses, staggering backwards and landing near his own corner. He was up at six and, just as his head started to clear, Reid jumped in with more hooks and a massive right hand dropped Michael again. Michael sank to one knee, his head bowed right down to the canvas. He was up at the count of three and kept his hands high as Reid tried to finish him off. But, by the end of this amazing round, Michael had regained control of the fight and again Reid seemed to be saved by the bell as Michael jumped on him, nailing him with a two handed attack that left Reid stunned and shaken.

The sixth round arrived and Michael looked exhausted, but he managed to draw the energy from the soles of his boots to hurt Reid again. However, whatever Michael threw at the Birmingham battler, Reid refused to go down. The seventh round would be the last. In the last minute, Michael trapped Reid on the ropes and let loose with a big two handed attack, forcing him to hold on tightly. The referee jumped in to part them, but Michael was straight back on him and Reid had nothing left. The fight was stopped. "I thought I was losing that fight points-wise. I'd sparred with Pele many times before. I know he's strong. I know he's got an awesome physique. I know he's a switcher. He's flashy and he's a banger at the same time. He knocked me down twice and it was a very good fight, but I said to myself, 'There's no *way* I'm losing to Pele Reid.' That's all that kept going through my head. I was determined. And as I leant back on the ropes, John was shouting, 'Come on! Come off the ropes!' and he caught me with a good right hand, and I went flat on my face. Everyone thought I was out, but I jumped straight back up. I went to a neutral corner and raised my hands up to say, 'I'm okay.' We carried on fighting and he caught me with another shot. I went down and Pele walked round the ring, thinking it was finished. As he turned around, he looked shocked when he saw I was back up. Some people were actually starting to walk out, thinking that was it! And I switched it around and I stopped him in the seventh with a number of punches, the last one being a left hook, and I heard him going, 'OOOhhhhhhh.' I caught him and he was out on his feet, and he went over to his corner and he had to sit down.

"I was happy, because there was no *way* I was losing to Pele Reid. I knew whoever lost that fight, it was going to be very bad for them. It was going to be much harder to get it all together again, and I was determined that it was not going to be me." For the record, Pele Reid had two more fights after Michael and then retired from boxing and turned to the martial arts sport of K1. After four years out, Pele made a return to boxing and is still at it today.

Garing Lane was a big, tough American journeyman. His nickname was 'Freight Train' and in July 2002 he took Michael the six round distance at Wembley Conference Centre. Lane weighed in for the fight at over 20 stone and his belly was hanging over his shorts. He is currently 41 years old and still fighting. "He's been in with Larry Holmes, Riddick Bowe, Ray Mercer, he's been in with all of them. He said to me that he'd heard that I was a come forward type of fighter, and as soon as the bell went and he saw me hold back behind the jab and moving, he thought, 'Oh no!' Because he obviously wanted me to trade with him so he could catch me with his big haymakers, but I wasn't having that."

After a September points win against Aberdeen born Derek McCafferty, a man who could only be described as an 'opponent,' and yet a man who never ducked anybody, Michael finished the year with a December stoppage over obese Hungarian, Tamás Fehéri in two rounds. They boxed at the Equinox Night Club in Leicester Square and as Fehéri, who weighed nearly 20 stone, sat in his corner at the end of the first round with his mouth gaping open, struggling to catch his breath, the bulging rolls of fat around his middle made him look like a balding and bearded Sumo wrestler who was about to keel over. I was there that night with another boxer friend of mine, David Wakefield, who boxed on the same bill, and we couldn't get over the poor shape that Fehéri was in. For that matter, neither could Michael. "Even people from the Boxing Board said they didn't know where they got this man from. Because at the weigh-in, they thought *he* was the manager and the other guy was the boxer. I couldn't *believe* it! I said, 'No! No way!' And Dean goes, 'Just get out there and take him out. Just get it over and done with.' But I always believe that you shouldn't write someone off from their looks. You just don't know, because although he's a big, fat man, he's still got the weight. He could be a tricky customer, so I didn't go out there straight for the kill. I just boxed him in the first round and in the second round I opened up. I'm cautious like that." When the end came, the Hungarian was sprawled on the canvas and incredibly he managed to beat the count but referee, Billy Aird, did absolutely the right thing in stopping this fight straight away.

January 2003 arrived and Michael started the year off in a sensational manner against Michael Holden at the Ponds Forge Arena in Sheffield. Holden, a part-time bodyguard who doubled as a film extra, was a former British Heavyweight Champion who incidentally never lost his crown in the ring; Holden was forced to relinquish his title when he pulled out of a fight with Danny Williams though illness. This fight with Michael was an unofficial eliminator for the British Heavyweight Title and Michael's performance was a pure job of work, technically efficient and a clinical demolition of the brave Northerner, who was stopped in the fourth round. Incidentally, this night was actually the first time I ever met Michael. I was at Sheffield with Tommy Eastwood, who lost a close points decision to Lee Swaby on the same show.

Michael continued his good form with a third round stoppage of Mark Potter at Reading's Rivermead Leisure Centre in March that year. I put it to Michael that Potter took a battering that night. Michael laughed, but not in an unkind way. "Again, that was down to John. John actually said that was the best fight he'd seen me have. Everything was right that night, everything! The jab, combinations, uppercuts. He said that was one of the best fights he'd seen me have, when I used everything." The fight was another eliminator for the British Title, along with Potter's Southern Area Title, which Michael took that night. The official reason for the stoppage was an awful cut over Potter's left eye that happened in the second round. The Walthamstow warrior had put up a typically brave fight, constantly coming forward right up until it was stopped. The laceration was in the soft tissue between the eye socket and the eyebrow and, when Mark came out for the third round, his face was soon a grizzly mask of blood. Referee, David Parris, stopped the fight to inspect the grotesque injury and decided that enough was enough. I have always felt that Mark Potter was the type of man who, if half of his head were hanging off, would still get up and fight if he could, and Michael fondly agreed. "He's a nice fella. He's got a bit of a streak about him too!"

In June 2003 Michael stopped tattooed, shaven headed Czech, Petr Horacek, in one round at the Ponds Forge Arena in Sheffield. Horacek, who was based in Maidenhead, was another one in poor physical condition. Michael had been originally scheduled to box Keith Long in a final eliminator for the British Heavyweight Title that night, but Keith pulled out five days earlier with a rib injury. "Yeah, all those so-called eliminators. I had Mark Potter, Michael Holden, then they said about Keith Long and I thought, 'This is unfair.'"

One of Michael's best ever performances came on the first day of August 2003. He defended his Southern Area Heavyweight Title against Colin Kenna, stopping the man of Dublin descent inside one round at York Hall. Kenna's record was eight wins and one draw and he was considered to be going places when he fought Michael. "That was a fantastic result for me. We were both training at Jim's and for that fight I had to leave the gym and go elsewhere, because they didn't want clashes in the gym. I did train there on some days when Colin weren't there, and then sometimes John used to take me to Runnymede Leisure Centre and we used to train there."

The preparation complete, fight night arrived and both boxers were in the York Hall ring now, ready for action. As the final seconds leading up to combat arrived, Johnny Bloomfield stood firmly at Michael's side, keenly chewing gum and calmly whispering last minute instructions to his charge from the corner of his mouth. Michael looked supremely confident and focused as the boxers were announced and, to me, Kenna looked only too aware that he had his work cut out for him. "It was his first title fight. It was packed out. You see, I'd had the experience of fighting in front of big crowds for titles. It was his first time and you get nervous, just like I was when I fought Harry Senior. I guess he was in the same sort of shoes as me really."

Kenna brought a lot of Irish fans with him that night and they made a lot of noise as their man piled in during the first minute. Michael covered up tightly before pushing Kenna backwards with seeming ease. When the stoppage came, it was a left hook to the body and another one on the chin that took the wind out of the Kenna's sails. In the heat of the moment, an impulsive war cry burst from Michael's lungs, and a split second later Kenna was down again. Michael did a brief dance of excitement before referee Richie Davies urgently directed him back to a neutral corner so he could begin the count.

I put it to Michael that he was in a wild mood that night and he laughed raucously. But, on the night of the fight, when Kenna went down, there was no laughing. There was no count. Kenna was flat on his back. Richie Davies dashed over to cradle the fallen fighter in his arms while Michael initially began to celebrate. Then, as Michael realized that Kenna remained on the floor, he quickly became still and concerned. The paramedics entered the ring and surrounded Kenna while he lay there for almost a minute as they tended to him. Eventually, Colin rose unscathed and Michael gave him a big hug. Everybody was fit and well and Michael's smile was radiant. "Oh, I was so happy. I'd been having all these stoppages, all these good wins. John had changed my style and I was punching a lot harder as well. For the Michael Holden fight, I woke up that morning and I thought, 'I'm going to stop him.' But, with Kenna, I thought I would have stopped him, but not as quick as that. We'd had some good spars and I think he fancied beating me, but I was so determined to keep hold of the belt. I think that was another eliminator as well."

Next on the agenda was Michael's second fight with Danny Williams. On the 26th September 2003 these two went head to head for Danny's British and Commonwealth Heavyweight Titles once more. Danny stepped into the lion's den that was Reading's Rivermead Leisure Centre and he stopped Michael in five rounds. But, this was a dirty old fight and a dirty old night, and the way Danny won the war was seen by many to be well below the belt, literally. I was there, and I was scared as Michael's hometown crowd vented their seething outrage when the end came.

But going back to the beginning, I spent most of the evening with my friend, former British, Commonwealth and European Light-Heavyweight Champion, Crawford Ashley. Incidentally, Michael has sparred with Crawf' in times past and told me, "He's a good fighter, definitely!" As I stood at the rail that surrounded the ring enclosure chatting with Crawford, somebody threw a missile and it hit me on the right temple. It was hardly a knockout blow, but it caught me by surprise and gave me the needle. As I stood glaring up at the sea of faces, blindly searching for a guilty one, Crawford gently but firmly took my arm and said, "Come on you, I'm taking you for a pint."

As we stood at the bar, a couple of men recognized Crawford and came over to talk with him. Suddenly the cheering of the crowd, the loud introduction music and charged atmosphere of the hall permeated through the doorway to the bar and reached us. This was the moment I had been waiting for all evening. I reached up and tugged excitedly at the sleeve of Crawford's tee-shirt. "Come on, Crawf!" I desperately implored, "It's starting." In complete contrast to my pogo dance of excitement, Crawford shook his head with the patient kindness of one who has been there and done it all before. He spoke calmly and kindly, as if to a child, "Hold on, it's only the introductions, and you've still got a full pint there." I soon changed that state of affairs, which made my huge friend smile, and we went out into the hall to watch the fight. I wanted to get back to our vantage point of earlier, but Crawford said, "No, because of those idiots."

In the opening minutes Michael and Danny stalked the ring, taking a look at each other, and then Danny threw a borderline punch, a left hook near the top of Michael's thigh. Referee, Terry O'Connor, spotted it and allowed Michael some time to recover while telling Danny to keep his punches up. Both boxers returned to their corner ten seconds early because somebody in the crowd rang a bell. Peter McCann, the timekeeper, signalled to the referee that the bell was not the real one, but Danny's gum-shield was already being removed and it was decided to end the round there.

Michael boxed carefully in the second, while Danny threw mostly big, single shots. In the final minute Danny jumped in to attack with an array of shots, but Michael shoved him away and poked his tongue out. Before the round was over Michael clobbered Danny, making him hold for a second, and then punctuated the end of the round with a spot-on right uppercut, right on the jaw and right on the bell. In the third, Michael stuck to his boxing, moving around, firing out the jab and not taking any chances. Danny did his best stuff when he got in close. There was one touchy moment when Danny banged two shots home to Michael's body, and Michael smashed him straight back in anger, as if to say, 'Don't you dare!'

The fourth continued along much the same lines, Michael moving and jabbing, Danny throwing single shots, looking for the big one. Michael got warned at one point for holding and hitting. Then came a low left hook from Danny. Michael complained and Terry O'Connor gave Danny a sterner talking to than he had the first time. The fight continued and then, at the end of the fourth round, another left hook from Danny landed below the belt. Michael automatically dropped his gloves to protect the assaulted area and, as he turned to protest to the referee, Danny let a right hook go, smashing into Michael's chin. Michael toppled forward and referee O'Connor had counted to six when the bell rang and Michael managed to climb to his feet. He was in agony as he limped to his corner. Apart from the minute between the rounds, Michael was given no extra time to recover from the foul.

Danny came out for the fifth with all guns firing, sensing that Michael was really hurt now, vulnerable. Michael held on through the attack and Danny hit him low once more. Michael's fists dropped to instinctively cup protectively around his groin and he appealed to the referee once more, his face a picture of pain and indignation. Terry O'Connor ignored his plight. Danny saw his chance and took it, sending a hammering blow through to Michael's unguarded chin and down he went, face first. The fight was over. Terry O'Connor finally waved the fight off - after 19 seconds had passed. The paramedics had been poised to come to Michael's side when he managed to get to his feet.

"The first time Danny hit me low, in the first round, I thought Terry O'Connor was going to give me time out, but he didn't, and I thought, 'Oh, I'll just carry on boxing.' So I carried on boxing, and then he done it again! I thought, 'What's going on here?' Then he done it *again*! And when he done it on the bell and I went down and I was, like, staggering over to the corner when the bell went, I was thinking the referee was going to give me time, because I was still wobbly then. I can't remember the fight really. I can't remember the low blows, or in which rounds, as such, but basically I thought the referee wasn't doing his job properly. And I thought Danny was trying to get himself disqualified, because he could *see* he was losing the fight. I was jabbing him and punching him, and his eye was closing and I could see he was looking really tired. And then it was like, 'BANG!' and he asked the referee, 'Am I disqualified?' So I thought, 'He's trying to find an easy way out, because it won't make his record look too bad if he was disqualified.'

"At the press conference, he kept saying I was trying to make excuses and I said to him, 'If that was the case, why did I keep getting back up to carry on? I would have stayed down and made a big deal about it.' He didn't have an answer to that. I thought that night he was trying to look for a way out and the referee was letting him do a job on me. In the end, he hit me well low. I looked at the referee to complain about the foul. I was like, aaaarrrrgghhhh! I was in agony, and then Danny did a horrible thing. He threw a massive left hook and he put me on the deck, and that was it really. And then Dan was asking the referee again, 'Am I disqualified? Adam Booth was in his corner and he was trying to talk to him, and Danny was telling him to 'F' off and things like that. I didn't know exactly what was going on. I kicked up a fuss afterwards. I was going mad."

The Reading crowd was seething as William's hand was raised, menacing chants of "Cheat, Cheat" resounding eerily around the hall. "Yeah, I know. I went back to my changing room and I could hear them." The hostile chanting continued with a vengeance while Danny was being interviewed from ringside. Bearing in mind the nature of the win and the mood of the crowd, the television people took an incredible chance by interviewing Danny out in the hall, out in the open. I suggested to

Michael that it would have been safer for everybody if they had conducted the interview back in Danny's dressing room. "Yeah. They were taking a big risk. I mean, anyone could have gone up to him, all those people."

Whilst I am well aware that the judging of a boxing match is a totally subjective process, I was at the fight and have studied the tape of the fight closely on several occasions. Therefore, as a writer, I have to call it as I see it and I want to declare here and now that, in my opinion, the referee's handling of that fight was totally unjust. I wrote to the Board of Control and asked for a comment on how Terry O'Connor was dealt with regarding his handling of this fight. General Secretary, Simon Block replied as follows:

> *"Referee Terry O'Connor was called before the Stewards of the Board under Regulation 26.9 (which is a regulation which entitles the Board to call any licence holder before it on any matter relating to the conduct of boxing but is specifically not a disciplinary Regulation.) Mr O'Connor was asked to give his explanation as to his handling of the contest between Danny Williams and Michael Sprott and following a videotape viewing of the contest and with Mr O'Connor having answered all the questions put to him by the Stewards, his explanation was accepted with no further action being taken."*

Today, Michael would not wish to see Terry O'Connor in the same ring as him again. "Oh, I wouldn't want him to referee one of my fights. I think I'd make a complaint, because it's just like he's blind or something. I don't know if he's got something against me or if that's just the way he is. Because before the fight they were saying, 'You've got Terry O'Connor, he's a good referee.' And then they said, 'Maybe he was having an off night.'"

Michael Sprott and Danny Williams completed their trilogy four months later, on the 24th January 2004. Danny was still holding the British and Commonwealth Titles and this was another fight to determine who would leave with the belts. For the record, the referee was Dave Parris. During the publicity build-up to the fight, Michael and Danny were dressed up in combat clothes and photographed looking moody and magnificent. The picture appeared in the Boxing News, accompanied by the headline: *'Now It's War"*. At the pre-fight press conference Danny was complimentary to Michael, declaring that he thought him to be the best heavyweight in the country, apart from him. On Sky Television Danny predicted that he would stop Michael in the third round. Johnny Bloomfield was interviewed for the same programme and, when he was asked about the previous clash, his sage words of wisdom were spoken with the serenity of truth. "They was low blows. *Blatantly* low blows. Whether Danny done them on purpose, or what, Michael should never have been beat the way he was beat that night."

The night this fight took place I was at Wembley Conference Centre, in the crowd with a bunch of friends rather than at ringside as a press reporter. We were sitting near the opening from where Michael would emerge, and when he entered the arena the whole place erupted with a surge of passionate energy. Later, I asked Michael how he was feeling as he came out to fight the man who he felt so strongly had fouled him so badly in their last fight. "Oh, I felt confident. I was looking for revenge. That's what I came there for. I didn't think about the low blows and I wasn't nervous that he was going to do it again. I knew that the Boxing Board and the referee were keeping an eye on him. It was just revenge for me really."

When Danny emerged from the opposite end of the hall the chants of, "Cheat, cheat, cheat!" filled the air, evoking a foreboding feeling of déjà vu. Michael told me, "No, I don't think he had a lot of support there, because apparently the promoter said that, if it wasn't for me selling so many tickets as what I did, the show would have been off or some of the boxers might not have got paid. That's what I heard anyway." Danny did not appear in the least bit ruffled about the hostile reception. He jogged up the steps to the ring and stepped through the ropes with the air of a man who was simply going about his business. He came in at nearly 19 stone but he still looked sleek and wore it well.

The storyline of this fight was Michael's faster hands and aggressive desire against Danny's smoother counter-punches, often delivered from the hip. Between them, the fallout of their last fight loomed large. Danny's performance was characteristic of what has become widely thought of as typical of this quiet yet temperamental ring artist. Danny Williams is the most personable man you could meet outside the ropes, and the fact that he is a highly talented boxer can never be disputed. But there are times when his actions inside the ring are nothing short of curious. Whether it is down to an ebb and flow of confidence, or emotional mood swings, only Danny himself knows, but when he delivers such a performance it makes him into the sort of fighter who is difficult for the audience to empathise with. Michael's performance was also characteristic in its honesty and determination - nothing flashy but, after their last fight, he was standing for nothing below the belt.

At the end of the first round there were the now familiar chants of, "Cheat, cheat, cheat." At the end of the second round the referee had to separate them as they stood head to head, literally, like stags with their antlers locked. The antics began in the third when Michael piled straight into Danny and, as Danny's arm got entwined across Michael's chest, he turned his back. In retaliation, Michael flipped him over onto the floor with his right arm. The referee sent Michael over to a neutral corner while Danny righted himself and then, when Dave Parris called them back together, Michael marched straight up to Danny and glared into his eyes. Battle resumed and Danny seemed unconcerned, continuing to box with his hands held down, flicking out that long, long jab of his. In the fourth, Danny started holding and Michael pushed his head down. The referee barked an order to, "Stop boxing!" and Michael released Danny and backed of with a good-natured, "Sorry", directed at the referee. Danny turned his back on Michael twice in the fifth round. But Dave Parris was having none of it, taking Danny to one side and asking him if he wanted to fight or not.

Michael told me, "I thought, 'What's he *doing?*' but he did say afterwards at the press conference that he was trying all this stuff to make me come, so he'd catch me out, but he said, 'He boxed clever and he stuck to his guns.' He thought he'd turn his back and, when I come rushing in, bang!

He'd catch me cold. But I wasn't having any of that. And he did say that he was really nervous for that fight. He's got mind problems, sometimes, Danny."

In the sixth Danny started boxing more conventionally. Then he went for the body and landed with a couple of borderline shots, and the crowd booed while he received a stern warning from the referee to keep his punches up. Before the beginning of the seventh, Johnny Bloomfield drummed it into his charge in the corner, "You've got to unload!" Towards the end of the seventh Michael smashed into Danny with a left, right combination that sent the Brixton man staggering backwards. Michael hit him again with a left hook as the bell went. Back in his corner, Danny looked tired as he sat on his stool, his nose streaming with blood. The eighth round arrived and, as they fought on, it was Michael who took the fight to Danny and Danny who seemed prepared to cruise through the rounds, seemingly without really trying very hard. Then Danny hit Michael on the waistband and a feisty exchange followed, ending with a left hook from Michael that knocked Danny backwards. Michael's fans rewarded him by chanting his name.

As Michael returned to his corner Johnny Bloomfield earnestly beseeched, "The man is ready to be *taken*. Michael, *please*, you can *do* this!" As Michael rose from his stool to go back into battle, Johnny urged him on one more time, "You can *do* this!" Two minutes into the ninth, Michael attacked and then tried to push Danny out of the ring. To the horror of the officials sitting at the ringside table, he nearly succeeded. At the end of the round the fighters hugged each other briefly before returning to their corners. I asked Michael if he remembered doing that? "Yeah, I do, yeah." I asked "What was all that about?" He grinned, "I dunno. It was a good fight wasn't it?"

Danny appeared dazed as he sat on his stool before round ten. When the boxers came out of their corners, it was Michael who looked the stronger one. And then suddenly, they both looked so tired, particularly Michael. Early in the eleventh round, Danny started to box properly and focus seriously, and then at the end of the round he started pulling silly faces, and the crowd showed their disapproval by booing and jeering the Brixton man. The final round came and went and we all sat and awaited the decision.

Sometimes in boxing, you can be at a fight, watching it live, and then you can see it later on videotape and it can look like a totally different fight. The reason for this could be down to dimensional perspective. I don't think anybody really knows why for certain. I got appropriately carried away watching this fight and enjoyed it immensely. That night, at the fight, I was fully convinced that Michael had done enough to win the title. I turned to my friend sitting next to me, a man who goes by the name of Creamy, and wildly declared, "If he doesn't get this, I'm going to storm the ring single handed!" Creamy, who for the record is Tommy Eastwood's father and has been a fighting man all his life, and is a good and objective judge of a match, nodded his head in solemn agreement. But, he warned, "You never know with some of these decisions though."

In any event, Michael's hand was raised at the end of the fight and we all rose to our feet, as one, to roar our approval, hands raised above our heads, clapping for all we were worth. There was, however, a lot of debate about Dave Parris' decision and, when I watched the re-run on video the following afternoon, I saw it as a much closer affair with Danny in a strange mood and seemingly more intent on showboating, swaggering and goading. Maybe this is why Mr Parris saw the fight as Michael's, favouring his solid and honest style of work rather than Danny's flashy tactics, and he awarded the fight to Michael by one point.

Michael explained to me, "It was hard for me because *I* thought I was doing all right but, in the corner, every time it came to the end of a round they were all, like, 'You're losing this fight. You're missing this and that. You're four rounds behind.' I thought, 'Hang on a minute, there's two rounds to go,' and it sort of put me off a bit. I think they were trying to urge me on, but it done the opposite. Afterwards when I had a look at the tape, I knew it was close but I thought I nicked it."

After the fight, Danny was interviewed from the ringside and declared, "That was disgraceful. That was more disgraceful than the last fight, when they said I hit him with the low blows." Then Michael came and sat on the ring apron next to Danny, and when asked for his opinion he replied, “I thought it was kind of close but, you know, these things happen. I’ve had a lot of bad luck and maybe luck came my way.” And so, Michael Sprott was finally British and Commonwealth Heavyweight Champion, and one remote spectator of his triumph was Terry Lawless who was watching from his home in Marbella. “Yeah, I speak to him after the fights. Dean rings him up and says, ‘Here you are. I’ve got someone who wants to speak to you,’ and he hands me the phone and it’s Terry. He always wants to know that I’m doing all right.”

Exactly three months after winning his cherished British and Commonwealth Heavyweight Titles, Michael’s first defence of his belts ended in defeat. On the 24th April 2004 he was stopped in the twelfth and final round by Bedford hard man, Matt Skelton. The week before, I had spent a bit of time down at Jim’s Gym while Tommy Eastwood helped Michael prepare for his fight in the sparring ring. This was the first time I had seen Michael since he became British Champion and I immediately noticed a different air about him. His personality had not changed, he was still the same man as he will always be, but he had captured the aura of a Champion. It is something that seems to happen to boxers as they make their way up the through the grades. Something indefinable. A subtle sparkle. An invisible, yet vibrant energy, just beneath the surface. I remember feeling very proud of him.

Fight night arrived and Skelton brought about a thousand fans with him. Although the fight was at the Rivermead Leisure Centre, it was as if Skelton was the man fighting in his hometown. Before becoming a professional boxer Skelton fought on the K1 circuit, a combat technique based on a mixture of martial arts. He had been big in Japan and once fought before an audience of 48,000 in the same Tokyo Dome where Mike Tyson got knocked out by James Buster Douglas on that unthinkable night back in February 1990. As a K1 combatant, Skelton had stopped 36 of his 52 victims. He had also competed in a combat sport named Vale Tudo, an animalistic form of ‘anything goes’ fighting that originated in Brazil. He is a self-admitted knockout craver and yet, he reportedly prays before every fight that nobody gets hurt. At the age of 37, the body clock was ticking away and he wasn’t wasting any time.

Since making his professional boxing debut a year and a half earlier, Skelton had notched up 11 successive knockout wins, along the way winning the inaugural English Heavyweight Title against Michael Holden in September 2003. Prior to fighting Michael, he went the distance for the first time against former British and Commonwealth Heavyweight Champion, Julius Francis, in a defence of the English Heavyweight Title.

While Skelton was the bigger, stronger man who was racing his way up the ladder three steps at a time, Michael was considered by many to be the most improved boxer on British soil. It was an eagerly awaited match between the talented and highly rated nice guy from Reading and the popular roughhouse switch-hitter from Bedford. Skelton was a clubbing and all-out sort of fighter, heavy handed and awkward. He also had an irritating habit of holding and hitting, perhaps an inheritance from his K1 days. Whatever the reason, he did not mind fighting dirty. Johnny Bloomfield said to me while we were in the gym, "I'm going to talk to the referee in the dressing room. I'm going to tell him he needs to look out for that holding and hitting thing. I'm not having that."

They billed the fight as *'Urban Warfare'* and Skelton was grinning widely as he marched to the ring, dressed in gold gown and gold shorts with a black stripe, flanked by members of the army, his fans chanting his name. Michael came to the ring, resplendent in black shorts with a gold stripe. There were no smiles from him; his expression was serious and focused. Skelton was ferociously hyped up and he was the mauler from the opening bell. He ran straight into Michael and shoved him to the canvas, both of them landing in a tangled heap. By the end of the first round referee, Richie Davies, had already warned Skelton twice for holding and punching the back of the head.

As the fight went on, Skelton kept charging in and slugging away relentlessly. As they fought their way through the gruelling rounds, Skelton's work became rougher and it looked as if he might punch himself out in the steamy arena, but he kept on coming. As the fight reached the halfway point, Skelton was indeed starting to wilt and Michael was beginning to get on top. By the seventh, Skelton was bleeding from the mouth and looking weary. Then in the eighth, he came alive again and threw Michael to the canvas. This was the third time in the fight that he had done that and Johnny Bloomfield became so enraged that he jumped up onto the ring apron to complain. Richie Davies promptly sent the irate trainer away. Commentating from ringside, Glen McCrory called the fight, "Something of a bar room brawl," which is exactly what it was.

The crowd provided the background scene, competing with each other to chant their boxer's name the loudest. Michael tried his best to negate the forest fire that was Skelton's marauding aggression for the next couple of rounds but the clubbing punches kept coming his way with a vengeance. As the fight was coming to a close, both boxers looked exhausted. The final round arrived and the referee called them together to traditionally touch gloves but Skelton attempted to move behind Richie Davies' back to get at Michael that way. Davies insisted they obeyed his command and the fighters grudgingly did as they were told. They returned to their corners, the bell went and Skelton came charging out to fight, piling straight in and putting Michael down with an avalanche of clubbing shots. Michael looked bewildered and broken as he sat on the canvas, his back against the ropes. Richie Davies started counting and Michael turned onto his hands and knees. He managed to rise to his feet but Davies waved the fight off. Michael did not know where he was, and his titles were gone.

"That was a fight that I shouldn't have taken. I should have listened to John. John said, 'You've just won the British Title. Enjoy yourself. You've got six or seven months to defend. Just enjoy yourself.' He said, 'You should have a couple of easier fights, and *then* fight Skelton.' John said I could pick my next fight out of the top ten and then the Board would tell me who to fight. I said to John, 'I'm confident of beating Skelton,' but John was getting all these doubts, telling me, 'You shouldn't be taking it.' He said, 'You've had two tough fights with Danny. You've been training hard. Your body needs a bit of a *break* now.' But I didn't listen. I just carried on training, training hard and, come the night, my body sort of went down. I couldn't get my punches up or nothing. I was static. I don't remember much about it while I was in there really. But, to give Skelton his due, he won the fight and that's all there is to it. If I had the chance to fight him again, I'd definitely take it. But I should have listened more to what Johnny was telling me really. Everything John taught me in the gym, nothing came out in that fight, and every time I came back to the corner, John was like, 'What are you *doing*! Do you *want* this fight!'" Michael sounds spookily like Johnny when he imitates his old friend. "After it was over John said, 'Don't worry about it. We'll come back.' But, at the end of the day, I didn't perform to what I should have done, and a lot of people said that really. I felt withdrawn, really knackered, like I'd left everything in the gym. When we both went on the floor, I thought, 'Oh, we've got 12 rounds of this!'"

Five months later, in September 2004, Michael boxed Robert Sulgan at York Hall. I was lucky enough to spend a few days down at Jim's Gym with Michael, Tommy and Johnny Bloomfield while the boys did their sparring thing. One day during that week, Michael was describing to me what he knew about Robert Sulgan and at the end he added, as if a complete afterthought, "Oh yeah, and he's Czech Heavyweight Champion." Michael stopped Sulgan inside one minute. "When we came out of the changing rooms he looked kind of strong. He's never been stopped, I believe." This was Sulgan's thirteenth fight and Michael was indeed the first man to stop him. "I felt good. I'd had a long break from the Williams and Skelton fights. I felt strong. As soon as the bell went, he came towards me and I was jabbing away, caught him with a right hand. As soon as I caught him with the jab he looked shaky and I knew I had his number. And John shouted, 'Throw one through the middle!' As he came forward I threw an uppercut and he went down. The referee started counting and I thought, 'Bloody hell!' But everyone said it was a cracking shot, and then, when I looked at it on the tape, I caught him with my elbow. I hit his throat and I caught his windpipe. When you get caught there, it's a killer."

The Sulgan fight was the last one that Michael and Johnny Bloomfield would share together. The last time I ever saw Johnny, it was the day before Michael's weigh-in for the fight. Tommy was scheduled to box at Wembley arena on the same night as Michael was fighting at York Hall and we had to go to separate weigh-ins. Tom and I wished Michael and Johnny good luck and we said our goodbyes. We had no way of knowing that it was to be for the last time. On the afternoon of Friday, 17th September 2004, Tommy's Uncle Champ rang me up to tell me the news and I will never forget the bewildered devastation in his voice. Johnny Bloomfield had suffered a heart attack and had died that morning.

Johnny Bloomfield was a big man, both in physical stature and human presence. He was one of those devoted trainers who was always there for his fighters, working tirelessly behind the scenes to get them as fit and sharp for their fights as they could ever be. He had an understated way of getting his point across and took a genuine interest in the people he liked. He was clever and he was funny. Whenever he was interviewed about one of his boxers fighting away from home he used to say, "A good cock will crow anywhere." If Johnny Bloomfield took you into his heart, you knew you were doing something right. And in the gym I knew I was watching an accomplished master at work. He was one of the old school. A class act.

Sitting in that coffee bar on the day of our interview, as we reached the part that we had both been dreading, Michael's big dark eyes welled up with sadness. Personally, I have always been an emotionally open book and, as we spoke about our mutual friend, I had to fight back the tears. Michael spotted my imminent distress immediately and gallantly swept his own grief to one side, his eyes suddenly full of concern. He quietly told me, "I was at my friend's house and Dean rang me up. He said, 'John Bloomfield has passed away,' and I was in shock. I said, 'What!' I couldn't believe it. Because Dennie Mancini died the same week and John was saying, 'Poor thing,' about Dennie, and then the following week John passed away. It was a terrible shock. I burst into tears. I couldn't believe what was happening. I was at Dennie's funeral, which was sad. And then I went to John's funeral, which was more sad. Then, when I came back from John's funeral, I came back to my sister's house, dropped her home, and I got *another* phone call saying that my other sister's boyfriend had died in a car crash, the same day! Me and my sister just sat there in the car for about half an hour. I didn't know what to think next. And people were joking around saying, 'Stay away from Michael. He's got the jinx,' and things like that."

Johnny's funeral was held at St Dunstan's Church in Feltham on the 27th September 2004. Hundreds of people turned out to pay their last respects to the gentle giant who touched so many hearts during his most valuable life. As the magnificent black, plumed horses drew the carriage containing Johnny's flower laden coffin to the entrance of the church, Michael stood out among the silent crowd, looking imposing in a smart black suit, standing tall and proud, a helplessly solemn look in the soulful eyes. "I did cry when I saw the horses. I burst into tears. The same thing with Geoff McCreesh. A lady said afterwards that she'd never seen so many men cry. We were all in tears. Because, you know, men would always hold it in. But that's the effect it had, his presence. A big man, a big man. The last words John said to me were that I've got to stand up for myself. And the same to my sister. John and my sister got on really well. What's so strange, it's like John was telling her everything before he went. It's like he was telling her everything before his time was up."

It was weeks before Michael could bring himself to walk back into Jim's Gym. "I didn't go up the gym for a while, and then when I did it didn't *feel* the same, you know? John's friends at the Runnymede Hotel, where he used to go down and have a sauna and a Jacuzzi and that, some of them don't go there no more because they say it isn't the same. They feel that they can't go back there. It's not the same, it's not the same at all. So, I'm training with Jim Evans now. Because I think if John would want someone to train me, it would be Jim, because John and Jim were partners for a long time."

On the 23rd April 2005, Michael travelled to Dortmund in Germany to fight for the vacant European Union Heavyweight Title against Cengiz Koc. The shaven headed, pale skinned German-Turk boxed in the Sydney Olympics the same year as Audley Harrison. As a professional he had a perfect record of 21 wins, 13 inside the distance. Michael and I did the first stage of this interview prior to the fight with Koc and I though he looked in marvellous shape, both physically and mentally. He had that special glow about him and an air of confidence that made me feel that he had a good chance of winning, despite the fact that he was fighting a German in Germany. Most of the people I spoke to referred to that old but true cliché, 'He'll have to knock him out to get a draw over there.' I am delighted to report that Michael proved me right. He became the first man to beat Koc.

The fight was decided on a split decision and, even though the crowd were obviously biased towards their countryman, there was no argument with the judges' decision. It was a tough fight and they gave each other all the trouble each could handle. "I knew what it was like in Germany. I knew how the system works over there. Everyone knows, it's tough to get the decision in Germany, but I had a good feeling that I was gonna win the fight. I was very nervous, because I hadn't boxed for the best part of a year since the Skelton fight. I was kind of restless really, but I know how to box over there. They don't like any holding or anything like that, so I kept it real clean. Every time we got in a clinch I tried to keep my hands inside his, or I put my arm on his arms, because I knew the referee was looking at me to get points off. It was the best show I've ever boxed on. The atmosphere was unbelievable. I've never boxed on a show like that before. He came at me with a left jab and I came back with a little bit extra and he was throwing one back and he sort of stayed with me. I got a stitch in the fourth round and it slowed me down a bit for the fourth and fifth rounds, but then I got back on the job again and, instead of me keeping my composure and picking my shots, I was just going ballistic. I guess he was just holding on, sort of thing, but I did catch him with a few good shots. He was strong. I wouldn't say he was a big puncher, as such, but where he's short and stocky, he was throwing in body shots and clubbing hands over the top.

"When they announced it was a split decision, I knew I'd done enough to win, but I didn't think I'd get it. After what happened with Timo Hoffmann, I thought, 'Oh, I haven't got this. They're gonna cheat me again.' And then Dean went over and he must have heard. He came back and said, 'It's yours.' So I knew I had the decision. Dean kept his composure. Obviously, he wasn't going to jump for joy. They announced the score cards in German and then, after the last one they said, 'The European Union Title to Michael Sprott,' and I thought, '*Yes!*' I didn't go ballistic or jumping for joy, I was just happy. And the Germans were all right to me. After the fight, when they announced the decision, no one booed, everyone clapped. The people who were near my sister, Germans, were saying it was the right decision and everyone said how good a fight it was.

"I carried the little laminated card that they gave us at John's funeral and I put it on the TV, and I mentioned that I did this fight for John. And I prayed some nights. I prayed really hard before I went in there. I'll do this for John, and for my boy, and I felt like John was there listening to me. I like to think that he's there looking down on me. But going in for that fight without him was quite tough. It was a bit difficult really, without John in the corner shouting, 'Come on Michael!'

"Jim Evans took control of the corner. Before the fight he told Dean and Jimmy Tibbs, 'You lot stay here. I'm gonna take him outside.' He said, 'I'll do the advice, you two do the cuts and water and stuff.' He said to them that he didn't mind them geeing me up when I came back to the corner, but he would do the advice. It was all good, because when I was coming back to the corner Jim was saying, 'Right, listen to me,' and, you know, it was just quiet."

As we go to print Michael is still boxing, still striving for his World Title. "I'll go on as long as it takes really. I'm determined to become World Champion, and I'll carry on going 'till I get there. I mean, obviously, if I was really getting bashed about or I kept getting knocked out, then there's no point in really trying because you'll get hurt. But I don't think I will get that way, so I'm going to keep on going really. See what happens. I might have had a couple of times when I've thought, 'Oh, I'm not doing it any more,' but I've always been a determined guy. I'm determined to become World Champion and that's what keeps me going, and the things I want in life really.

"I've always worked. As soon as I left school I went straight to work and I've been working ever since. I was a hod carrier for seven years, and I've done removals for seven or eight years. I've always been active work-wise. I've gone back to it now. And for relaxing I like to go out to restaurants, or chill out at bars, or a sauna or a Jacuzzi, just chill out really and do nothing."

Former WBU Lightweight Champion, Colin Dunne, always describes Michael to me as the Evander Holyfield of British boxing. I once asked him why and he told me, "Because he's a small heavyweight who has fought everybody. He's fought all our top guys. He's never ducked anyone." So I found it fascinating when I discovered that Evander Holyfield is Michael's favourite boxer of this era. "He's my idol, yeah. My favourite boxer of all time is Muhammad Ali. But if you said a *fighter*, then it would be Mike Tyson."

And the biggest influence on his life? "God. I haven't been to church that much lately, but I do pray. I'm trying to get back into it. I'm not as strong with it as I used to be. I haven't been to church for a long time. My mum always took us to church with her from a young age. I was confirmed, the whole lot. My sisters go to church every Sunday. I'm the only one who doesn't go, but I do pray. I pray for my boy, my niece, my family, people with diseases around the world. I try and pray for everyone really. I pray, because kids growing up now, they're going to grow up in a bad place. But, you know, it's a good world, because of the people in it."

* * *

As I am preparing to put this book to bed, I would like to add the following footnote. After I interviewed Michael, he went on to have five more fights, in Germany, Austria and Scotland, along the way bagging the European Heavyweight Title for his trouble. But, for me, his true moment of glory came on the 17th February 2007. Michael returned to fight on English soil and he challenged Audley Harrison at Wembley Arena. I use the word "challenge" as if Harrison was the one who was defending when, in fact, it was Michael's European Title that was on the line, together with the vacant English Title. However, despite Michael being the defending Champion, he was considered to be the underdog in a big way.

In all honesty, when I discovered that my friend was taking this fight, I was concerned that Harrison would maul and spoil. I felt that he might use his rangy southpaw tactics to frustrate Michael out of the fight and take it on points. Then, on the Wednesday before the fight, I went to Jim's Gym with Tommy Eastwood and Michael was there. After a great big hug and the most mutually cheerful of greetings, I stood back and took a look at my friend. It immediately struck me that the aura was back with him, that radiant glow that came upon him when he won the British and Commonwealth Titles from Danny Williams back in 2004. It was at that moment that my worries went away. Now, I was in no doubt that this was a fight that Michael could certainly win, and I am delighted to report that he proved me right. It was one of those wonderful times in this world when the underdog, who just happens to be one of the sweetest men in boxing, came through in fine style and emerged victorious.

There were anxious moments in the first round when Michael went down after being caught with a right hook to body and a left to the head, but he was straight back up and undeterred. Harrison piled into Michael on the ropes and Michael just charged straight back out again, chasing Harrison across the ring before the bell went to end the round. Six minutes later, right at the end of the third round, Harrison went in with a left uppercut and Michael countered with the left hook of his life, which caught Harrison square on his jaw. Harrison went down like a tree, and it was all over. Michael had done what he set out to do.

I was at home that night watching the fight on the television, and I could not help but feel sorry for Audley when, once he was back on his feet and the result was announced, the crowd booed at the mention of his name. But, at the same time, my heart was bursting with warmth for the winner. I shed more than a few tears that night, but they were tears of joy, for this was a triumph that was never more deserved.

After the fight, Michael went away to New York for a well-earned holiday. When he returned, I rang him up and we had a lovely chat. Obviously, one of our main topics of conversation was the fight, and he told me, "Oh, I was over the moon, really over the moon." As he said the words, I could hear the sparkle in his voice, and then suddenly the tone became solemn, like the sound of an aching heart. "That win was for Johnny Bloomfield. I really, really wish he could be here now. You know, he wasn't just a trainer. He was a friend and a father figure. But I know that he is with me in spirit."

Jim Evans is still in Michael's corner, loyal and true, and when I asked him to tell me how he felt about Michael's win against Harrison, he replied, "You can say that Jim says, sometimes nice guys do come first."

Whenever I think of Michael Sprott, it is his fabulous smiling face that always springs straight to mind, and his smile was never more stunning than in that ring at Wembley Arena. But, that night, I am certain there was an angel in heaven with the pads on - whose smile was just as bright.

CHAPTER SIX - MARK ROWE

We had such a hard fight. It was a really ferocious fight. Actually, the referee wanted to stop it but it showed favour to me that he didn't. I would say that Mark Rowe was the strongest amateur that I ever boxed." **(Jimmy Tibbs)**

When I wrote *'Sweet Fighting Man'* one of the first subjects I interviewed was Jimmy Tibbs. It was during my research for Jimmy's chapter that I started to learn all about Mark Rowe. These two met in an ABA Championship match back in the 1960's and their fight was one of the all-time classics of British amateur boxing history. The 5,000 strong crowd present at the Albert Hall were on their feet from the beginning to the end of this epic clash, which incidentally Mark won on points. As I read the reports and studied the photographs, I became captivated by the concept of the dark and menacing Jimmy Tibbs doing battle with the blond and charismatic Mark Rowe. I learned that Mark went on to win an Empire Games Gold Medal, and then turned professional, becoming British and Commonwealth Middleweight Champion in 1970. Initially, he took the titles from Les McAteer, stopping the Liverpudlian in the fourteenth round. Then he controversially lost his belts in his first defence against Bunny Sterling on a questionable cut eye verdict. In a final challenge to regain the British Title from Sterling, Mark was defeated on points. This was his final fight.

Going back to the days when Mark was a sparkling young amateur, so much was expected from him by the media and by his army of fans. These days, Mark firmly believes that he never fulfilled his true potential. He explained to me, "I didn't really live up to what the fans wanted and I didn't live up to what I wanted to do myself. I never really achieved what I should have done in boxing. I think it was because I wasn't really happy a lot of the time. I was never, ever settled. It was all up in the air, which was a shame." He spoke the words in a matter of fact fashion, but I detected in his voice the most distant note of yearning for what could have been. It seems to me that it is often the special people in this world, those who give so much of themselves, who end up wishing that they could have given more.

Mark's style of fighting was relentless. He was always prepared to take the shots himself, without bending, without breaking, refusing to go down, just so that he could get to where he wanted to be, up close so that he could unleash his phenomenal body punches, to the detriment of many of his opponents. His ferocity in the ring, together with his golden persona, earned him the hero worship of the fight crowd of the time. Having got to know Mark as he is today, the words I would use to describe him would be calm, capable and kind. He is not the most talkative of men, definitely not one to brag. Put him on the spot about his boxing fame and he instinctively retreats behind a guard of bashfulness. His face, which is unmarked by battle scars, remains instantly recognizable from the days when he was hailed as the glamour boy of the ring.

The first time I actually met Mark was in the summer of 2001 at the Angels with Dirty Faces annual Boxers versus Blind golf tournament. During these matches a number of blind golfers challenge their sighted opponents, many of whom are boxers. The blind golfer has a guide who becomes the eyes of the partnership. When the golfer is lined up and his club is in the right place, the guide steps well back, right away from the swinging club, and the blind golfer does his thing. During the day, the Angels raise money to keep their charitable events going and spread their special kind of happiness wherever they can. Unbeknown to me, my first visit to this event was to be very much a hands-on experience. My friend, and Angels stalwart, Bob Paget, telephoned me to invite me along and during that conversation he introduced me to Tommy Mulholland. "Here's Tommy," said Bob, "Have a chat with him." Tommy is one of the event organizers and he is also one of the blind golfers. We finished our conversation that day, happily looking forward to meeting up the following week.

The following Wednesday, when I arrived at Wandsworth, Bob and Tommy broke it to me that I was, in fact, to be Tommy's guide for the day. I agreed to take on the task but I was more than a little apprehensive. I had never been on a golf course before in my life and, although Tommy was not eager to win the tournament as he had taken the top slot for the previous two years, he was not too keen on coming bottom either! We walked out onto the course on that sunny June morning, me in front, Tommy's hand on my shoulder, and I was praying that he wouldn't feel the vibrations of my pounding heart. I had no idea where to start and I was petrified that I was going to let him down.

Fortunately for me, Mark Rowe was the boxer on our team. I explained my predicament to him and he was typically patient and generous, showing me the teeing off procedure and explaining how it all worked. His kindness really settled my nerves and, by the time we reached the third hole, I jovially asked him, "Shall Tommy and I tee off first this time?" Mark looked down at me with a quizzically raised eyebrow. "You're getting a bit confident, aren't you?" he asked. To which I replied, "Well, you might as well get hung for a sheep as a lamb." While the rest of our team, including Mark, stood by in mystified silence, Tommy and I took our place on the third tee and we were off! When it goes right it is brilliant to watch and there were times during the day when I found it impossible to contain my enthusiasm. And thanks to the guidance of Mark Rowe, Tommy and I came second – which was perfect.

Mark and I arranged to meet for this interview in August 2003 at his farmhouse in Kent. The week before, I told Reg Gutteridge that I was going there he warned me, "It's a lovely place, but you'll never bloody find it." With this in mind, Mark kindly suggested that we should meet at a garage near his home that is easy to find, and then he would guide me through the rural country lanes. However, shortly before I got there, I managed to take a wrong turning off one of the roundabouts and I pulled over into a dual carriageway lay-by to ring Mark. "Oh dear," he sympathised, "You'll have to go all the way to the next roundabout and turn back. It's quite a way." "Don't worry," I assured him. "There's no mid-section here, so I'm going to wait for a break in the traffic and do a U-turn." *"What!"* came the shocked reply, "You be careful!"

Thankfully, no harm was done and I found the designated garage without having to demonstrate my daring driving skills any further. Mark came out to meet me and, as I followed him home, I saw what Reg had meant. I could not have found 'The Grove Farmhouse' if my life had depended on it. The farm itself is no longer in operation, but for many years it was a pig farm, originally started by Mark's father, Bill. As we walked into the house I mentioned to Mark that I often saw him described in his boxing days as the handsome, blond pig farmer from Kent, which made him laugh. "Well, I'd been doing the pig farming since I left school at 15, and I used to run in the morning and go in the gym in the evening. So I kept it going from when I left school until I was 19, when I turned professional." When he retired from boxing Mark returned to the pig farming and continued to run the farm until 1990, a job that he enjoyed very much. "Pigs are lovely animals. They're very inquisitive you know, very nice they are."

Reg Gutteridge once told me that he remembered visiting the farm one time to talk to Mark's father. At the end of the day Bill asked Reg if he would like "a bit of bacon to take home." Reg duly accepted the offer and told me, "I thought, I'll have a nice piece of ham to take home to the wife. Anyway, before I could blink, he'd put a whole dead pig in the boot of my car!" When I related this story to Mark, he grinned, "Yeah. That was my dad."

Mark's wife, Sandra, was in the kitchen when we stepped through the door and she welcomed me warmly and offered me some lunch. Mark and I sat in their sunroom, which looks out onto the back garden, and I was surprised to see some bovines in the adjacent field. They were blankly staring in at us from across the lawn, which alarmed me slightly as, I have to confess, I am rather scared of cows. "My goodness, look at those!" I exclaimed. Mark smiled and informed me, "Oh, they're all right. They're only bullocks." Our interview began and I soon forgot the bullocks were out there and enjoyed our chat.

Mark Rowe was born in Camberwell on the 12th July 1947. "I started boxing when I was nine because my father wanted me to be a boxer. He was in the army and Randolph Turpin was around at the time. My father was a PT instructor in the army and he used to tell me, when he was in the army they used to just put them in and say, 'Right, you're boxing him,' and he just wanted me to be able to defend myself I suppose. So that's basically how it started, when I was at school, because they had a boxing team there." Mark is a firm advocate that Britain would be a better place if they brought boxing back to schools today. “Yes, definitely. It would definitely teach the boys some discipline and respect and things. I started boxing at Northfleet Boys School, Colyer Road School. I was about ten when I had my first amateur match. I went from there to Brixton and District Boxing Club for about a year and a half, and then I went to Fitzroy Lodge when I was 12 years of age.”

As Mark settled down at Fitzroy Lodge, he matured into a light-middleweight and it was there that he met a man who would become a key character in his story. His name is Bill Chevalley. Mark explained, “I was with Bill from when I was about 13. When I went to Fitzroy Lodge, Vic Andreetti started to look after me, and then for some reason, I can’t remember why because it was a long time ago, Bill took me over. After that he trained me all the way through the amateurs, and then I turned professional and he stuck with me. Bill wasn’t exactly my manager in that sense, but he was, if you know what I mean.”

I have used plenty of Bill Chevalley’s words of wisdom in this chapter so, in an effort to make smooth and comprehensive reading, I have printed his words in italics. Therefore, whenever you see *italic* print, it is Bill who is doing the talking.

Bill Chevalley is a man who was no stranger to the boxing ring himself in his youth. He never turned officially professional but he had 187 fights, many of which took place while he served his time in the Royal Navy. He was knocking around the professional boxing gyms when he was no more than a lad. He started as a flyweight and finished up as a featherweight. When he finished fighting he turned to training and, looking back at it all, he believes that possibly two or three hundred boxers passed through his hands, but he was quick to add that number was *“a pure guess.”*

Bill, Mark and myself are all members of the London Ex Boxers Association (LEBA) and it was at one of the LEBA meetings that I asked Bill if he would give me some words for Mark’s chapter. He generously replied, *“I’ll be happy to help in any way that I can.”* The following month, Bill and I got together at the post-meeting drink downstairs in the bar. We took ourselves off into a quiet corner and we made a lovely tape. *"I was a trainer up Fitzroy Lodge, and there was Vic Andreetti, Kenny Field, all that lot were down there. We had a very, very strong team down there. Anyway, from the moment I started training Mark I took him along very, very slowly, in a fashion, like, 'Oh, that's good, but why don't you try it this way?' I worked with him on his technique.*

"By the time he was 14, he was working like a pro. See, I taught all my fighters to fight as if they were pros, so that if they did turn pro they wasn't going from there to there. I myself was in a pro gym when I was 14 years of age. I mean, Mark knocked two pro's out in the gym when he was an amateur because they started taking liberties, and one of them was a very, very good fighter." Bearing in mind the historical reluctance that the amateur authorities have always shown to allow their boxers to mix with those who punch for pay, I asked Bill how his relationship was with the ABA in those days. Was he allowed to mix his methods without getting penalized? *"No, no, no. I just done it. The ABA, oh, they didn't like me at all.*

"The thing was with Mark, he done as he was told, always. He had space down the farm and he used to work hard down there. What you taught him on the Thursday, by the Monday he was getting there. He was very easy to teach. Even as a kid, he used to come up from Kent to either the 'Beckett or Fitzroy Lodge. I used to see him four or five days a week. He only lost two junior fights and on both of them he was robbed, diabolically. It was spite, 'cos the ABA just didn't like me."

In 1963 Mark lost the National Junior ABA final to Tom Imrie, a labourer from Leith with black curly hair and a lob sided grin. Bill Chevalley remains bemused to this day that the judges awarded the decision to the Scotsman. *"How they gave him the verdict at the Albert Hall, I just don't know. Again, I think it was spite. The ABA just didn't like me. Not that I wanted to be liked. I just wanted to train fighters."*

Mark went on to win two Junior ABA Titles before joining the senior ranks. I found that, even in those early days, he was a regular feature in the amateur pages and often the front page of the Boxing News. I asked if he felt the pressure of that. "Not particularly, no. I don't think I was in there that often, I think maybe just a couple of times, probably when I got beat by Imrie in the ABA finals, and when I went to the Empire Games." I adamantly stood my ground, "No, you were in there all the time." He laughed, "Was I? Well, to be honest, I didn't used to buy the Boxing News every week. I used to get it sometimes but not always. I must have missed some of them."

These were the days when amateur boxers were given so much more freedom with their style, before the introduction of the much disliked computer scoring system which encourages our young talent to throw single, heavy shots rather than go for exciting flurries and hooks to the body. Also, the fact that the boxers did not wear head-guards back then meant that the audience could see the boxers' faces and really identify with them. Mark's handsome looks combined with his fearless approach made for a potent combination, and the fans loved him.

The thriller that Jimmy Tibbs describes at the top of this chapter is still discussed today in boxing circles, and many regard it as one of the best amateur contests ever. It was the 1966 North-East London ABA tournament and they boxed at the Albert Hall. Jimmy still maintains that Mark was the strongest amateur he ever boxed, and the feeling is mutual. "Well, I maintain the same thing. That's my favourite amateur fight too. I boxed him when I was about 12 at West Ham and he beat me that night. Then, when I was about 18, we boxed again and it was spoke about a lot, you know, so I suppose there was a bit of pressure there at that time. Because it was, like, you both really wanted to win. And it was a good fight, me and Jimmy, a good fight."

When I reminded Mark that, although the bout went the distance, the referee came close to stopping Jimmy because of facial injuries, he seemed surprised. "Was he? I don't think so." I confirmed that Jimmy's version of events testifies to this fact. "Well, he's the man who should know, but I can't remember doing it. It was ever so close. I only wish I had the film of it. The atmosphere was a bit electrified. Then, when I got back in the ring in the evening to fight Ronnie Smith, the crowd really roared and the atmosphere, it sort of took you back a little bit. That was the London Finals. That was the first time I boxed Ronnie Smith. I boxed him again the following year. Anyway, I won the Londons that year, but I didn't win the finals."

The night of the National Finals arrived and, when the Boxing News came out the same day, the front page was dominated by a photograph of Mark, looking resplendent in a dark satin gown, gloves on, holding a trophy aloft. The tournament was held at Wembley Pool and in the other corner was Tom Imrie. Imrie was seen very much as the underdog. In fact, the Boxing News did everything but actually write the words, "Mark Rowe will win this fight."

The most dangerous weapon that Imrie possessed was his phenomenal punching power. While I was putting this chapter together I was chatting on the telephone one evening with my great friend, Sylvester Mittee. Sylvester and I got talking about this fight and he reminded me, "They used to call him Tom 'TNT' Imrie, and do you know why? Because he had dynamite in both gloves."

Battle commenced and, just as it looked as if Mark's destiny was about to be fulfilled, something happened that had not been in the script. "Yeah, I got knocked out by Tom Imrie. He caught me with a right hand at the end of the third round." As Mark lay on the canvas, Imrie's delighted team-mates jumped into the ring and, one by one, they leapt over Mark's motionless body. The doctor was called into the ring and Mark was soon up again. The first thing he did was congratulate Imrie on his victory.

Bill Chevalley was never a man to treat his boxers with kid gloves. *"It was his own silly fault. I mean, Imrie was all over the show. He was falling to pieces. I said to Mark beforehand, I said 'Take your time and do as your told.' I couldn't go in the corner with him because I had a pro licence. Imrie just shut his eyes and threw one. It was just a lucky punch. Mark wasn't hit, he just walked into it and, I mean, they couldn't believe it. This is why they all stormed into the ring afterwards. Mark did exactly what I told him not to do."* Suddenly, Bill's whole demeanour softened. *"But I didn't make an issue out of it. I mean, he was in shock, the kid, more or less. He couldn't believe it, because he was so far in front. I told him, 'Don't worry about it. You've earned what you've earned. Now, don't throw away what you've learned.' The thing is, see, if he'd have beaten Imrie when they boxed at the Albert Hall, then he wouldn't have been so excited to get rid of him. It was sort of like, 'You've cheated me once. You're not going to cheat me a second time.'"*

After the fight, back in his dressing room, it took Mark a while to regain his bearings. "I remember I went back to the dressing room and I didn't know what had happened. I was saying, 'When am I on? Am I on next?' And they said I just got knocked out. I said, 'I haven't boxed yet.' So I didn't even know. I sat there for a quite while and then, as I had a shower, bits of the fight started to come back to me. But, for that while, I couldn't even remember being knocked out. I couldn't even remember the punch. You never can, can you? You don't see it."

Later that year Mark was picked to compete in the Empire Games in Jamaica, a memory that evoked a sunny smile. "Oh it was lovely; really nice. Beautiful place. It was lovely to be there, taking part with the other athletes." In those days the Empire Games generated the same sort of excitement as professional title fights do today. The public really got behind it. The proprietor of the Thomas A' Beckett pub, Tommy Gibbons, held a benefit night to raise spending money for the boxers and Mark has fond memories of Mr and Mrs Gibbons. "My relationship with Tommy Gibbons and his wife Beryl was very good, yeah. I was training up the Thomas A' Beckett so I used to see them nearly every day, so my relationship with Tom and Beryl was brilliant.

"There were quite a few good fighters using the Thomas A' Beckett at the time. Oh blimey! I remember Vic Andreetti was there, Kenny Fields and Billy 'Kid' Davies. Henry Cooper came up there some times. Dave Charnley was up there sometimes; he was a good fighter. I can't name many people really who should have been World Champion but, if anyone should have been, Dave Charnley should have been." During his career, the Boxing News often compared Mark's style with that of Charnley, something that pleased Mark when I pointed it out. "Yeah, there was quite a few fighters there. I used to spar with quite a few fighters all the time. I thoroughly enjoyed that. Good times."

One man who I know used to share the sparring ring with Mark was popular veteran fight figure, Steve 'Columbo' Richards. Steve once placed the palm of my hand on his left rib cage and demonstrated that the bones actually move. As I jolted my hand away in horror, Steve leaned forward and sagely informed me, "See that? That was Mark Rowe, that was." But there are obviously no hard feelings about it, as Steve had a big smile on his face at the time.

Mark returned from Jamaica with the Empire Games Gold Medal at light-middleweight, winning the final against Tom Imrie. "Third time lucky. After the fight was over and I'd won the gold medal, Tom just said to me, 'You won the one that matters.' Because he'd won the Junior ABAs and the Senior ABAs but *I* won the one that mattered, and I remember him saying that to me." I asked Mark which was best, beating Tom Imrie or winning the gold medal. He laughed. "Both, I think. It was lovely. I'd love to go back and do it again, but I can't because it's too late now. You can only do it once, can't you? But it was lovely." For the record, Mark became the first British boxer to win a Gold Medal since Brian London bagged a Gold in the Vancouver Empire Games in 1954.

In September 1966, at the age of 19, Mark announced that he was turning professional. "Well it's what I wanted to do all the time really, from when I was a young teenager. I always looked up to Joe Louis. He was my favourite boxer of all time. I met him once, in Germany. He was ever so nice. I was having a photo taken with him and then somebody came walking across, and he told them get out of the way while we had our photo taken. He was a nice chap." Although the top managers were approaching Mark, he chose to sign with a virtual newcomer to boxing management, a former professional boxer, 28 year old Johnny Arrow. "Well, it wasn't really down to me. It was more down to Bill Chevalley. He chose Johnny Arrow."

Bill considered this issue for a moment before he told me, *"I gave him the freedom to go with a manager. I wasn't his manager, as such, but I was, if you know what I mean. When he was an amateur, I did it to protect him from the ABA. When he turned professional, I used to sort of make sure his money was okay, and Johnny Arrow was a good manipulator. He knew how to get salt out of a saltcellar when it was damp."*

Mark received over £8,000 to turn professional. This lucrative offer put him up there, in boxing terms, with the likes of Billy Walker, 'Blond Bomber' and international superstar. Mark laughed modestly, "I was nothing like that; no, definitely not." But, despite what he says, the boxing media had bestowed on Mark the same name as his heavyweight contemporary, 'The Golden Boy.' I put that to him and his face lit up. "Oh blimey! I think they started calling me that as an amateur, when I won my medal. It was quite nice, yes." Bill Chevalley was quick to emphasize, *"All the fighters that I handled, I always made sure their feet kept on the floor. Every fight was a different problem, because every opponent was a different opponent."*

In order to join the paid ranks, Mark had to move up to middleweight, as the professional light-middleweight division did not exist in those days. "I think they brought in the professional light-middleweight division in about 1971, so I fought as a middleweight and I was only about 11 stone, three. I didn't mind, but naturally, I suppose, I would have been a light-middleweight." Mark's professional debut arrived on the 25th October 1966. His opponent was Hugh Lynch. The charismatic Brixton based Jamaican southpaw was no pushover, but it still caused massive shockwaves when Mark lost the fight by a quarter of a point over six rounds. "Yeah, I got beat on points. It was my first professional fight and I remember going in, and when they said my name and that, there was quite a roar, you know. It took me back a bit, because it's a strange feeling when you're in there having your first professional fight. That was a little bit of pressure, I suppose.

"And boxing at the Albert Hall as well, that was a great place to fight actually. I was always a bit of a slow starter and nerves made a big difference. Sometimes, if you were a bit nervous, it could take you a bit of time to get going. I used to control the nerves quite well. Maybe when I was younger ... But it's the same for everybody, isn't it, no matter who they are? I used to go in the dressing room and think about what I was going to do the next day. On the day of the fight, I'd go out and watch a film or something, try and concentrate on that and not really think too much about the fight." Eager to dispel the disappointment of his debut, three weeks later Mark blew away his next opponent, East Ham's Chris Jobson, in 65 seconds. "That was at the Hilton and I stopped him in one round. Then I fought Dave Wakefield, didn't I?"

It really is a small world, and never so much as in the boxing world. I know David Wakefield very well, as I am close to his son, who is also called David and is currently a professional welterweight, and his daughter-in-law, Caroline. I am also Godmother to one of his grandsons, Mark.

In December 1966 Mark Rowe stopped David Wakefield senior in three rounds. "I remember hurting my knuckle. I went to hit him to the body and I caught his elbow, and they weren't a brilliant pair of gloves. The padding was really bad on one side and I done my knuckle. I had to have a cortisone injection before the next time I boxed." They used to call David Wakefield the 'Hackney Nobbins King' and that night his bravery was a clear indication of how he got his name. But bravery was not enough to overcome the force of Mark Rowe and, in the third round the referee, Harry Gibbs, stopped the fight to protect Wakefield from 'taking further punishment,' as they say in boxing. But, all the way up to that point, David Wakefield was as brave and game as they come, and I can confirm that he still is today! I made Mark laugh when I told him that, in my opinion, David Wakefield would still fancy a rematch. "Oh, really? He was a brave man."

1967 arrived and, in January, Mark stopped Glaswegian, Derek Cowper, in another sweeping third round victory. This one was at the Albert Hall and on top of the bill was the late, great Howard Winstone who that night fought and beat American, Richie Sue, on points. "Yeah. I knew Howard. He was ever so nice, Howard. He was a really nice chap. I didn't watch them that night because, by the time I went back to the dressing room and had a shower, it probably would have been all over, and I just used to go home then. I wouldn't necessarily go out and watch the other fights.

"But it was very sad when Howard died. I mean, he was only 61, wasn't he? That's no age at all really. I met him quite a lot of times and I saw him box quite a lot of times as well. I watched him when he boxed Vicente Saldivar at Earls Court. It was a great fight. Saldivar never stopped throwing punches. He was ever so busy."

A couple of weeks later, Mark was back in business. He stopped Joe Falcon in the fifth round. "That was at Bermondsey Baths." They called Falcon 'The Iron Man,' and he was vastly experienced. Mark agreed, "Yeah, he *was* a bit sly in the ring. He'd been around a long time and he knew all the tricks." Even though Falcon had lost many points decisions, Mark became only the second man to stop him in 56 fights. As the rounds slipped by, Mark steadily built up the pressure and in the fourth round he drove the Midlander all over the ring. Falcon had to be saved by the bell. Mark attacked with venom as the bell began the fifth and it was all over bar the shouting when the referee, Pat Floyd, stopped the fight. "I met Joe Falcon a few times since, just recently. I say recently, about three or four months ago. He's all right Joe, yeah. He gave me his address."

On St Valentine's Day 1967 Mark performed at the Albert Hall, but there was no love affair between he and Nigerian, Ernesto Musso. "Yeah, I remember. I stopped him in four rounds." A month later, Willie Fisher of Craigneuk was stopped by Mark in the first round at Wembley's Empire Pool. "I got him with a left hook to the body. I remember he caught me on the shoulder. I just turned and he hit me on the shoulder and it went BANG, and it went numb, it did, for a few seconds. I remember thinking I was glad he hit me on the shoulder, not on me chin! Because if he had, I think *I'd* have been on the floor rather than him actually, because he was a good puncher."

Three weeks later Mark avenged his debut defeat against Hugh Lynch. "Yeah, it was a bit of a score settler. I boxed him at Manor Place Baths and beat him on points. He was a big southpaw, quite a big lump. I fought quite a few southpaws. I think it was probably a bit easier fighting orthodox boxers, but it didn't bother me really. When I took the gloves off after boxing Hugh Lynch that time, my hands were all swollen. I don't know why, because they were all bandaged up properly."

It was around this time that Mark was featured on the old ITA television, on a sports series. "Oh, was I?" Mark seemed keen to sweep this aside, and when I asked him if he got on the television much, he replied, "Not really, no." Having said that, many of the reports I read about him called him a "TV star."

But, back to the boxing, next in Mark's firing line was Belgian Light-Middleweight Champion, Roger Van Laere, at the New St James' Hall in Newcastle in May 1967. By the end of the first round Van Laere was reddened around the face and body and, as he rose from his stool to come back out, he had the look of a defeat about him. That brave Belgian had been down three times in the second round when his corner threw the towel in, but referee, Fred Wintrip, kicked the towel back out of the ring and ordered the men to keep boxing. Van Laere's corner, desperate to stop the hammering that their man was taking, threw the towel back in, but this time the referee failed to see it. Moments later it was obvious, even to Mr Wintrip, that this boxing match was turning into a one sided beating and he stopped it in the final seconds of the round. Poor old Roger Van Laere left the ring to a booing crowd and the memory made Mark sympathetically shake his head. "He didn't deserve that. I mean, the bloke's come over here to do his best, and I think he did try. It wasn't as if he wasn't trying."

As Mark's career was progressing he was becoming more and more of a boxing star, despite his earnest protestations to the contrary. In June 1967 Mark boxed another natural crowd pleaser, in the shape of Pat Dwyer of Liverpool. Just like Mark, Dwyer had been an exciting amateur. His idol was Terry Downes and, when he reached the senior ranks, he used to delight the crowds by imitating Terry's ring antics, something he would never have got away with under today's amateur regime. The fight with Mark had come close to being called off when Dwyer had a warm-up bout against Bermuda's Freddie Thomas and was stopped in 90 seconds. Because of that loss, the bookies had Mark down as the strong favourite to win. Dwyer was 21 at the time, two years older than Mark, and he had twice as many professional fights under his belt. Because of the high profile of both men, this fight captured the interest of the national newspapers and television cameras in a big way. The pressure was on.

The fight took place at the Albert Hall. As Mark thought back to that night, his voice became more hushed now, his face set in a serious and thoughtful expression. "He stopped me in the fourth round, yes. I was nice and fit for the fight. I saw Pat box several times and I didn't think he would jab and move when I fought him, and when the bell rang and I came out, he started back-pedalling and jabbing and it really honestly took me out of my stride a little bit; it really did. Then he caught me in the fourth round and I went down. It marked me up a little bit and when I got up, instead of getting hold of him, I went to have a fight and I got caught again. But, that's what threw me, because where I thought he was going to come out and have a fight, he never.

"I remember reading about Gene Fullmer fighting Dick Tiger, and the same thing happened there. Gene Fullmer didn't come forward like he usually did and he took Dick Tiger out of his stride for a little bit. I know it sounds silly but that's what happens." I assured him that it didn't sound silly at all. "Well, like I say, Dwyer put me down, and I got up too quick and I got caught again, and eventually I got stopped. Because he caught me with a couple of good punches, and when I got up my head wasn't clear. I should have stayed down really and took a count. But I wasn't out cold. I was still conscious, whereas with Tom Imrie, I just didn't even know what had happened.

"Anyway, it was the end of the season and I had a break for a few months. Then I fought Tommy Bell at the Grosvenor House Hotel. He was quite cagey. I didn't let the stoppage against Pat Dwyer affect me. I just boxed Tommy Bell as I normally would, and I stopped him in the third round." Anxious not to let the grass grow under his feet, three weeks later Mark stopped Jackie Cailleau in the fifth round at Manor Place Baths. When the end came, the Frenchman was trapped in a neutral corner and Mark dropped him to the floor with a blizzard of shots. Cailleau staggered to his feet but raised his hands, seemingly in a sign of surrender, and walked back to his corner. All the fight had been knocked out of him. Mark gently acquiesced, "I boxed quite well that night, yeah."

Mark began 1968 with a January six round demolition job on Henry 'The Turk' Turkington who had travelled over to London from Belfast to box

Mark on a wintry Tuesday night. Turkington was a game, all action fighter who, prior to his fight with Mark, had been the distance with both Les McAteer and Bunny Sterling, drawn with Pat Dwyer and held a points victory over Harry Scott. "Oh yes, that was at the Royal Garden Hotel. That was for Tommy Gibbons and Beryl. That was quite a good fight. He was ever so strong, Turkington. He was a tough nut, but I didn't know he'd boxed all those."

1968 brought with it turbulent times in Mark's corner. He had a new manager, Arthur Boggis, a man who Mickey Duff once described as "The gamest manager who ever lived." Boggis and Bill Chevalley were not seeing eye to eye and the effect of the unrest took its toll. Mark and Bill went their separate ways for a while. "For a while, yes. It was silly really. I hated all that. Because, when you've been with a trainer for such a long time, it leaves you feeling unsettled, you know? You've got to know each other and you suddenly find yourself in a different place, and it upsets you a bit. I went with Freddie Hill, Al Phillips, I was all over the place. I actually went with four or five different trainers at the time. I was never settled, and it was like that all the time. It was a shame really."

But the show must go on, as they say. In March 1968 Mark forced Paris-based Lebanese southpaw, Assane Fakyh, to retire in six rounds at Manor Place Baths. Training duties that night were taken up by former professional featherweight, Charlie Tucker. When Mark stepped through the ropes to take his place in the ring, the thousands of fans who cheered and chanted his name had no idea of the conflicts that clouded the mind of their hero. "That wasn't a very good fight. I didn't box all that well. I can't remember if I stopped him or if I won on points." When I confirmed that Mark stopped him in six rounds, he replied, "Did I?" Fakyh was saved by the bell at the end of the fifth round, but he failed to come out for the sixth and referee, Harry Gibbs, declared him disqualified. This was a sad ending because, in fact, Fakyh was cut badly inside his mouth, an injury which later needed three stitches.

"Then I boxed Nojeen Adigun [in May 1968]. That was at York Hall. I liked boxing at York Hall. It's a nice, cosy little place, like Manor Place Baths and all those little places. A lovely little place." Mark looked to be on his way to another victory, almost punching the muscular Nigerian out of the ring in the third round, but in the fourth Mark suffered a gruesome cut to his face. Referee, Harry Humphreys, stopped the action to inspect the injury and called the fight off. "I used to bleed quite badly, but there's nothing you can do about that really. If you get cut, you get cut. But I can't remember if it was his head or not. I know some of them, they'd used their head, they done it on purpose, but with this fella I can't remember if it was accidental. But, you know, I was a bit disappointed being stopped like that. I don't think I was boxing my best at that time, not at all. My mind was all over the place and I wasn't focused. I'd run hard and train hard in the gym, but there was so much turmoil going on outside and I tried to block everything out, but I couldn't do that, and you've got to have that. You've got to be fit physically, but you've got to be right in your mind as well. You've got to be right in both. I used to always be training. I probably did too much. I used to keep myself fighting fit all the time."

Bill Chevalley returned to the fold, and in September 1968 Mark stopped Larry Brown in two rounds at Wembley. Mark grinned happily as he told me, "I boxed well that night. It was good. Because I'd been away from Bill for a while and I think this was the first one where he was back with me, and I just felt good." The following month, Mark stopped popular Londoner and Southern Area Champion, Johnny Kramer, in three rounds. With seven years between them, it was a case of Kramer's talent and experience against Mark's youth and powerful aggression. The fight began and Kramer used the ring to his advantage, putting his fine boxing skills into play. Mark was out early to meet Kramer in his own corner at the start of the second and he threw caution to the wind, taking jabs to the face which he didn't seem to feel in order to get in close where he could make his mark with pounding fists to the body. When the third round arrived, Kramer discarded his clever boxing tactics and decided to have a fight. It was a bad move and, before the round was over, Mark had beaten him to the floor with a body assault. The Canning Town boxer remained on one knee as he was counted out. "Yeah, I boxed well, but Johnny Kramer was a good boxer, a good mover. Me and Johnny are good friends. We were out playing golf yesterday at Hendon Manor. Me and

Johnny Kramer versus 'The Toffs.' They're known as 'The Toffs' they are, against the boxers. It's a good day out. Johnny's a nice chap."

I had the opportunity to speak to Johnny at a LEBA meeting before this book went to print, and he was quick to repay the compliment. "Oh yes, Mark and I are good friends. He hit me in the belly and stopped me. I'll never forget that, after the fight, the referee told me that he had been thinking about stopping Mark at the end of the round because of a cut eye, but that's life."

Three weeks later Mancunian warhorse, Nat Jacobs, was Mark's next victim. For Mark's part, it was an assault that was brutally perfect in its intensity and, despite being cut across the right eyelid from a head clash in the second round, he forced the referee to stop the fight in the third round. "Well, at this particular time, there was Larry Brown, then there was Johnny Kramer and then Nat Jacobs. I felt much more happier in myself, and I knocked Nat Jacobs out in three rounds. I remember that one. It was a good fight. I felt more a lot happier, more comfortable in myself.

Mark saw out the year of 1968 in style with a points decision over former British and Commonwealth Welterweight Champion, Johnny Cooke, and then a seven round stoppage against St Pancreas based Jamaican, Len Gibbs. Gibbs was another one who had fought the top of the crop, including Les McAteer, Kevin Finnegan and Maurice Hope. I noticed on the photos that Mark's blond locks had been hacked into a severe crew cut. "I always had it short when I was boxing, and when I packed up I let it grow. But, at this stage, I was more together, and things were rolling along nicely, you know. There wasn't so much turmoil and problems going on at that particular time. I boxed well that night. I'd say that from 1968 to 1970 was quite a good time."

Mark's first fight in 1969 was in February against French based Tunisian, Pascal Di Benedetto. "That one was at the Albert Hall. I stopped him in four rounds, didn't I? He was a good boxer." Exactly a month later Mark swept away the first American opponent they put in front of him, Jimmy Ramos, the Boston boxer in no state to continue in the seventh round at

Wembley's Empire Pool. Next in the firing line was another American, Bob Herrington. He came to London to box Mark in April 1969 at the Albert Hall. Just like his countryman before him, the man from Louisville was rescued in the seventh round. It was a torturous experience for Herrington as Mark's body shots hit home time after time and the American's gum-shield came out several times, a classic sign of a boxer in distress. Yet, he was still game to fight right up until the end and, when the end came, it was a blessing. "Yeah, I remember the chap. I remember his face."

Two weeks later Mark was back in the ring, this time with Paris based Dramane Ouedrago from the Ivory Coast. They topped the York Hall bill and Mark won the fight on points over eight rounds. He knocked Ouedrago down in the first round and almost knocked him through the ropes in the second. By the third, however, Ouedrago started to get more into the fight, forcing Mark to chase him round as he used his feet to stay out of trouble. Mark was cut near the right eye in the fifth, a problem that was occurring more and more often, and he was forced to protect the injury for the rest of the fight. "I didn't box too badly. It wasn't a particularly hard fight, but I got cut again."

That York Hall show was promoted by the legendary boxing promoter, Mickey Duff, who is another regular at LEBA. Mickey and his elegant partner, Gloria, are two people who I am always pleased to see and Mark feels the same way. "Oh yeah, I get on very well with Mickey. We just saw him in Spain in September. About three or four times we went out for a meal with him in the evening, me and Sandra. He was always all right to me when I was boxing. He was always good to me really. I think it was the first fight with Tom Bethea, Mickey was so pleased with the fight that he gave me another £250. And he was a good matchmaker."

Doug 'Dub' Huntley came from Los Angeles to box Mark at the Albert Hall in May 1969. "Yeah, that was on points that I won that one. He boxed Carlos Monzon, didn't he?" Huntley did indeed box the outstanding Argentinean World Champion the year before and got stopped in four. Mark had a grisly sense of déjà vu in the fifth round when his right eye got cut, the same injury from the Ouedrago fight three weeks earlier. There were tense moments in the Rowe corner when Harry Gibbs carefully inspected the gash at the end of the round. The sight of blood injected new enthusiasm into Huntley's work and the fight was stopped momentarily in the sixth for Gibbs to inspect Mark's bleeding face once more. The fight was allowed to continue and Mark went on to win by the tiniest margin of a quarter of a point.

Cuts take time to heal and Mark needed a rest. It was October 1969 before he stepped through the ropes once more, this time to stop brave Belgian, Lionel Cuypers, in four. "I boxed him at the Hilton. I boxed well that night. I think he'd just fought [former British, Commonwealth and European Champion] Ralph Charles before he boxed me. He was ever so strong." Back in harness and anxious to move on, a few weeks later Mark fought New York based Matt Donovan, who was Trinidad and Tobago Welterweight Champion at the time, and for the record he went on to win the Middleweight version of the same title in 1972. Donovan was brave and resilient, but he was giving away half a stone and Mark was firing on all cylinders. By the sixth round, the crowd and even the press reporters, who usually remain professionally impassive, were calling out for the fight to be stopped, because all they could see was a needless hammering of a brave but outclassed fighter. Referee, Wally Thom, eventually stopped the beating in the ninth round. "That was at the Albert Hall. I stopped him in nine rounds. He caught me with his head, but I think it was unintentional. I caught him with a body shot, a left hook to the body I think it was, and his head come right down with the punch and hit me in the face and closed my left eye. But, I'm sure, positive, that he didn't mean to do it. It was definitely accidental. That was quite a hard fight. He was a good boxer, a good mover. I was quite tired the next day. I remember I stayed in bed for a while."

It is usually the referee who issues stern warnings, but that night it was Wally Thom himself who received a damn good talking to, from Bill Chevalley. *"That American was a very, very good fighter and a very, very good pro. Mark took him to pieces, hitting him with body shots. The fella was on the floor. He was groaning. As he was lying on the floor, Wally Thom counted up to about eight, and you know what he said to the fella? He said, 'Come on, get up. You're not hurt,' and there's pools of blood down by the side of him! In between that and the next round, I walked over to him and I said, 'Here, if you don't stop this fight, do you know where you and I are gonna be?' He went, 'Go back over to the corner.' I went, 'No, I'll tell you where we're gonna be. We'll be in the Coroner's Court.' Honestly, he could have died. I mean, one of the journalists who was sitting next to me, he was smothered in blood from the kid. The Secretary of the Board of Control at the time, he walked to the middle of the ring said to Wally Thom, 'Don't you think enough is enough?' 'Cos he'd already seen me go out and have a row with him over it. Now, this perpetuated itself on the Sterling fight."*

As this story unfolds, more controversy crops up between Mark and this particular referee. Stating the seemingly obvious, I pointed out to Mark, "Wally Thom didn't like you, did he?" The answer came back in a flash, "I didn't like him either." The voice remained gentle but the blue eyes blazed, and for a split second the fighter inside Mark Rowe laid himself bare. "Because, I mean, in the Sterling fight, [which we will get to soon] he should have disqualified him really. And a couple of other times when I boxed and he was refereeing, he was telling me no hitting behind the elbow, and I didn't *hit* behind the elbow. He was always laying the law down to me, and I knew straight away that he wasn't a referee who was going to do me any favours, do you know what I mean? He didn't like me, and for no good reason, because I never, ever spoke to the guy really."

Mark's next fight was in January 1970. He boxed Pat Dwyer, who had beaten him two and a half years earlier. Spookily enough, Mark fought him on the same day of the month, they fought at the same venue, the Albert Hall, and it was another fourth round stoppage. Mickey Duff was the man who made the match and Mark was now being hailed as the number one contender for the British Middleweight Title, held by Les McAteer. There had been yet more upheaval in the Rowe training camp, as a result of which Mark had no official manager, but Bill Chevalley was still very much in his corner, giving wise counsel in and out of the ring. The sports reporters were making regular journeys to watch Mark at work in the Thomas A' Beckett. They all confirmed that he was looking the business and the bookies had him down as firm favourite to win the fight.

Fight night arrived and, as Dwyer marched down to the ring sporting a Beatles style moustache, he firmly believed he could beat Mark again. He even had special tee-shirts made up to that effect. The first bell went and Dwyer was fast and hard to get hold of. He made Mark miss often, but the punch power ratio was heavily loaded in Mark's favour; in other words, one of Mark's punches was worth several of Dwyer's. By the end of the first round Mark was in control. No matter how many jabs Dwyer threw, and many of them landed, he could not keep Mark at bay. At the end of the fourth round Dwyer's corner called referee, Harry Gibbs, over and seconds later the Bootle man was retired on his stool because of a suspected fracture of his jawbone. "Oh, Pat yeah. I was happy about beating him. I didn't necessarily want to break his jaw, but I stepped back and hit him with an uppercut and I caught him on the chin. I didn't mean to do that, but it happens."

In March 1970 Mark boxed in an official eliminator for the British Title with Welshman, Dick Duffy, at the Hilton in Park Lane. The Cardiff boxer had started his professional career back in 1965 with a long string of wins, but time took its toll and he ended up becoming a journeyman. However, prior to his fight with Mark, Duffy had scored an eight round points victory over Bunny Sterling and he knew all the tricks of the trade. The stubborn Celt went to the canvas five times during the fight, but he fought valiantly right up to the final bell. Mark won the fight but he did not emerge unscathed. By the end of the sixth round he was cut beneath the left eye and bleeding from a graze across the bridge of his nose. "That was a points win. I didn't box brilliant that night, but I didn't box too badly. He was a bit cagey. I don't think I was maybe as forceful as I had been before. It wasn't the same sort of fight."

Good things usually come to those who work hard enough and, on the 12th May 1970, Mark got to the opportunity to challenge British and Commonwealth Middleweight Champion, Les McAteer, for his titles at Wembley Pool. McAteer was born in Liverpool and he came from a traditional fighting family. His cousin, Pat McAteer, was British Middleweight Champion in 1955 and won a Lonsdale Belt outright. His brothers Neil and Gordon were tidy professional boxers too. 24 year old Les was a skilful boxer and a hard man.

Promoter, Harry Levene, was the man to recognize the star potential of Billy Walker and he saw the same potential in Mark Rowe. Levene knew that glamour sells. I put that to Mark, and he smiled, "Possibly, yeah." Bill Chevalley was adamant, *"Of course he did!"* Harry Levene went by the nickname 'The Merchant of Menace,' and along with rival promoter of the time, Jack Solomons, he was a very powerful man. He intervened in a scheduled box off between Harry Scott and Bunny Sterling in a final eliminator for the British Title, the winner of which would have fought Mark for the right to fight McAteer. Then, completing his strategy, Levene made McAteer a financial offer that he could not refuse and the Board of Control sanctioned the match, providing the winner forfeited the six month grace period afforded to British Champions to give either Scott or Sterling their crack at the title. The business was done and the fight was on.

It was a ferocious battle between two fired up young men with everything to prove. Mark came forward with his usual relentless persistence, while McAteer boxed in his own natural way, counter-punching and boxing cleverly. Mark and Bill Chevalley reasoned that Mark's greater strength and relentless body punching would win them the day and they stuck to their guns. In the first two rounds, despite McAteer's jab pounding into Mark's face at every opportunity, Mark was on the Birkenhead boxer's body like a flee on a dog and McAteer was warned by the referee for holding. As they arrived in the third round, McAteer's boxing was lovely, but Mark's persistence was already paying dividends, the body shots smashing into their target with sickening regularity. The fourth round moved the crowd to a deafening roar as McAteer jabbed and moved and Mark stormed forward, attacking to the ribs over and over again. "Sometimes I used to hear the crowd, but not really that much, because you just used to concentrate on what you were doing, you know, when you was actually in the ring." Blood made its grisly appearance in the fifth round when a cut opened beneath Mark's left eye. He fought with this face to get past McAteer's jab so that he could get to the body, and all the while McAteer was aiming for the gash.

When the sixth round came, McAteer did something that, for some reason, so many natural boxers did when they faced Mark Rowe; he cast his boxing skills aside and went in to have a fight, and Mark made him pay, at one point making McAteer audibly gasp with a left hook to the body. By the eighth round McAteer seemed to be slowing, Mark forcing him to cling on as he hit home with lefts and rights to the ribs. In the ninth 'The Mac' came back. He re-opened an old cut on the bridge of Mark's nose, and both fighters returned to their stools bleeding. They got into the trenches of the eleventh round and Mark started to really close in on the Champion. The crowd roared as McAteer tired, his earlier precise boxing skills dulled by desperation, and he looked stunned as he trudged back to his corner at the end of the round. Mark marched out for the twelfth round and he took the fight by the scruff of its neck. McAteer was splitting blood before the round was over. But the man from Liverpool answered the bell for the thirteenth round and fought for his very livelihood. Mark showed no mercy and in the fourteenth McAteer was smashed to the floor for three long counts, the last of which ended the battle.

As McAteer was being counted out of the fight, he sat on the floor with his back up against the ropes, legs stretched out in front of him, gloves resting on his thighs. It was all over, and Mark Rowe was the new British Middleweight Champion. "I remember Bill Chevalley saying to me in the corner, 'You're going to have to stop him to beat him because he's too far in front.' So, going out for the eleventh round, he just said, 'Go out there and try and hit him on the chin with the right hand,' which I did. I hit him on the chin with a right hand and he wobbled. And then I hit him with a hook off the jab, which put him on the floor, and then I ended up stopping him." So, at the age of 22, after 29 fights, Mark Rowe became the first Londoner to win the British Middleweight Title since Terry Downes stopped Phil Edwards 18 years earlier, back in 1958. "I was well pleased. It was just what I wanted. All I wanted to do was defend it a couple of times, and then I could have kept it. But, some of my fights after that, there was just something missing. I don't know why, but I couldn't seem to get going. In fact, I think that was coming when I fought McAteer, to be honest. Instead of me getting to the top and carrying on, it just dropped. It just went. There was too many distractions, that's what it was. And then I fought Bunny Sterling."

As every Champion knows, winning a title is an exhilarating experience. For our British boxers, winning the Lonsdale belt is often the most important one of all. But that is only the beginning. Titles must be defended. On the 8th September Mark defended his titles against London based Jamaican, Bunny Sterling. Sterling, like Mark, was 22 years old. He had lived in Britain since he was seven years old. He was managed by the late George Francis, who had become so frustrated with boxing politics that he once declared that he would not take on a Commonwealth fighter again because of all the hassle. Francis once said of Sterling, "If it had been anyone else, I would have advised him to pack it in. But I've known Bunny since he was a kid. He's so keen and we'll see this through together."

At Wembley's Empire Pool, where Mark had won his titles from Les McAteer, Bunny Sterling stopped Mark in four rounds and took the British and Commonwealth belts away. "I knew Bunny Sterling was awkward to handle. He was awkward to fight because he was gangly and all over the place. But I didn't box too badly; a little bit slow maybe, at times. I caught him with a good left hook off the jab. I blocked his jab and counter-punched with a left hook and made his hair stand on end, and then he came straight back and butted me. That was in the third round, and then in the fourth he came rushing out, jabbed across my right shoulder and come straight back in with his head again. I can remember standing with my back to the ropes and just shouting out, 'Watch your head!' I remember saying it." By this point, the crowd were shouting the same warning, irate that their Champion was being fouled and sliced up in the process. "But the referee, Wally Thom, never said nothing at the time. He just let it go on. I don't know why he was like that, because there was absolutely no reason. I never said two words to the man. I didn't even know him. He was in the ring refereeing me, and he never knew me and I never knew him, but I could tell he didn't particularly like me. I knew that because of his actions in the ring. I remember when he came into the dressing room before the fight, he kept telling me, 'No hitting behind the elbows.' And it wasn't even an illegal punch, because that's a legal target down there. You've got to get behind the elbows."

Wally Thom walked over to Mark's corner at the end of the fourth round, looked at the facial damage and shook his head. The fight was over. Bill Chevalley, who felt he had patched up the injuries more than adequately, went berserk. *"All I know is, that cut, I could have spat on me finger and stopped the blood. It was just a dribble. I've cut myself shaving and the cut was no worse than that, but he stopped the fight. The judgment was out of our hands."* As Bill spoke, his face expressed all the naked incredulity that he felt at the time. In all fairness to George Francis, he asked Master of Ceremonies, Nat Basso, to announce that they would give Mark a quick return whenever he wanted. As Sterling realized that Wally Thom had called an end to the fight, he jumped in the air and jigged around the ring in delight. Across the ring, Mark sat on his stool in a state of utter disbelief and devastation. "I was gutted. Absolutely gutted. To lose it like that. I just couldn't believe it. I was just absolutely choked. I don't mind if I lost it fair and square, but that *wasn't* fair and square, that's the thing. I still feel the same way about it now."

One of the things that I love about boxers is their unique ability to face their worst nightmare and walk straight back into the firing line, as brave as ever. Less than two months after losing his titles to Bunny Sterling, Mark stepped back through the ropes to demolish plucky Puerto Rican, Danny Perez, in the four rounds at the Albert Hall. Perez fought out of New York and topped many bills over there. "I was just thinking in my mind that I was going to get it back again, you know, and I boxed well that night. He was a brave man." When Harry Gibbs stopped the fight, he declared of Perez, "He was a game fighter but I couldn't let him take any more punches." Perez said afterwards, "Rowe is a great fighter and very strong. He whipped me and no complaints. He could be World Champion."

Four weeks later Mark was given an unenviable job. His name was Tom Bethea, an awesome looking black man from New York with big sideburns and a moustache. Earlier that year, Bethea had stopped Nino Benvenuti while the fierce Italian held the World Middleweight Title; however, this had been a non-title fight. In Bethea's next fight, which was for Benvenuti's World Title, the Italian returned the compliment and stopped Bethea. Two fights later, the American and Mark got it on at the Albert Hall.

Bethea took the beginning of the fight, Mark took the middle and Bethea came on strong in the end. It was a blazing show and a full on brawl, one of those fights where it was a shame there had to be a loser, and when Harry Gibbs scored it to Bethea by a quarter of a point it could not have been any closer. The crowd gave both boxers a massive ovation. "Tom 'The Bomb' yeah. I lost by quarter of a point over ten rounds. I mean, the referee could have made it a draw. I remember the fight. I started a bit slow for about two or three rounds, but I didn't box too bad that night. I thought it was quite a good fight. He was quite a strong chap, quite a strong fighter, and he come forward a lot. I reckon he had a half a stone on me before we started. But he just nicked it off me. He made a bit of a show in the last round, but that's the way it goes. And a quarter of a point is quite close really. You can't get any closer."

It was around this time in his life that Mark journeyed across the Atlantic to visit Cus D'Amato. Mark stayed with the revered boxing guru at his Catskills home with a view to possibly moving out there for a while to learn from the man. "That was the idea. I stayed there for four days. It was brilliant. He was a really nice man. I think that Lennox Lewis is a good boxer, but Mike Tyson, he was something else. He was the best boxer, while in his prime, that I have seen for many, many years. Anyway, I thought about moving to New York to live with Cus. But, I mean, when I moved to Black Heath, which was only down the road from where we lived, my dad said, 'You're not going all that way?' So you can imagine if I'd moved to New York! Anyway, Cus Damato was a really nice fellow and he was very kind to me."

The Mark Rowe success story continued and in February 1971 he fought a re-match with Dramane Ouedrago, stopping the Frenchman in six rounds at the Albert Hall. The following month, Mark out-pointed fast, slippery Italian, Sauro Soprani, at Wembley's Empire Pool. Top of the bill was Joe Bugner's controversial points defeat of Henry Cooper for Cooper's British, Commonwealth and European Heavyweight Titles. Harry Gibbs' unpopular score of a quarter of a point in favour of Bugner remains a talking point in boxing gatherings to this day. Mark was there to watch it. "Yeah, I come out and saw that actually." My next question was obvious; who won? "I'd just come out of the shower and, I think, by the time I came in, about five or six rounds had already gone, but I think Cooper won it."

Three weeks later Mark drew over ten rounds with American, Fate Davis, at the Albert Hall. This was the main event and a punishing job for both boxers. "I was on the floor a couple of times, when I lost my concentration. I *tried* hard enough, and I was fit, but my mind was not co-ordinating with my body, you know? Anyway, after that fight I had to have an operation. I had all these loose bone chippings removed from my left elbow. Just jabbing too much. I think it's an injury that a lot of fighters got. When I used to jab, if I missed, it would lock. It was a right shock, it was, when it used to happen, but once I had it done it was fine. After the operation the surgeon give me this little plastic bottle and he said, 'Look at that lot in there,' and no wonder it hurt! There was about eight or nine little bits of bone in there, all floating about. Bloody loads of it, honestly, so I had to have it done."

By September 1971 Mark had recovered sufficiently to step back through the ropes to dismantle late Liverpudlian substitute, Ronnie Hough, in three rounds at York Hall. Hough was a fighter who had become a journeyman, but he could still prove a force to be reckoned with (he stopped Kevin Finnegan in two rounds, two fights before Mark). However, he was not in Mark's league and he went down twice in the second and once in the third. His knees sagged and he was ripe for a fourth knockdown when referee, Sid Nathan, jumped in and rescued him. "That was quite a good performance actually. The elbow was all right. I'd been sparring with it and everything, and it was okay."

The following month, Tom Bethea returned to fight Mark once more at the Albert Hall. This time the rugged part-time bouncer from Harlem stopped Mark in the ninth round. In the fifth round Bethea's lowered head caused a cut on Mark's scalp, for which Harry Gibbs gave him a stern warning. But warnings do not heal cuts and Mark bled throughout the rest of the fight, his face becoming a garish red mask of grim determination. As Mark sat on his stool at the end of the ninth round, his head bleeding and his left eye swollen shut, Bill Chevalley decided to pull him out. "But I was all right. I wasn't on the floor or nothing like that. This side of my face was all closed. My eye was completely closed, because he boxed the sort of fight. He had half a stone on me at the weigh-in, so really, on the night, I was probably fighting a cruiserweight, and I wouldn't have been any bigger than I was. But I'm not giving out excuses.

"What it was, I couldn't box going backwards. So when I boxed him the second time, what he done was he kept his hands up high and he kept pushing me back all the time, kept right close to me, throwing jabs to me chest to keep me off balance, keeping close all the time, and then he come in with his head. Harry Gibbs warned him a couple of times, but not enough. Because when you looked at me the next day, you couldn't see the left side of my face. It was all black, and he done that with his head when he was inside the clinches. But he fought the right kind of fight and you can't take it away from him. They pulled me out in the ninth round, but he didn't have me on the floor or knock me out or anything. They called it a TKO." Mark was back in the ring one month later and he shrugged off a cut forehead, which bled continuously from the second round, to immobilize Frenchman, William Poitrimol, in five rounds at Wembley's Empire Pool. Jerry Quarry knocked out Jack Bodell in 64 seconds of the first round on top of the bill. "I saw that one."

1972 arrived and, in January, Mark came a cropper and shocked the crowd when he fought Howard Sharpe at the Albert Hall. The 24 year old Jamaican, who had come in as a late substitute, demolished Mark in one round. Sharpe was a decent boxer with a strong punch, but he was not in Mark Rowe's class and nobody could believe what they were seeing. The first bell sounded and Sharpe was right on Mark, knocking him down onto his back with a right to the head. Mark looked shaky as he got up, but he managed to hurt Sharpe with a left hook. Sharpe came roaring forward with swinging hooking shots and, before Mark knew it, he was on the floor again. Referee, Harry Humphreys, let him have one more go, but Mark was out on his feet and, as Sharpe hammered him back to the ropes again, Humphreys jumped in. Mark's expression became distant as he told me, "I can't explain it really, but I wasn't *in* the Albert Hall that night. My mind wasn't *there*. He caught me with a good right hand. I got up. He caught me again, and that was it. But it just felt like I was somewhere else at the time. I know it can happen, a boxer can get caught, but something had gone. It wasn't like it was in the earlier days. It didn't matter how hard I tried. I just couldn't seem to get it back."

In April 1972 Mark returned to his winning ways and earned a points decision over eight rounds against Jimmy Mitchell at the Albert Hall. The 24 year old Canadian looked to be carved from ebony. As he faced Mark, he was unbeaten in eight fights. During the middle of the match Mark seemed to labour against the man from Montreal, and one ringsider could be heard clearly shouting, "Come on Mark, like it used to be." There had been more changes to the team and Terry Lawless was now Mark's trainer and Jarvis Astaire his advisor. Mark liked both men and told me of Lawless, "I got on well with Terry Lawless. I was more settled then. He was with me then up to my last fight. We saw Terry in Spain in September. We went out to dinner with him. He's a very nice man."

I do not know why Mark and Bill Chevalley parted company at this stage in their lives. They have never told me and I have never asked. All I do know is that they are good friends today, which is really all that matters. When I attended the LEBA awards lunch this year, I had the pleasure of sharing a table with Mark and Sandra Rowe and, as soon as Bill's name came up in the conversation, they answered in perfect unison, "If Bill says it, it's got to be right."

The following June, Mark was back at the Albert Hall to face 'American Bulldog' Skip Yeaton. Mark looked strong and confident and he blew Yeaton away in one round. The American was down for a few minutes before he was able to rise and be helped back to his corner. September came and Mark won a points decision against Carlos Marks at Wembley's Empire Pool. Carlos Marks, who hailed from Trinidad, had been a professional on the unforgiving American circuit for seven years. He was a journeyman who had won half as many as he had lost, but he had mixed in good company, including the likes of Emile Griffith and Bennie Briscoe. He survived the fight and he looked rather slick at times, but he was in a sorry state at the end, his mouth and nose streaming with blood. Mark won it by half a point. "I think, to be honest, I was definitely not the same fighter at that stage. I didn't know it at the actual time but, looking back, you can tell that there was just something missing." Mark rounded off 1972 with an October six round stoppage against German mauler, Werner Mundt, at the Albert Hall.

In January 1973 Mark claimed an eight rounds points win over French hard case, Gerard Cola, at the Albert Hall. "That was a hard fight. He was a very tough man and my focus had gone. I was all right in the gym with Terry Lawless, but there were other distractions going on outside, domestic things." The following month, Mark knocked out Tony Berrios in six rounds at the Albert Hall. In the final moments, Mark knocked the defiant American's gum-shield out with a left hook. But, almost immediately afterwards, Mark emerged from some infighting with a cut on his right eyelid. The blood was streaming down his face and Mark realized that it was going to be now or never. He steamed in, knocking Berrios all over the ring. A huge right to the jaw sent Berrios back to the ropes and he slumped, his eyes glazed. Mark stepped in and continued to attack and the referee leapt between them. When it was over, the crowd gave both boxers a standing ovation.

On the 17th April 1973, Mark Rowe stepped through the ropes to fight for the last time. His opponent was his conqueror of two and a half years earlier, Bunny Sterling. This fight was for the British Middleweight Title, which Mark had lost to Sterling back then and Sterling still held. They fought at the Albert Hall and Mark lost it on points over 15 rounds. It was a fitting tribute that Mark's last fight was at this fabulous arena, where he had produced so many of his best ever performances. As Sterling walked to the ring he was jeered by some of the crowd, a cruel greeting by ignorant people for any fighter about to step through the ropes. Battle commenced and the crowd cheered loudly every time Mark made an aggressive move. "Yeah, I didn't do a lot in the earlier rounds and then, in the last five rounds, I knew I really had to do something and I truly pushed myself to get into the fight. The crowd was really roaring, which was nice. The fans stayed loyal to me, right up until the end of my career."

The first half of the fight was claimed by Sterling, who looked dominant as he snapped Mark's head back with jabs again and again. Mark was cut on the left eyebrow in the fourth and at the side of the right eye in the seventh. Coming into the eighth round, Mark turned up the heat and suddenly he was just as dangerous as he ever was, coming on and bringing the fight to Sterling, hurting the Jamaican with heavy body punches. Sterling countered with flashy flurries and moved away, sometimes hurt but staying out of serious trouble. A banging of heads caused a cut on Mark's scalp in the thirteenth round and he finished the fight smeared with blood, but his performance in those last few rounds was fabulous. However, there was no controversy about butting this time around. Sterling was completely innocent.

Mark made the decision that night that his boxing days were over. "It was gone, you know? Whatever I had, it was gone. So it was best to say, 'Let's call it a day.' But I was 25, almost 26, and I think it was for the best. I could have stayed in there. I know I could have gone on. But I knew I was finished, so I made the decision and that was it. I was so disappointed. I tried, but I remember saying to Mickey Duff, I said, 'Mick, you could have come to me in the corner and said, I'll give you two million pounds if you could do a bit more work, and I just couldn't have done it.' I knew then that the enthusiasm that I had when I was younger had just gone out the window. That's definitely what it was. I can't put it down to anything else." For the record, this was possibly the best performance Bunny Sterling ever gave in front of a London crowd and he declared afterwards, "Maybe they'll give me a better reception next time."

All too often, when a boxer decides to retire, as time passes the yearning to go back and relive the glory years becomes too strong to resist. Sylvester Mittee once described it to me (when talking of his own comeback) as "a feeling of unfulfilled potential that refuses to go away." That never happened to Mark. When he decided it was over, that was it for him. "But, you know, I had a good career really. My favourite times were when I won the Gold Medal at the Empire Games and when I won the British Title. They were really good times." As he thought back to those heady days, Mark's eyes twinkled. "After I decided to retire, I come home, I bought a load of pigs, put 'em down the bottom of the farm and I looked after my pigs and I looked after my dad's pigs. That's what I did up until 1990."

At the age of 60, Mark is still very much a regular face on the London boxing circuit, particularly in charity circles. Aside from regularly attending the Boxers versus Blind event mentioned earlier, he is also a staunch supporter of the Angels with Dirty Faces 'Sorta' Boxing' events, where the Freddie Mills Club team, who are mainly people inflicted by Down's Syndrome, get in the ring with a boxer. The rule is that the boxer always loses within three rounds, by knockout. The boxers eagerly compete for 'Dive of the Night' and the Freddie Mills team have a whale of a time, proudly showing off their victory medals at every opportunity. In fact, Mark was the first man to go in with one of the Freddie Mills Club team. "Oh blimey, I've been going there since 1966, when it all first started. You need to confirm that with Bob Paget, but I think it's that long." Bob Paget, the man who introduced me to Mark for the first time at the Boxers versus Blind golf day, was happy to confirm, "Oh yes. Mark was the first one to do that. It was at the Drill Hall in Victoria, 1966. That was when it all started."

Mark also makes himself available to attend any other social activities the Angels invite him to, including their Christmas party, when the Freddie Mills Club members love to show off their marvellous sense of rhythm on the dance floor. Mark is always there, always the same, quiet and unassuming, always willing to help in any way that he can. He is such a regular face at these events that I wondered if he has an official role on the committee. "Not necessarily, no. They ask me to go along at times and I always try and get to as many events as I can."

I came away from this interview with the strong feeling that Mark Rowe is a man of two halves. From the boxing point of view, he is painfully hard on himself, but he has no regrets. "It's too late to have regrets now, isn't it? I think I could have done a lot better, but it can't be helped. I'm fit and well, that's the main thing." Aside from the boxing, Mark comes across as being totally at peace with himself. "Are you religious?" I asked him. He thought for a moment. "Yes and no. I do believe in something." And when I asked him who the biggest influence on his life has been, there was no hesitation at all. "My dad."

Our interview came to an end and it was time for me to hit the road again. I bade Sandra goodbye and thanked her for her kind hospitality. I asked Mark if he would mind guiding me back to the garage, from where, I assured him, I could easily find my way back to the motorway. But Mark was having none of it. He was adamant that I would be performing no more dramatic U-turns that day and, as we left the house, he called back over his shoulder, "Sandra, I'll be back soon. I'm just guiding her straight back to the M25."

CHAPTER SEVEN - JANE COUCH MBE

***"If they want to fight, let them fight. It's not right to stop somebody doing something they love, whether it's a man or a woman. It's something all of us fighters were born to do. It's as simple as that."* (Crawford Ashley)**

She has a fighter's eyes and a sunny smile, but she is best recognised for her corkscrew curls. My mum would call them ringlets. She was born in Fleetwood, but she has made her home in Bristol and she is a hugely popular figure there. But there are no opponents for her in this country, so if she wants to perform for her British fans she is forced to box imported fighters, often from Eastern Europe, and nobody ever remembers their names, because Jane Couch is the one they have all come to see. Despite her massive capacity to attract the spotlight, she is not somebody who courts fame and publicity. All she wants to do is box at the highest level. In order to do this, she regularly packs her bags and jumps on a plane destined for America so that she can box the best. She has become one of the most experienced female fighters in the world today. In the United States, she rubs shoulders with the likes of Arturo Gatti and Mickey Ward. In fact, she has boxed on the same bill as the latter.

Sadly, despite being a World Champion at both lightweight and light-welterweight, the money that she earns for these far-flung excursions runs into hundreds of pounds rather than thousands. She is the epitome of the boxer at the bottom of the food chain. And the reason she puts herself through all this? She loves to box. It is as simple as that. Boxing has changed her life and she is now the consummate professional. She radiates an air of supreme fitness and she comes across as a woman who is totally at peace with herself. When I interviewed her, I found her to be warm and kind, with a wicked sense of humour and an engaging turn of phrase. Then we got onto her boxing and she started to talk about hurting people. The Northern voice remained gentle, but the level gaze became compelling in its intensity.

The first time I met Jane Couch was in the beatific surroundings of Spaniorum Farm, where she lives with her trainer, Tex Woodward, and his wife, Pat. We were doing a piece for the British Boxing Board of Control Yearbook. She was then, and still is, the only female boxer I have ever interviewed. As I drove down the M4 on that Saturday morning in July 2004, I wondered if the gender issue would make a difference. The moment I met her, I realised immediately that it would make no difference whatsoever. Jane Couch is a fighter, just like any other boxer I have ever met. Did this surprise me? If I am to be totally honest the answer is, yes, it did a little bit.

This was my first time to take a close look at women's boxing. Before I met Jane, I had never watched a woman's boxing match from beginning to end. In the past, when I have studied photographs of two females in the ring, I have never found any beauty in it. When men box, some of the most grotesque images can become strangely beautiful in their garishness, but I have never felt that with women. It is just an instinctive feeling. No matter how hard I tried to open my mind and look at it objectively, an inner reluctance remained within me to accept that a woman should be a professional fighter. And then I met Jane Couch.

I started putting the Yearbook article together and transcribing the tapes was a joy, but at the same time it made me feel a little sad. You see, the Boxing Yearbook is a most valuable part of British boxing culture, but it is a bit like the Church of England answer to boxing writing, if you like. Nothing taboo. You must not stray too close to the mark. Therefore, because of Jane's naturally open approach, much of our interview would end up wasted. Suddenly, I had a brainwave. I immediately telephoned Jane and wildly enthused, "Jane, apart from doing this Yearbook article, how about we do a piece for *'Sweet Fighting Man – Volume II'* as well?" She was delighted but slightly perplexed at my suggestion and patiently pointed out, "Mel, that's a lovely idea, but I'm not a man. I'm a *wo*man!" I replied, "Yes babe, but surely that is a statement in itself, and you deserve to be in there anyway." To this, she modestly acquiesced and the seed was planted. The following chapter is a harder hitting combination of exerts from that first interview, together with subsequent conversations between Jane and myself, and some insightful input from some of Jane's male contemporaries.

SHE WORKS HARD FOR THE MONEY

Jane's first fight in the ring was against London policewoman, Kalpna Shah. Jane was promised £150, but she never got paid because the promoter said he had lost too much money. This type of thing sometimes happens in the male boxing world as well. However, the difference is that, when it happens to men, it is invariably those who box at the bottom end of the bill on small hall shows. Although Jane has fought her way up the ladder to World Champion status, for her nothing has changed.

The one that shocked me the most was the paltry purse that she was paid when she won her World Light-Welterweight Title from Jamie Clampitt in America in June 2004. I sat and watched the fight on video with her and she gave the performance of her life. "I got paid $2,000 but, by the time we converted the money, £700 is what I came home with. They paid for two of us to fly over, but the rest of me team paid their own way out there. Twenty-two million viewers they had! But, there you go. I don't do it for the money. Good job I don't, isn't it?"

I nearly choked on my cup of tea when I heard that figure. I reasoned, "I would have thought they had missed a zero off the end there. I mean, I know men who get paid more than that for having four-rounders." Jane agreed, "Yeah, I know, and not going all that way to America. But, like, these girls that have got promoters behind them have got sponsorship deals. The promoter pays for the training camp, so she's probably got no bills to worry about, and they're just lucky enough to have a promoter like that. I mean, I'm on telly in America and not my home. All it's down to is a big promoter. It's just getting the big boys here to take an interest, you know, but I've just got to respect their decision that they don't want to do it. You're not gonna change that. You just can't change it. It's one of them things. I'm not bothered."

COME AND HAVE A GO IF YOU THINK YOU're HARD ENOUGH

Occasionally, when male journalists have gone to interview Jane, they have wanted to actually get in the ring and spar with her. This is something that surprised me, and not in a good way. I can understand the concept of her sparring with her fellow male boxers, but a journalist who has never laced a glove wanting to get into the ring with a woman of Jane's calibre seems to me to be a pointless exercise. Jane grinned cheerfully as she confirmed, "Yeah, they do!" Now, the day Jane Couch needs the likes of me to stand up for her against anybody will be a cold one, in hell. However, this information deeply offended my sensibilities as a woman. I mean, if these men were going to interview, say, Colin Dunne or Crawford Ashley, they would not dream of or dare to turn up with a kitbag and say, 'Right, I want to spar with you.' I have never seen myself as a feminist but I found myself becoming quite militant. "How dare they!" I raged. I asked her, "Who do they think they *are*? Do you think that these men feel the need to prove some form of latent male supremacy, or are they just simply liberty takers?" Jane smiled calmly and shrugged her shoulders as she replied in the most nonchalant fashion, "I dunno, mate." It then became obvious to me that my new friend really had not wasted too much time thinking about it.

Jane continued, "I don't know why they would want to do it. Maybe they must just see women boxers as different. We *are* different. Men and women *are* different. You can't get away from that. I always liken women's boxing to women's tennis. Men's tennis is about the power of the serve and women's tennis is about rallies. Well, in the boxing, there's not as many knockouts in women's boxing because we haven't got the muscle mass that men have got. But what they don't understand is that, if they're not a trained boxer, like, if you've got a journalist who's never trained in a gym in his life, I'm *going* to be stronger than an average normal man. I wouldn't be stronger than, say, Colin Dunne, because when Colin was training he was fit and strong, but someone who's never been in the gym of Colin's weight, I'd be stronger than him and they probably don't *see* that."

I put this concept of journalists and boxers sharing a sparring ring to former WBU Lightweight Champion, Colin Dunne, and he explained, "It's not unique. I have had that happen once to me, but I think Jane does get singled out because they're all intrigued by her. Personally, I would never spar with Jane, or any other woman for that matter. Because there is always the possibility that she could catch me, and I mean *really* catch me with a good shot, and I could get the eye of the tiger. To be honest, I wouldn't want to be responsible for the consequences of that, although I'm not saying that Jane couldn't handle it and retaliate just as vociferously. It's just that I wouldn't want to go there. Because sparring is, in essence, all about learning, but every now and again things can flare up in there and it can become extremely competitive. And don't forget, there is always the possibility that *she* could get one over on *me,* and how am I gonna live with that?"

Crawford Ashley, who is former British, Commonwealth and European Light-Heavyweight Champion, sparred with Jane in the days when he was still boxing. I rang him up to speak with him about it and he confirmed, "Yes, and I hit her! When you're in the boxing ring you're *gonna* get hit. I'm not going to hit you hard or knock you out, because I've got nothing to prove, but I *will* hit you. I went down there to Bristol to spar with a cruiserweight that Tex was training and Jane asked if she could spar with me. I told her, 'Okay, I will spar with you, but don't come in there trying to knock my head off, because I *will* hit you. When you're in a boxing ring with me and you drop your guard, you *will* get hit. Otherwise, how are you going to learn?' Afterwards she thanked me and she told me, 'That were really great.' If I remember rightly, I think I broke her nose, but you'd have to check with her on that one. But I think I did. I didn't mean to do it, break her nose, I mean. But she dropped her guard so I hit her. Not hard, but I did hit her, because when you're in a boxing ring these are the things that can happen. I like Jane. She's all right, and I hope I helped her to become a better fighter."

Having spoken to Crawford, I asked Jane about the experience of sharing the sparring ring with him. She told me, "It was Leighton Morgan who Crawford came to spar with. He went on to win a series on Sky Television called 'Britain's Hardest.' Crawford was lovely. He didn't break my nose, by the way. He just made it bleed. He was really helpful and he let me know when I made mistakes, but he didn't take the piss."

NO WOMEN PLEASE, WE're BRITISH!

Jane and I are both casualties of the 'men only' rule imposed by the Boxing Writers' Club. Subsequently, we are both banned from attending their annual dinner at the Savoy Hotel. This is one of the most prestigious British boxing gatherings of the year and it did used to upset me that I was not allowed to attend. I have dedicated my life to the sport that I love, and yet my gender prevents me from being there. However, these days, I feel that I would never wish to be a member of a club that doesn't want me.

The first time that Jane realised that she was not welcome, she was not happy either. "Tex told me, 'Right, I'm going now.' I said, 'Where're you going?' He said, 'The Boxing Writers' Dinner.' I said, 'Right, I'm coming with you.' He said, 'You can't.' I said, 'Can't! Just fuckin' watch me!' He tried to get me a ticket and I nearly took it a bit further, because I thought, 'Wait a minute, this is wrong.' So I spoke to my solicitor about it. She told me they can't stop it. It's sexual discrimination." Jane was adamant that, as a boxing writer, I should be allowed to be there. "People like you *should* be there. You've got a *right* to be there. I think that should be your next step. You should be the first woman to get into the Boxing Writers' Club. I mean, for you, it's also restriction of trade, because it's your trade, it's what you do. If you started proceedings against them they'd cave in. You should *do* it mate! You could do it in a real subtle way. You could just shame them."

Moments earlier, Tex Woodward had joined us in the room. As he sat in an armchair, he started to chuckle away quietly to himself. As Jane and I turned our attention to him, he said with a smile, "I'm just amused by the use of the world 'subtle.' The words 'subtle' and 'Jane' don't mix!" Jane waved his remark aside, "I'm not talking about me. *I* couldn't, but *she* could. She knows all the writers anyway. They'd all be on her side." Eventually Jane and I sensibly and reasonably concluded that, as far as we are both concerned, the men who insist on keeping us out are just afraid that, if they let us go in, they would have to let their wives attend and, really, we feel that they are being quite silly. Tex was theatrically indignant as he gave me a sharp look. "Be careful, young lady. Remember *I'm* one of those men!" His remark caused Jane and I to simultaneously giggle behind the backs of our hands.

HISTORY IN THE MAKING

Jane Couch paved the way for licensed women's boxing in this country. She fought on unlicensed shows nine times before, in June 1997, she applied to the British Boxing Board of Control for a professional boxing licence. She was refused. I contacted the Board at the time of my interview with Jane and spoke to Simon Block, who told me, "I wasn't General Secretary at the time, but I remember the Board's position clearly. Jane applied for a licence to box in this country and the Board replied, stating that they were not in a position to consider taking responsibility for women boxing in this country at that time."

Jane decided to fight the Board's decision and she took them to court on the grounds of sexual discrimination and restriction of trade. The reasons that the Board provided in opposition were based on medical grounds. They felt that premenstrual tension could make women more liable to accidents, more emotionally unstable and prone to injury. They also cited painful periods, fluid retention and risk to an unborn baby. Jane found herself a solicitor and took the Board to an industrial tribunal. The case took six months to prepare and proceedings began at the Montague Court Building in Croydon on the 12th February 1998. The case was heard over two days and Jane had to wait a further six weeks for a decision.

The battle made huge waves in the media and was covered by all the national papers and mainstream news programmes. Many of the headlines openly ridiculed the reasons given to prevent Jane obtaining a licence. In Jane's corner were solicitor, Sarah Leslie, and barrister, Dinah Rose. Dinah Rose took no prisoners in court. She remained cool and lethal as she put the Board of Control Chairman, Leonard Read; the General Secretary, John Morris; and the Chief Medical Advisor, Dr Adrian Whiteson, on the back foot on several occasions. I was stunned when Jane informed me that this strong and successful lady was only 26 years old at the time. "If I ever got to be a quarter as clever as her. What a diamond, a fucking diamond. It was unbelievable what she did. She says to the doctor, right, she says, 'Excuse me, but if you were going on holiday and you found out the pilot was a woman, would you get on the plane and fly?' And he went, 'Not if she was due on her period.' Well, even the Chairman, he just took his glasses off. Dinah asked the Doctor, 'Why's that?' And he said, 'Because women are un-stable at that time.' And Dinah said, 'Well, God forbid that women should ever look after children then, if they're unstable.'"

I asked Jane how she would answer the question of risk to an unborn baby. "Well, there *is* a risk to an unborn baby, isn't there? But, there again, you've got to be professional enough to know that. You get pregnancy tests days before, so there's no way you *would* be. But there's always a risk that you're going to get caught, isn't there, if you're not using protection? The other thing is to abstain. That's what most people would do. That's what *I* would do, anyway. I mean, you could always use Durex, but it's just not worth it. You've got to be professional enough to know what you're doing yourself and, like I say, with the rules about the pregnancy tests the way they are, you're always going to get caught anyway. I mean, God, you really wouldn't want to do that, would you? It would be really bad for the sport. I mean, any sport, not just boxing, but rugby, football, the women have got to be professional enough to know what they've got to do. You can't." In 2004 I contacted Simon Block to enquire as to the rules regarding female boxers and pregnancy tests. He told me, "A female boxer applying to appear on a show in this country would need to produce a negative pregnancy test result that has been certified by a medically qualified person. The test must have been done within seven days of the contest."

In March 1998 Jane was made aware that the court had ruled in her favour. She described to me the day that her boxing licence finally arrived. "It was wicked! It was all I ever wanted. I love boxing and all I wanted was my licence, and now they've finally realized that, they're brilliant with me. Honestly. We're on first name terms. At the time when I got my licence, I had little old ladies coming up to me and saying things like, "Go for it!" I asked her if that kind of thing still happens. "Yes, but people come up to me now and say, 'Well done for beating up Michael Barrymore,' and that's all they remember. They've never seen me fight. They've never seen me train. But that's the thing with TV, isn't it?

"When I took the Board of Control to court, I stood outside the courtroom and said, 'Look, I'm not some sort of lesbian, left wing boxer. I'm not doing this for women's rights. I'm doing it for *me*. I'm doing it because *I* want a licence. It's not about what other women want.'" She continued, "Like, with me, I've been striving to achieve, achieve, achieve, all the time. Even now, after five World Titles, you don't realise what you've done. I think, when it's all over and it's gone, because it's a short career, that's when it will hit home. What you did for the women, what you did for the sport. I mean, all right, it didn't take off in this country, and to be honest I never really expected it to because we haven't got the grounding."

On the 25th November 1998 Jane Couch made boxing history when she stepped through the ropes at Caesars Night Club in Streatham to become the first ever woman to box on a Board of Control licensed show in this country since the Board's formation in 1929. The venue was packed out with a crowd of 1,500. "I didn't really feel any different because, when you're doing it, you don't realize you *are* making history. Even now, I don't realize that I have. But that fight wasn't any different to any other. You feel built up and ready to go, and scared. I was thinking, 'Why are all these photographers here? It's only a fucking boxing match. What about all the other people on the bill?' That's what really annoys me."

Boxing News reporter, Simon Euan-Smith, was covering that show and he told me of the media circus that covered the event. "Oh, there were photographers there from *'Vogue,'* and television cameras, all sorts of people. Us boxing journalists couldn't get *near* the ring because there were so many of these people, all there for Jane. It was impossible. And then, as soon as Jane had boxed, they all left. It was a mass exodus." When this happened, Jane felt very strongly for her fellow fighters on the show. "Boxing is boxing. They shouldn't just give one boxer on the bill all the recognition. They *all* should get it. I think with me though, over the years, it's been overkill with journalists and photographers and that. I don't even do anything now, no interviews, nothing. I just took a step back from it because it was, like, every newspaper you picked up, every time you turned on the TV, I was on. And it got to the point where I said to Tex, 'I can't *cope* with it. I don't *like* it. It's not my *way.*' People see you as something different, that you're *craving* the publicity. So I've took a step back this past few years, just stepped right back out of it. Because I don't like that world. I don't like what it brings with it."

Jane's opponent that night was Simona Lukic, an Economics student from Frankfurt. It was a mismatch and Jane stopped her in two rounds. My good friend and stalwart corner-man, Lenny Lee, was in Simona's corner that night. He told me, "It was intriguing. That's how it felt. It was kind of a weird sensation. Maybe it's psychological, because don't tell me for one minute that women are the weaker sex. Don't tell me that for one minute. I've got the greatest respect for Jane Couch and everything she does. But it was just the feeling inside. Watching that German girl getting punched, it made me feel sorry for her. Because she was quite pretty really, and one would question her presence in that situation, that maybe she shouldn't have been there. It was like you were watching something that you shouldn't have been watching. I've done the corner for literally thousands of male fights and if someone gets hurt you think, 'Oh, that's tough.' But, because it's a man, it's all right. But watching that girl getting punched, it just made me want to rush to her aid."

A happy footnote to this episode is that, in July 2004, the Board of Control celebrated their 75th Anniversary with an opulent dinner at Cardiff City Hall. British Boxing Champions from the past and present attended in their droves, and Jane was delighted to be invited. "It was an honour to be there with all the other Champions. They were all so nice and they made me feel really welcome. To be in a room with so many Champions is the sort of stuff you dream about, and I didn't expect to even be invited. It was great." For the record, Jane wore an elegant black dress that night and everybody that I know who attended expressed their opinion about the way she looked. The universal word used to describe her presence was "stunning."

THE CLOSEST THING TO DEATH

One of the most poignant stories that I have ever heard was of the aftermath of Jane's fight with French kickboxing star and WIBF Light-Welterweight Champion, Sandra Geiger. Jane fought Geiger in Copenhagen in May 1996 and they battled over ten gruelling rounds for Jane to take the decision. That night, both women sustained horrible injuries. Jane finished up with a battered face and a broken cheekbone. Sandra sustained a broken nose, a broken rib and a broken hand. She was out on her feet at the end of the fight and had to spend the next three days in hospital to recover. Today, Jane maintains "without a doubt" that Sandra Geiger is the toughest woman she ever fought. Tex confirmed, "I said after that fight, 'You'll never, ever have a harder fight than that.' It was a war! Geiger was something different, and she could *hit*!"

Jane told me, "I didn't want to box again after fighting her. I was hurting for *months*. We were in the bar afterwards and Sandra's trainer and her manager were in there, but we couldn't see her anywhere. They just *left* her!"

Tex went looking for Sandra Geiger and he found her in her dressing room. She was lying in the foetal position on a massage table, shivering and crying softly, hiding under a towel, alone in the dark. He told me, "The lights were out. I thought she was dying." Jane continued, "The Commissioner came out, he'd been in to see her, and he said, 'Can you be a bit quiet? This is serious.' He went, 'I think she's gonna die.' He even said that to us."

Tex explained, "I was in there before that and I went back in, but the trouble was I couldn't *speak* to her, because she couldn't speak English and I couldn't speak French. So I just held on to her hand." Jane continued, "He just sat and held her hand. She was just lying there, and her fucking trainer just *left* her. And then I was outside the arena, and *I* was crying." I asked Jane why she was crying. "I don't know why I was crying. I think it was all the build-up. And he's just sitting in there, holding her hand."

Tex laughed the laugh of a man who remembers trying to cut himself in half at the time so that he could be in two places at once. He was determined to acquit himself, "But I came outside and sat with you on the bench." Jane was quick to respond, "Yeah, and then you went back in and held *her* hand." Tex shrugged his shoulders helplessly, "I was trying to look after *both* of you!" Thankfully, Sandra Geiger fully recovered. As far as I am aware, she had one more boxing match the following year, which she lost on points, and she then retired.

JANE COUCH, THE BOXER

"Boxing is different to street fighting. Anyone can street fight. With boxing, you've got to think about it every day. It just changes you as a person. I think, if anything, it *stops* you from street fighting, because you've got more about you then and you know it's just *not* the way to do it. I wouldn't fight in the street or anything now. I don't even go out!" I asked her if she still likes a drink. "Yeah, but not like I used to. Obviously, you can't with the training, but I do, yeah. I had a couple last night. Two or three, and I'm pissed then. I drink them alcopop things. But, I mean, I've got to be back in training on Monday.

"I'm just more for the farm now. I've got me chickens, and the horses, and I'm quite happy. I never thought I'd say it, but I like being away from everyone, just being on the farm. It's wicked. I don't like going out. I wouldn't go into a bar or a nightclub or anything. There's no point." Jane is so recognizable and I asked her if she has ever experienced drunken fools challenging her to a fight. "It has happened once or twice. That's why I don't go out, because I think, if you put yourself in that position, you're leaving yourself open to it. So I don't bother. I just think it isn't worth it, because you're always going to get some knob-head with a glass, and it could end your career. I go out to dinners and boxing shows and that, but I don't go to nightclubs." I put it to her that I hate nightclubs because they are just like cattle markets. "They *are* cattle markets. That's bang on, isn't it? I just think my career's more important, and the training."

On the 12th June 2004 Jane travelled to America to box Jaime Clampitt for two World Light-Welterweight belts at the Foxwoods Casino, Connecticut. During our interview, Jane played me the tape. This was the first time I have ever watched a female boxing match from beginning to end and it was a quality affair, made extra special because Jane was sitting next to me at the time. The first thing I noticed was how at home she seemed as she shadowboxed for the crowd in her striking black and gold garb. She had her hair plaited close to her head and it really suited her. "Yeah, I always do, because it looks so unprofessional when you're hair keeps coming out. Anyway, she came out to *'World's Greatest,'* by R.Kelly. I mean, how egotistical is that? Usually, as the opponent, you don't get asked what music you want; they just put any music on. I just said, 'Oh, put 'owt on,' and they just put some rock music on. I wasn't bothered, to be honest. But *she* came out to *'World's Greatest,'* and I'm in the other corner shitting meself."

Tex pointed out, "You weren't bothered." Jane countered, "I was. I was so nervous." I asked Jane if she suffers badly from pre-fight nerves. "I'm not normally too bad, but for this fight I *was* nervous, because it was my last chance at top level. I was well aware of that. Because when you've been to the top of the world once, you can't *keep* going."

Jane pressed the play button and, as we watched battle commence, Tex remarked, "At least the referee let them fight. That's something. Those ones who say 'break' all the time, they get on my nerves." Jane fought a brilliant fight. I thought her movement was smooth and her combinations were swift, and I told her so. "Yeah, it's not bad is it? They say in round six, 'Jane Couch is a *machine*.'" I asked Jane if she likes watching herself and she shook her head. Tex was straight in there, "Yes you do!" Jane considered this for a few moments, "I like watching *this*, but you tend to watch it for mistakes rather than just to enjoy it, and that's annoying. I want to analyse it all the time and I shouldn't *do* that."

Jaime Clampitt was right in front of Jane all the time, but as the fight went on into the later rounds the Canadian was starting to look as if she didn't want to be there. "Yeah, I think I won it in the last two rounds. She was very strong on the inside, but I caught up with her later on though, when she got tired." As the American commentators make their remarks, Jane joyfully imitated them, delighting in their complimentary comments. I remarked that Jane had a lovely uppercut developing that was highly evident in this fight. "I catch her with a lovely one towards the end. But I was a bit of a twat actually because, in the tenth round, I hadn't knocked her out and I didn't think I was going to get the decision. I knew I'd won the fight, but it still wasn't over and I was doing all that." She raised her fist in the air to demonstrate. "I never do that, but I was just thinking, 'I know you're going to rob me, so I'm gonna tell you I know that I've won.' And then, when they gave it me, I felt such a twat."

Tex chimed in, "It was an absolutely *stupid* thing to do, because one punch could turn it all around again." When the tape reached those final moments of the fight I grabbed the tape-recorder and adopted a commentator's tone, "For the benefit of the tape, she's showboating," to which Tex remarked, "She got some showboating when she came back to the corner, I can tell you!"

On the 10th December 2004 Jane was scheduled to return to America and defend her title against Jaime Clampitt back at the Foxwoods Casino. Eight days before they were due to box, Jane promoted a show in Bristol and boxed Ukrainian, Larisa Berezenko. It was a tall order for Jane, but our girl was prepared to take the risk. The Bristol fight proved to be a gruelling struggle. "It were a hard fight. She was really awkward and she didn't make it easy." Due to the huge problems in the Ukraine after recent presidential elections, the transport system there had come to a virtual standstill. As a testament to Larisa's toughness and fighting spirit, she had to walk six kilometres through the snow with her luggage to catch the aeroplane to England.

Jane won every round but, a few days later, she was struck down by a ruthless combination of the flu and impetigo, a vile skin infection that leaves open sores all over the body. Jane tried her best but could not beat the count and she was devastated when she had to pull out of the re-match with Jaime Clampitt. "Even though I sent them photographs of my face, which was really horrible, that wasn't good enough for them. They stripped me of the title. I couldn't believe it. Then she fought Eliza

Olson instead. That was supposed to be an easy win for her, and she only went and drew with her. So now the title is still vacant and I'm the number one contender." When I rang Jane up and she told me about what had happened, I put it to her that maybe her body had taken matters into it's own hands. She was absolutely exhausted, physically, mentally and emotionally, and nobody can keep up that pace indefinitely. Everything happens for a reason. She agreed. "Yeah, I think you're probably right there. Anyway, I can't wait to fight her again. I'm going to stop her next time."

THE DIRTY MAC BRIGADE

Within male boxing the structure is all there, the boundaries clearly defined. You have Champions and contenders. Not everybody can be the shining superstar, but they all try their best and are respected for that. However, the world of women's boxing is an ambiguous one where the opportunities for exploitation are frightening. At the most basic level, I have heard horrendous stories about women getting into a ring to box who have never received a day's training in their lives. The audience have no interest in their ring prowess. They just want to see two females battering each other. It is the cheapest of thrills.

When I look at Jane Couch, I see this outstanding fighting machine who lives for her boxing and trains like a demon. When you meet her you know she is special. Jane Couch is such a chasmic world away from the farcical and dangerous set of circumstances I described above. And yet, that gap between the two is heavily populated with women who have earned absolute fortunes compared to our Jane. "Oh yeah. If you do it right it's a hard game. And then you get the ones who are going into it to get their tits out and all that. It's a different game for them. The trouble is that the promoters don't want real fighters. They want girls to look like models. They want them to have big boobs. But, where the top girls are, it really is a different game altogether. But a lot of girls won't even find that out because a lot of promoters, what they do, they get the girls and they just use them like an exhibition, like a showpiece thing. So they never really want the girls to get that hurt, which don't do the fans any good and it don't do women's boxing any good.

"The top women have got that respect, but the ones who say things like, 'I beat her up and I kicked her ass,' that's not the *way* is it? It's just shit. But that's how a lot of women are, and some of the men are like that too; not all of them, but some of them are. I trust most boxers with me life, but you're always going to meet one or two. But I think all the top women, the ones who have been there and done it, have got respect."

As I did my research for this interview, I discovered that even the 'Women Boxing Archive Network' website, which is one of the top fact bases for female boxing, has a section called 'Hot Hot Hot Photo Galleries.' It is a complete mirror image of human nature really. I have often been accused of being involved with men's boxing because of all the muscled men in their shorts. And yet, glamorous images of women in boxing gloves are shamelessly flaunted on one of the top women's websites, and I suppose you cannot blame them really. At the end of the day, some of these women are fabulous to look at, and the images are, after all, harmless.

As I surfed the internet for information on Jane, of which there is an abundance, I also did searches on other women boxers who Jane has fought. I was horrified when my search logically led me to some websites that were pornographic. Within these forums, bona fide women's boxing is grouped under the same umbrella as mud wrestling, topless boxing and catfights; and I mean *real* catfights. One of the most disturbing things I found was an advert for a video of two women who were going to fight each other, but there was no boxing involved. I'm talking about ripping each other's hair out by the roots and kicking each other full force, in the face. The winner would be the last woman standing. And all this in the name of 'entertainment.' I made this discovery early one Thursday morning, and what I saw on the screen made me feel sick and depressed all day. When I told Jane about it, her gentle compassion and empathy really helped me. Her understanding of my shock and concern gave me comfort. "Yeah, and you risk your fucking life for 700 quid, and then you see that. It just does me head in. It is really sad, but that's how a lot of men would look at it." She shook her head sadly.

AND IT's GOODNIGHT FROM HER, AND GOODNIGHT FROM HIM

Jane's trainer and manager, Tex Woodward, cuts a tall, elegant figure. He has white hair, a wise and knowing face and his concise words are spoken with cultured accent. He has strict standards and he can't abide bad language or uncouth behaviour. He boxed for the RAF in the mid 1950's and was also an RAF PT Instructor. He had 20 professional fights at welterweight between 1956 and 1964. At a glance, these two appear as different as Prince Charles and Lorraine Chase, but they are so close that they actually share each other's sentences. Jane explained, "It's love, hate really isn't it? I call him granddad, because that's what he's like. He's like my best friend, like my soul mate. And other days I hate him. But I tend to be on the side where, if they're a bit older, they know so much more about the game, and he does.

"He's been coaching for about 50 years. He's a good trainer, and he's really helped me. He's the only one who *has* helped me, out of the whole boxing world, when I first started. He's the only one that was there. Even now, we do row and that, but I know that, out of all the people in this world, he's the only one I can trust. He's the only one who's really there for me. I dunno, it's like a weird relationship with a trainer isn't it? I'd never go with any other trainer, ever. I mean, I've been offered loads of times. I've been offered to move out to America, but I just wouldn't. It's just that loyalty thing as well. But I don't know, it's a weird one. You have to ask Tex about that really." So I did. His eyes twinkled mischievously, "Love, hate I would think. More hate than love. It's a funny word, that four letter word, 'love.' We get on well together, sometimes."

Jane continued, "I think he was the only one who could have controlled me early doors, because I was a bit of a handful. I still am a bit of a handful, but I'm more humble now. I used to be like, fuck it! I'd do anything. I've got a lot more respect now. Its just age though, isn't it? It's got to be age." I put it to Jane that we all have to calm down, eventually. Jane is 38 and I am 44 and we both like it when people think we're younger than we are. As we discussed the age issue, I suggested that you can use all the face-creams in the world, but you will never escape from the fact that we are all getting older and it is all down to having a happy heart and being truly at peace with yourself inside. "Mind you," I confessed, "I couldn't *live* without Plenitude," which, for the unaware, is quite an expensive moisturiser that I use under my eyes. Jane laughed, "I use Vaseline, me! But seriously, I think it's how you feel inside."

Tex got the final word in at this point. "When it comes to accepting fights for my boxers I usually work on a 'need to know' basis, but with Jane I'm a bit firmer, because she's crazy!" He laughed affectionately. "One minute she'll say 'Yes,' and then a hair's out of place and she'll say, 'No!'"

FIGHT NIGHT

On the 25th February 2006, Jane boxed Galina Gumliiska, who came over from Bulgaria. They fought at Whitchurch Leisure Centre in Bristol and I was ringside to watch Jane Couch live in action for the very first time. I was there with Tommy Eastwood, who was having his first title fight and was top of the bill. Earlier that afternoon I'd been out in the market square and, when Galina came into our vision, Tommy's wife, Pearl, pointed her out to me. "That's her, Mel. That's the one your friend's fighting." On first impressions, I thought she looked rather nondescript, quite ordinary, nothing special.

We arrived at the venue and I bumped into Jane outside Tommy's dressing room before the show started. She looked fresher and younger than ever. Her hair was braided prettily and she looked radiant, superbly fit and happy with herself. Tommy was boxing Dean Francis for the vacant English Cruiserweight Title that night, a fight that Tommy lost narrowly on points. Jane made a point of visiting Tom's dressing room before and after his fight, and on the way home he told me how much he had appreciated that.

I went out into the hall to get myself a ringside seat and found myself sitting next to professional light-middleweight, Danny Gwilym. He told me, "I've been Jane's sparring partner for 15 years. Basically, she's been battering me for all that time! But Jane's a really good friend. When my little boy, Jake, was born prematurely, Jane came to see him in his incubator. I'm telling you now, she's his future Godmother. She's one of the most down to earth people I've ever met in my life. She's a special person, Jane."

When Jane came out to box, the 2,000 crowd raised the roof. She strode into the ring and danced happily around, totally at home in her territory, beaming out at her adoring fans. Galina looked diminutive and pale by comparison. The bell went and Jane came forward in the crouching American style that she has become so comfortable with. She landed with speed, power and skill, and her experience shone out at every twist and turn. Galina was not on the same level and, when the referee jumped in to stop it in the third round, I think everybody was relieved. *I* certainly was. The Bulgarian lady was well out of her depth from the first bell, but the defiant bravery that she displayed that night in the face of Jane's rapid firepower made me feel ashamed for thinking of her in such a dismissive manner when I had seen her in the market earlier. As Jane walked from the ring she gave me a big smile as she passed by and I stood up to give her a hug. She said, "Watch it mate, I'm all sweaty," but I didn't care. I am no stranger to a boxer's sweat. As she walked on, her supporters lined up to congratulate her warmly.

The show came to an end and it was time for Tommy, his family and myself to head back up the M4, back home. Before we left I made a quick pit stop to the Ladies. Jane walked in while I was washing my hands. We had already said our warm goodbyes earlier, but I had one final question. I asked her, "How long are you going to go on boxing, Jane?" She grinned at me, spread her arms in a gesture of supreme confidence and asked, "How do I look to you?" I said, "You look fantastic." She replied, "Well, there you are then!"

* * *

Shortly before this book went to print, Jane Couch was included in the Queen's Birthday Honours List and awarded an MBE for Services to

Sport. She told me, "I were stunned! It was an absolute shock. Can you believe it?" I asked her what she would say when she meets the Queen, and she replied, "I dunno, but I've got to buy a dress and I'm practicing me curtsey!" Ladies and gentlemen, I give you Jane Couch MBE.

CHAPTER EIGHT - IVOR 'THE ENGINE' JONES

"I have been promoting at the Albert Hall for 20 years and I have never known anyone with the drawing power of this kid. He doesn't stop punching from the opening bell to the last, and the racing boys idolise him. Trainers, jockeys and owners drop everything and rush to see him whenever he appears. If only I had another couple like him, I would be able to post 'House Full' notices at every show." **(Mike Barrett)**

They say it is the quiet ones that you have to watch, and those words could have been written for Ivor 'The Engine' Jones. I met Ivor for the first time quite a few years ago. On first impressions this thoughtful Welshman can come across as rather reserved, and I remember back then mistaking his taciturn manner for a sign of shyness. However, it did not take me long to realise that Ivor is simply a man who likes to test the water before he opens up. Just beneath that strong and silent surface lies a sense of humour that is as sharp as the punches he used to throw during his ring career. At the same time, Ivor is a man of strong principles and he is always prepared to speak his mind, but only if he feels it is worth it.

I have been told by many promoters that boxing is all about 'putting bums on seats' and it is largely down to the boxers on the bill to ensure that those seats are filled. Ticket selling is usually a thankless task and it puts a lot of pressure on a boxer whose mind is filled with the thought of a fight. For Ivor, selling tickets was the least of his problems. Outside of boxing he was virtually an unknown quantity, but during his career Ivor's army of fans were a phenomenon in themselves. He had a massive following out of Holloway, the place where he made his London home. Coach loads of Welsh friends and family would regularly make the journey to come and watch him fight. On top of that, the Newmarket racing fraternity never forgot Ivor 'The Engine' Jones and how hard he tried, and they came to support him in droves.

When Ivor stepped through the ropes all pumped up for action, he made the boxing ring his own territory. As he entertained the crowd with his swashbuckling style and fearless fighting spirit, enthusiastic Welsh voices would fill the smallest of halls to the Albert Hall with the emotive sound of powerful singing, *"Ivor Jones, Ivor Jones, we'll support you evermore,"* to the tune of that most stirring of hymns, Cwm Rhondda (otherwise known as Bread of Heaven) and I am certain that many English voices joined in too! And after 'The Engine' had done his stuff, the nobbins would rain into the ring like April showers.

At this point, I should point out a powerful link between my first book and this one. Those of you who read *'Sweet Fighting Man'* will know that in Colin Dunne's chapter there is a very prominent character, a loveable Londoner called Colin Lake, fondly known to his many friends as Lakey. Before the days of 'The Dynamo,' Lakey was the man in Ivor's corner. Like both Ivor and Colin Dunne, Lakey also started out as an apprentice jockey and went on to become a professional boxer, issuing a brave challenge to Jimmy Anderson for the British Junior-Lightweight Title in 1969.

Lakey and Ivor first met when Ivor was a teenage stable lad at Newmarket. Over the years, these two have stuck together and they remain inseparable. Therefore, it was only right and proper that Lakey should take part in the following chapter. Our interview took place in April 2006. We had been planning to do it for ages and, when the day arrived, Ivor and Lakey came to collect me at Highbury & Islington Tube Station and took me to a friendly pub nearby called The Duchess of Kent. In my first book, Lakey's words were printed in italics. I've done the same thing here, in the interests of both uniformity and comprehension for the reader. Ivor and Lakey interact all the time, so remember, Lakey is the one in *italics*.

Ivor William Jones was born in Holyhead on the 8th April 1954. He left home when he was 15 and his ambition was to become a jockey, but along the way his dream took on a new direction and he decided that boxing was his game. As an amateur, Ivor started boxing at light-flyweight and over the years he grew into a natural bantam. I was surprised when he told me that he walks around at ten stone these days, because he looks much lighter than that. He has dark hair and a fine looking face. The fighter remains in his green eyes, and they are the eyes of a man who I would trust to the ends of the earth. I once saw those eyes go a shade darker when he thought a friend was being bullied. Luckily, the situation blew over with no harm done and, when Ivor recognized that his friend was not in any danger, he calmed down with the sort of split-second timing that he displayed as a boxer, the smile firmly back in place. For the record, the friend that Ivor was looking out for was me.

One does not have to look very far to understand where Ivor inherited this fierce instinct to protect, for he is directly descended from a man who is bravery personified. "My dad's name is William. He was Coxswain on the Holyhead Lifeboat for many years, and he was the Holyhead pilot. He used to bring all the ships in. That's what he did." At this point, I thought that Ivor meant that his father was an aeroplane pilot, but he clarified the point. "No. You know when all the big ships came into the harbour? He'd take over and guide them in. He'd go out on his boat, jump on the big ship and bring her in. He did that for a long time, and he used to work on the railway before he did that. When he was on the lifeboat he was awarded a silver medal and two bronze medals for saving people."

I asked Ivor if, when he was growing up, he was aware of the danger that his father regularly faced. "Not really. I was too young. But I do remember in 1966, he got a medal. They went out to save this Greek ship. There was a hurricane, and it was really, really wild. [The ship's name was Nafsiporos. The date was 2 December 1966 and ten crewmembers were rescued.] My father and one other man were okay, but all the others were sick. My father, he saved one man, and you know on the big ships, they have the ship's lifeboats? Well, when they were back on the lifeboat, one of those boats fell and crashed right into the lifeboat, and my father jumped and pushed this fella out of the way, and that was the man he had saved earlier. Oh, that was some sea, that was. I mean, I was small and I didn't really understand, but I'll never forget it because all the roofs were going everywhere. It was really a bad wind. I think my dad was on the wheel for 24 hours that night."

William, who is now 80 years old, was awarded his silver medal for his part in a rescue mission that took place in 1977. He and his crew ventured 23 miles from the Holyhead coast in a force ten gale. There was a yacht in trouble and four men were snatched to safety. During the rescue, the lifeboat men had to literally pour oil onto troubled waters in an effort to dull the ocean spray and tame the ferocious waves that tossed them about on that wild and windy night. "When my dad used to go out on the lifeboats, my mother used to sit up at nights. She used to be worried sick, listening to the radio to find out what happened. But I didn't realize, because I was too young. Me and my dad, we get on brilliant, absolutely brilliant. We're best friends."

William was with the Royal National Lifeboat Institution for 30 years. During the preparation of this chapter, Ivor loaned me a photograph of his father for the book. When I saw it I exclaimed, "Gosh Ivor! He's so like you." Ivor chuckled and gently corrected me, "No, Mel, I'm like him!" Ivor's father has always been behind him in whatever he has chosen to do, be it racing, boxing or anything. "And my mum, ah, she's beautiful. Her name is Elizabeth. She's a diamond. And I've got one sister and two brothers, Sharon, Colin and Robert.

"My uncle, Llewellyn Jones, was also a professional boxer. I think he had about two fights as a pro. That was a while back. He's dead now. When I boxed he used to follow me everywhere. He was all, 'Ivor this, Ivor that.' I remember just after he died, it was when I fought Kelvin Smart at the Albert Hall. Afterwards, I made a speech in the Albert Hall that night. Llewellyn had just died, and after my fight I grabbed the microphone and I just said that fight was for him. That night I was firing. Frank Bruno was top of the bill. I think Bruno knocked his man out. Me and Bruno were in the same dressing room that night.

"I left home when I was 15. Went to Newmarket. I was an apprentice jockey and I done six years apprenticeship there. I was with Fred and Robert Armstrong. I used to ride out on all the gallops alongside Lester Piggott, Willie Carson and Jimmy Lindley. They were all right. I got on well with them. That was a good time really."

Racing and boxing have always gone hoof in glove, so to speak. Jockeys have clocks in their heads, just like boxers do. As Ivor says, "You have to think when you're gonna make your move. I believe good jockeys will always make good boxers, and vice-versa." It was during his time as a stable boy that Ivor began to develop an interest in the art of boxing. "It wasn't compulsory but, you know, it was a couple of days out of racing. It was a couple of days rest so I thought, 'Right, I'll do it.' The first time I went in I got slaughtered, and I started training and running then. That's how I met Lakey.

"I was about 18 when I met Lakey. He kept seeing me at the old Exeter House Stables. That was really rough place, that was, and you've got to put in this book. We didn't have no gym when we was at Newmarket. The gym was only open one night a week, so we used to spar in the loft up at Exeter House Stables. Before we could start, we had to sweep up the straw first. There was an old ring in there, and all the lads, we used to spar with each other. We used to have wars! There was no one there to say 'You're doing this wrong' or 'You're doing that wrong.' There was no trainers there or nothing. I was useless, but Lakey said he could see a bit of potential there, and I didn't know who Lakey was from Adam! I thought, 'Who's he, telling me what's what?' And then I found out that Colin Lake was Mr Boxing."

It goes without saying that Lakey was more than happy to provide me with reflections of his first memories of Ivor. *"Well, he was sparring with this kid from Armstrong's Stables and Ivor used to spar with him regular. His name was Jimmy Daniels, and they used to knock hell out of each other. I was training Ian Ramage then. He turned pro with me and had four undefeated. He's a friend of mine now. Anyway, Ivor seemed keen and that, you know. So I said to Ivor and Jimmy, 'Is anyone training you two?' They said, 'No.' I said, 'You're killing each other. You'll end up blowing bubbles, the pair of you.' Anyway, I used to take the lads running regular and I said, 'You can come with us if you want.' So they did, Ivor and little Jimmy as well. I remember the first time Ivor caught me with a good shot. We were sparring in the loft and he hit me with a good left hook. That was the first time I realized that he could bang a bit."*

Ivor enlightened me, "The lad that Lakey is talking about, Jimmy Daniels, he used to live in the same place as me when we was in racing. I lived with a couple, Mr and Mrs Brammel. Actually, their son was a good amateur boxer. I lived with them until they died, actually. I thought the world of them. I used to come home and there was always big dinners there, you know. They used to really look after you. When I was racing, I was getting 25 pence on a Monday and 25 pence on a Friday. That was it. That's what they used to give us. They paid our living expenses to the people we were staying with, but you never even seen that."

"I could see straight away that Ivor had a lot of bottle, but I had to teach him defence as well. What a lot of people didn't see was that his attack was his defence. Because when you're attacking, attacking, you can't just throw yourself at them. You've got to work out a way how to do it. There's all the moves that you do, the shoulder feints, the head feints and body feints. They seem to have forgotten all these things now. You've gotta teach kids not to let the opponent know what you're gonna do. This game is a sneaky game."

"And I've been taught these things by Lakey, and that's what I teach the kids now. You've got to read the fight. I think boxing is like a game of chess. Every fighter is different."

Lakey developed a strong stable of boxers at Newmarket. Twice a week, he would take his charges to Brookside ABC in Borehamwood in order to provide them with proper training facilities and allow them to enter the ABAs. Eventually, Lakey opened the Cheveley ABC, near Newmarket, and Ivor won three consecutive National Stable Lads Titles there. He also won the Home Counties Light-Flyweight Title in 1974-75 and the Eastern Counties Bantamweight Title in 1978-1979.

I was interested to learn how Ivor's day as an apprentice jockey and amateur boxer would pan out. "Well, I used to run first thing in the morning, and then we'd go to work in the stables. We used to finish at one o'clock, so then you'd rest 'till four o'clock. Then you'd go back to racing, and then it was evening stables until seven o'clock. After that you'd go boxing training. It was a lot of hours really. I'd be in bed about ten, and then I'd be up about half-five the next morning. It was hard, but I was young and I wanted it. That was my goal, to be a jockey, and then after a while, boxing took over, absolutely. Boxing was the love of my life. It still is."

During their time together at Newmarket, Ivor and Lakey cut quite a dash with the locals. *"Did you know we used to clean windows in Newmarket? Everyone knew us. We had a little Morris Minor. It would only go in reverse gear and we used to go around the town with the ladders on top, going backwards. Everyone was in stitches.*

"I remember one time, we were followed by the police after coming out of a pub one night. Ivor hadn't had a drink. I had, but only one or two. They followed us and stopped us, but Ivor's door was permanently locked and he couldn't open it. Anyway, they chased us and they caught me. They tested me, but I wasn't over the limit. And Ivor got away. He was too fast for them."

Ivor grinned, "Another time, I was up one ladder and Lakey was up another ladder, and he threw the scrim at me." Ivor then explained for my benefit that 'a scrim' is something that you use to clean windows. "He threw it at me, so I ducked and it landed on a lorry, and we end up chasing this lorry to get our scrim back!"

"Yeah, well it was worth a lot of money! We didn't catch him. In the end we had to buy another scrim, didn't we? That was when the strike was on." The stable lads strike of 1975 was a bitter uprising that lasted three months. As with all major industrial disputes, the wide division between the classes that had always been quietly accepted and tolerated suddenly became a turbulent battleground of anger and discontent. That year, just before the Two Thousand Guineas Race at Newmarket, two prominent jockeys became involved in the hostilities. One was dragged from his horse as he was about to take part in the race. The other then led a mounted charge at the protesting stable lads. Ivor knows because he was there, and he remembers being in the crowd when they were charged at. "We just got out of the way." In the end, Ivor confirmed that the stable lads emerged with some sort of victory. "We come out of it with £1.26 a week."

"They made sure you wouldn't get very fat anyway! They were strict in those days, and they were even more strict in my day."

"And I'll tell you another little story as well. Lakey made me a belt out of the old floor polish tins that were full of lead. When I was riding horses out on the gallops, I used to wear it under my clothes so they couldn't see it. It's all about finding out how good that horse is that's underneath you. Anyway, one day I was wearing the belt and I fell off."

"That belt was about a stone or more in weight. The thing is, with the extra weight, you're gonna find out the best chance the horse has got. I mean, with horses, even three or four pounds will make a lot of difference, so if you're carrying an extra stone ... Anyway, one day he come off he couldn't get up by himself, so they had to lift him up." Ivor chuckled at the memory, "The trainer went, 'You're putting on weight aren't you?'"

We got back onto the boxing. "I remember I got through to the finals of the Stable Lads Championship at the Hilton, and I fought Billy Nicholson. He was the hot favourite." Nicholson had won the Stables Lads Championship once, and he was also Schoolboy Champion at the time. "Yeah, and he'd beaten the best. Lakey was in my corner and it was funny, it was. I was slapping like an old woman and the referee warned me about five times. Coming out for the last round the referee said, 'You do that again and you're out.'" Lakey was quick to interject, *"And I screamed at him, 'If you do that again, I won't fucking be here when you get back to the corner!'"*

"Anyway, I went out and I hit him with the left hook, knocked him spark out. It was unbelievable; it really was. Everyone was round me and I got a big picture in the Sporting Life.

"I fought the best in the amateurs. Whoever beat me in the Championships won the final. But I was always more of a pro anyway. I was a pro when I was amateur really. It didn't suit me, the amateurs. It was too short. I'd be just starting to warm up and then it would be over. That's how I got beat a lot. I don't know exactly my amateur record, but I had a lot of fights. My last year in the amateurs, I fought Renard Ashton in the quarter-finals of the ABAs. He beat me on a majority decision. I had him all but out, and I think he knew that he got the decision because he was an England representative. Afterwards, he had to give me and Lakey 20 quid to get us home! But he gave us his address and we sent the money back to him. In the final he beat Jim McDonnell on a majority decision."

For Ivor, turning professional was always a foregone conclusion and, by mid-1979, the time had come to make the break. Ivor and Lakey packed their bags and left the picturesque surroundings of Newmarket to head for Holloway in North London. Lakey sorted Ivor out with some lodgings and set about establishing his status as a professional boxer. Ivor was initially managed by the late Danny Vary, who had trained Lakey while he was a professional boxer, along with many other fighters, including Terry Downes. When Lakey qualified for his manager's licence, he officially took over as Ivor's manager and trainer, but nothing was ever actually signed between them. This was a gentleman's agreement. *"That's all we needed. I trust him and he trusts me."*

One of Lakey's many fortes has always been coming up with ring-names for his fighters. "It was Lakey that gave me the name, 'The Engine', which was good because I was a come-forward fighter, just like an engine. Mind you, that was more my defence actually, going forward, bobbing, weaving and throwing punches all the time. A lot of people used to think I used to have wars, but I didn't really. As Lakey says, my attack was my defence. There's a right way to attack and a wrong way to attack; that's the thing to learn. And, I mean, I did get cut. I used to get cut all the time, but Lakey was in the corner and he used to stop it straight away."

Despite his aggressive style of boxing, outside the ring Ivor was positively angelic to look at. When he stepped into a boxing ring, he truly did become a completely different person. He was happy to jump in the sparring ring with anybody, and when he performed in front of his fans he relished every moment with focused venom. Because of this, the lads in the gym gave him the nickname 'Crippen', after the infamous wife-murdering doctor whose quiet and unassuming manner concealed his dark secret, before his wife's headless and filleted remains were discovered buried beneath his coal cellar floor. He was hanged for her murder in 1910. Ivor smiled darkly when I reminded him, "Old Crippen, yeah."

Many boxers relax between fights, and then whip themselves back into shape when they know they have a fight on the horizon. For Ivor, fighting fitness was built into him. "I used to love the training. I used to always go running up Hampstead Heath. I did hundreds of miles up there. I would say it's the best place a fighter can run, because it's all hills and it's brilliant for stamina. I used to go there before work every morning. Then I used to go to work as a roofer, and then I used to finish about four o'clock and go to the gym." Today, Ivor still enjoys regular runs on Hampstead Heath. I asked him what he thinks about when he goes running nowadays. He laughed, "I don't know. Work perhaps, or training the lads at the Angel Boxing Club.

"When I turned professional, I had to go for my medical and this doctor was trying to find my reflexes. He kept hitting me on the knee with the hammer and nothing was happening. Anyway, I was getting fed up with him hitting me with his hammer, so I just kicked my leg out. The doctor said, 'I knew I'd find his reflexes,' but he didn't find nothing! I'd just had enough of him hitting me, that's all."

But there was nothing wrong with Ivor's reflexes on the 17th October 1979, the night he made his professional debut at the Lewisham Concert Hall against Carl Gaynor. The Rochdale man was a good five inches taller than Ivor and he was rated as a featherweight, compared to Ivor being a bantam. "I felt great. Oh yeah, I really wanted it. My mum had seen me box once, but she didn't like it. But my dad and my sister were there, and my sister was only a little kid then. Everyone was nervous but, you know, I was confident and I wanted it. He was a nice little boxer. I stopped him in the third round." Ivor's fans went wild with joy, sensing that this was the beginning of special things to come, and they were right. A month later Ivor was back in the ring at Lewisham, this time against Stuart Crabb. He was another featherweight and another man who Ivor stopped in three rounds. "He was about six foot. He was really tall and thin."

"Ivor was a body puncher anyway, so he didn't mind if they were tall. He was a good body puncher, and he had a very awkward jab. You don't think it's there but it gets to them. Ivor's jab was similar to Terry Downes' jab. Terry Downes was not known for his jabbing, but when he jabbed he was effective with it. His opponents never used to think it was gonna get there, but it got there. It was one of them sort of jabs. It was a deceiving jab."

Ivor's next fight was in January 1980 and he won on points against tough Swansea trier, Bryn Jones, at the Hilton in Piccadilly. Six weeks later, he won another points decision against Norwich featherweight, Robert Hepburn, at Wimbledon. "I boxed him as an amateur in the ABA quarter-finals at Cambridge and I had him down five times, and when they give him the decision the crowd didn't like it." Lakey shook his head sadly as he remembered that night of violent reaction at the amateurs. *"They wrecked the place, they did. They totally wrecked the place. It was awful. We never wanted that, not whether he won or lost."*

After two more points wins, one against Neath featherweight, John Griffiths, and another exactly a month later, against London based Jamaican, Iggy Jano, on the 19th October 1980, Ivor experienced his first loss as a professional boxer. He was beaten on points over eight rounds by Central Area Bantamweight Champion, Steve Enwright, in Birmingham. "That was a very close decision, but I was ill at the time."

"He come back from the third round and usually he's buzzing to go, but this time he wasn't. It was two days later when he told me that he felt tired after the first few rounds. I wish he'd have told me that at the time, because if he had I would have pulled him out. After that he had to have nearly a year off. He couldn't move. They diagnosed him with a blood disorder, but it was actually an under-active Thyroid gland. They never discovered that until years later, well after he retired. At the time, we didn't know what was happening to him. As time went on, he packed up boxing and he was starting to slur when he spoke."

"And I put on weight, because the Thyroid was under-active. I was slurring and everyone thought I was going punchy! They didn't know what it was. Even at the hospital they didn't even know. I thought I was cracking up."

"I was saying, 'How can he be punchy? He never fucking hardly took a decent shot!' But for ten months there was no life in him."

"Eventually, after I retired from boxing for good, I went to Homerton Hospital and I seen this doctor, and he was brilliant. I can't remember his name, but he asked me if I got tired and if anyone in my family had got anything similar. I didn't know, but my Nan had it, and now my sister's got it. Anyway, this doctor said, 'From what you've told me, I know exactly what's wrong with you.' So now I'm on tablets for the rest of my life. I take one tablet a day. That's all it takes."

After months of rest, Ivor's health started to improve and his desire to return to the ring took over. Eleven months after his last fight, he managed to recover his fitness and strength sufficiently to box again. On the 22nd September 1981 Ivor stepped through the ropes at York Hall to make a gruelling comeback against Carl Cleasby. "York Hall was my favourite venue to box. That was where I fought for the Southern Area Title." Ivor won on points over eight rounds, but the Leeds southpaw was a tough man. He spat his gum-shield out in the sixth round and fought on without it. He put on a fabulous show in the last round and forced Ivor to dig really deep. "He was a tall southpaw, but I didn't mind fighting southpaws. If you stand off them and let them pick you off, they're hard. But, if you keep close to a southpaw, it's all right."

"He's had all the education, you see. You know, a lot of people, they used to think he was just a come-forward fighter, but you've only got to listen to him talk now to know that he didn't take many shots."

Ivor had two more fights during the next two months. In October he stopped fellow Welshman, Steve Reilly, in three rounds at York Hall. Referee, Paddy Sower, jumped in when the Newport man had nothing left to give. Sower was never off his feet but he lacked the power and stamina to keep Ivor off. Lakey commented, *"Too strong."* Ivor countered, "Too good." The following month Ivor scored a six round points decision over George Bailey at The Hilton, Park Lane. The red haired Bradford boxer had had 33 fights when he fought Ivor for the first time, and he went on to have 60 fights in 13 years. "He was a nice fella, actually. He'd had loads of fights and he knew his way around the ring." Lakey nodded sagely in confirmation, *"George Bailey was a tough little bugger."*

After that, there should have been a re-match between Ivor and his only conqueror in the professional ranks so far. The fight was arranged and the venue was to be York Hall. "Then we tried to get Steve Enwright again, and what happened? He didn't turn up for the weigh-in at one o'clock. It was a one o'clock weigh-in on the day before the fight in them days. Anyway, they said they'd weigh him that night."

"You see, the thing is, I wanted to see him weigh in, so I sent Ivor home. I waited there all day and I had the money with me as well. I had nearly six grand in my case, so the matchmaker said, 'Don't you want to hand the money in?' I said, 'No, I'm waiting for him to turn up.' He said, 'It ain't your money.' I said, 'It ain't your money either!' Anyway, they phoned up and said that Steve Enwright was on his way."

But Ivor still doesn't believe that Steve Enwright had any intention of fighting him again. "His missus phoned me and said, 'He's broken down on the motorway,' and I think he was sitting right next to her, to tell you the truth."

"Ivor had sold over £5,000 worth of tickets, and in those days that was a hell of a lot of tickets! To cut a long story short, the place was empty 'cos they all went and got their money back. I waited outside and explained as they arrived that Steve Enwright wasn't turning up. All the Newmarket lads, they don't get a lot of money, so everyone got their money back. There was only a few that stayed on. The place was empty. They had all come to see Ivor, hadn't they? He wasn't on, so that was it."

Ivor began 1982 in explosive style with a three round stoppage of Joe Park in January at York Hall. Park had agreed to step in as a late substitute for this fight the day before. The Scottish southpaw stepped off the train from Glasgow hours before the fight and for the first couple of rounds he gave it a good try. He had Ivor touching down in the first round for a few moments. Lakey conceded, *"He was quite awkward for the first couple of rounds. He was a nice little boxer."* But as soon as Ivor settled down to the fight and started working to the body, destiny ran its course. In the third round, Ivor caught Park with a crunching body shot and the Scotsman sank to his knees, his face contorted in agony. The referee, Roy Francis, did not even bother to start a count. He just marched straight over to the stricken boxer, helped him up and led him back to his corner. Ivor told me that Joe Park was a good amateur but this professional fight with Ivor would be his last. Lakey and Ivor have no idea why. Ivor shrugged his shoulders in a matter of fact fashion, "You don't know what happens to them, do you?"

A month later, Ivor scored another six round points decision in a re-match George Bailey at York Hall. Ivor pressurised all the way and made Bailey's nose bleed from the first round onwards. However, Bailey did manage to get a sneaky but neat left hook in at the beginning of the second round that put Ivor down. Ivor bounced back up before the referee, Roland Dakin, had time to begin a count and went straight back to work with both fists. "He didn't hurt me, but he caught me with a good shot."

"It was more a case of Ivor being off balance than a punch that put him down." Ivor thought about it for a second, and then agreed, "Yeah, I was more off balance, definite. But, you know, he was a good little fighter; there's no doubt about that." I often think that, when a boxer shows a trace of vulnerability, it excites the crowd and that helps to make the boxer a bigger draw. At this point in our interview, I asked Ivor if he agreed with that philosophy, and I used this particular fight to stress my point. But he just smiled and shook his head, "I think I was more embarrassed. It was the first time anybody had ever put me down like that, and I was definitely embarrassed."

On the 20th April 1982 Ivor lost a points decision over eight rounds to former Northern Irish Bantamweight Champion, Davey Larmour, at the

(Photograph - courtesy of Derek Rowe)

Bill Chevalley & Mark Rowe - A winning team

(Photograph - courtesy of Derek Rowe)

Mark Rowe - British Middleweight Champion

(Photograph - courtesy of Derek Rowe)

Mark Rowe with the two Bills - his father and Mr Chevalley

(Photograph - courtesy of Derek Rowe)

Mark Rowe & Bill Chevalley - Strategic planning

(Photograph - courtesy of Rebecca Harley)

Jane Couch - She works hard for the money

(Photograph - courtesy of Rebecca Harley)

Jane Couch - Pretty in pink

(Photograph - courtesy of John Stadnicki)

Jane Couch - Come and have a go if you think you're hard enough

Ivor 'The Engine' Jones - In training

Ivor 'The Engine' Jones & Colin Lake - That's my boy!

William Jones - Hero

Father & Son - William and Ivor Jones

Tony Booth with Nigel Benn & Jimmy Tibbs, training in Tenerife - Happy days!

(Photograph taken by Action Images)

Tony Booth - Tough guy!

(Photograph - courtesy of the Daily Star)

Colin Jones - Don't mess with him!

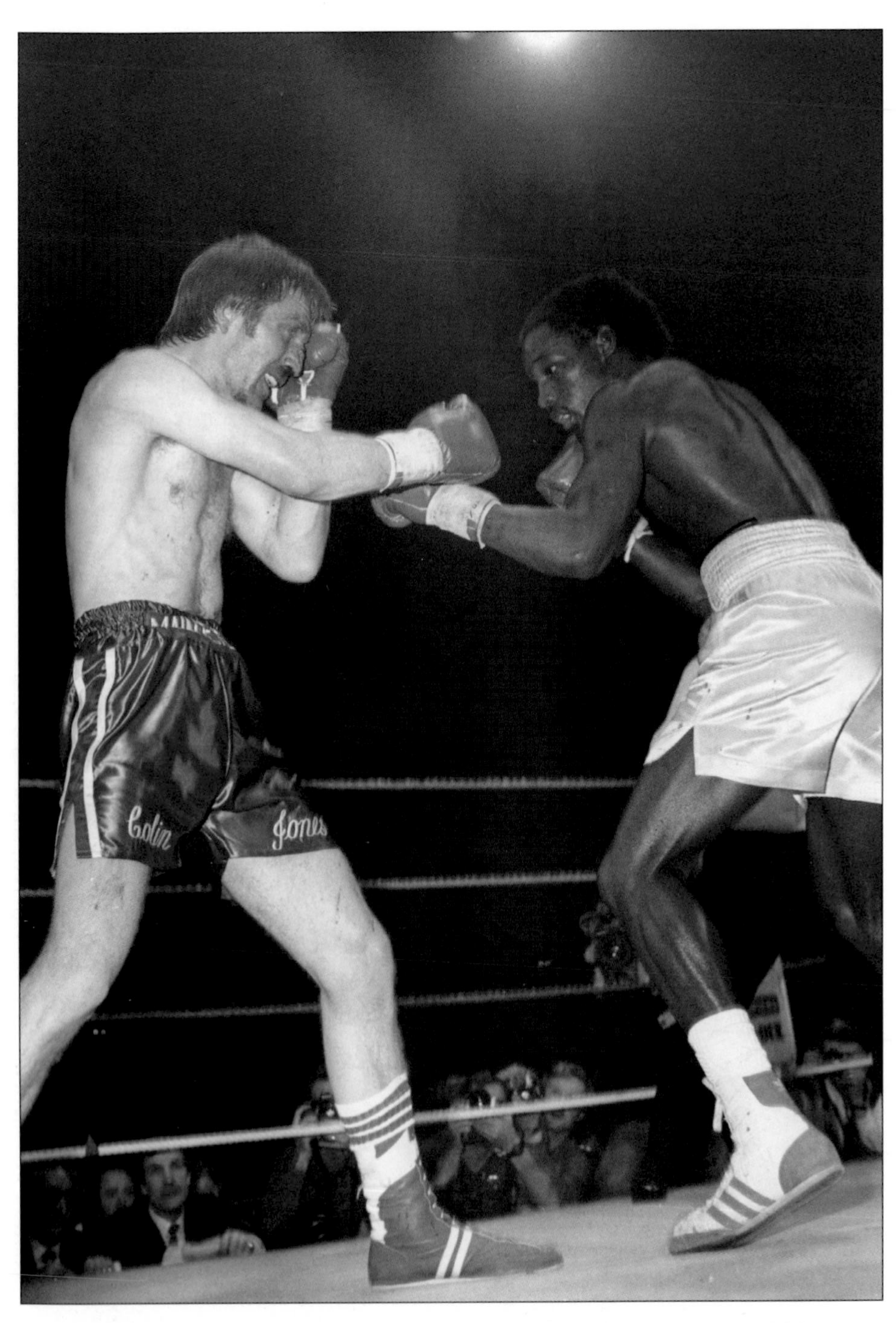

Colin Jones v. Don Curry - Boxing for the World Welterweight Title

(Photograph - courtesy of the Daily Star)

Colin Jones hard at work with Gareth Bevan and Eddie Thomas - The Welsh Wizard watches over them

James Cook MBE!

Royal Albert Hall. Ivor kept punching and marching forward, but the Belfast boxer took the referee's decision by one point. Ivor blames himself for this defeat. "I was cruising and I don't know why, but I nutted him. At the time, I remember Lakey said, 'What are you doing?' I lost the fight through that, and I didn't even know that I'd done it. I still can't remember doing it, but Lakey said, 'You definitely nutted him.' I couldn't believe it, 'cos it's not my temperament to nut someone. But he was a swarm all over you type, holding and grabbing. I suppose I got frustrated and I didn't realize it, but I nutted him." For the record, Dave Larmour went on to regain his Irish crown and he won the British Bantamweight Title in March 1983.

A month after fighting Dave Larmour, Ivor experienced another loss, this time a devastating sixth round stoppage at the hands of Jimmy Bott at Wembley's Empire Pool. Bott came from Liverpool. He was tall, lean, and he had black hair and a big moustache, which was drenched with his own blood from the first round onwards, courtesy of Ivor's unyielding fists. In the sixth round Bott caught Ivor with a right hand counter-punch. Ivor went down, got up again and fought back, but the referee, Brian Anders, decided that he had seen enough and stepped in to stop the fight. Ivor remains adamant to this day that the fight should never have been stopped. "It was unbelievable really. He knocked me down. I went down, got up, and how the referee stopped it, it's unbelievable. It was a liberty. I was so far in front."

"He was so far in front, the only way he could lose was to get stopped. He did get caught with a good shot, but he was okay. He touched down heavily, that's all, and all of a sudden the referee went, 'Right, that's it.' I couldn't fucking believe it! And Ivor couldn't believe it either." For the record, Ivor was never stopped again.

A month after the stoppage by Bott, on the 1st June 1982 Ivor knocked out Neil McLaughlin in four rounds at the Royal Albert Hall. The Derry man had won the Northern Ireland Bantamweight Title in 1977 and in 1980 he fought for the Commonwealth Flyweight Title, a brave challenge which he lost on points over 15 rounds to Ray Amoo. McLaughlin was another one who never fought again after boxing Ivor. During his eight year career, McLaughlin boxed Johnny Owen four times, drawing the first time and losing on points the other three. Ivor's green eyes became distant when I mentioned this. "It was so sad what happened to Johnny Owen. I met him once when we were in the Albert Hall. At the time, he was rated number one and I was about number five. I wouldn't have minded fighting him, of course. That would have been a hell of a fight, because we were similar sort of fighters. Because, you know, he was aggressive; he was there! That would have been a war. But it didn't happen." Lakey conceded, *"That would have been a hard fight for Ivor, but what a fight that would have been."*

During his career, Ivor had two fights with John Dorey of Eltham. The first one happened on the 28th September 1982 at York Hall and, having watched the tape, I have to say that it is one of the most exciting fights I have ever seen. This time, Ivor scored an eight round points decision over the man from Eltham. Dorey had a record of five wins, one loss and one draw and he was considered a bit of a hot prospect, but Ivor knew all about that. "Me and John used to spar nearly every single day up the Thomas A' Beckett and we were good friends. But, when it comes to boxing, it's business."

Aside from being friends, these two were made for each other in boxing terms. Dorey was an upright, correct sort of boxer who was brave and unafraid to try a vast array of different shots. Then you had Ivor, crouching, dangerous and furiously unwilling to be put on the back foot. 'The Engine' was firing on all cylinders that night. As they waited for the preliminaries to be over, Ivor flexed his muscles, kicked up his legs and danced about the ring. As the MC introduced the boxers from each corner, the crowd drowned him out with chants of, "Ivor, Ivor." The first bell sounded and Ivor and Dorey provided non-stop action from the beginning of that fight until the very end. The crowd never stopped calling, "Go on, Ivor," or "Go on, Johnny boy," but it was by far Ivor's fans who made the most noise, all the while stamping their feet to a partisan tattoo that made me think of Roman soldiers marching.

After the first round, the MC attempted to announce that there was a car causing an obstruction in the car park, but the crowd drowned him out with their enthusiastic singing. As the rounds slipped by, both boxers seemed to become more energetic rather than tiring, and the crowd stayed with them, even louder than before. For a fight that was fought with such ferocious intensity, I noticed that there was never a single shot thrown after the bell. By the seventh of this eight rounder, the boxers were finally starting to feel the frantic pace, but both refused to surrender to fatigue, determined to slug it out until the bitter end. When the end finally came, Ivor and Dorey were hugging each other before the bell had finished ringing. Ivor finished the fight with a cut over the left eye and across the bridge of his nose, and he won the fight by half a point. The two of them received a standing ovation and the most generous cascade of nobbins. "But I didn't care about money. I only cared about winning. I would have fought for nothing. Money was never an issue for me, never ever. I just wanted to win. If I'm going do something, I'm going to win."

"Winning and losing were so important to him. After all the work he put in, losing would bring him down for weeks."

In boxing, sometimes it is said that one boxer has 'the Indian sign' over another. This means that, no matter how many times the two will box, the result will always be the same, but not always for the same reasons. On the 16th November 1982 Ivor boxed Jimmy Bott again, this time at York Hall. Bott, the only man to ever stop Ivor, won on points over eight rounds. As we started to talk about this fight Ivor shook his head in an adamant indication that, even today, he finds it difficult to accept that Jimmy Bott won their second fight. "Again! He beat me again! I couldn't believe it."

I have to declare that I could not believe it either. When I sat down to watch the tape of this one, there were no notes on the cassette sleeve that Ivor had given me and I was uncertain as to whether it was the first or second of Ivor's fights with Jimmy Bott. The fight began and Ivor stalked his prey throughout, keeping Bott on the back foot for most of the time. Bott countered well and his footwork was excellent, but when Ivor came in close he negated the Liverpudlian's boxing skills and the crowd got loud every time.

There were anxious moment's in Ivor's corner when he was cut over the left eye in the third round and referee, Mike Jacobs, led him over to his corner for the doctor to inspect the damage. Straight after that, Ivor piled straight back into the fray. As I enjoyed the tape, I came to the conclusion that it must have been their first fight, because I felt that Ivor was so far ahead on points that it was only a stoppage that could win it for the man from Liverpool. And then, they were into the seventh round and I realized that this was the one that Bott won on points. I watched in wonder as, in the final round, 'The Engine' nearly ran Bott right through the ropes and out of the ring. Throughout the fight, Ivor's fans had made their presence felt. The menacing foot stamping was always there, like jungle drums.

The referee gave the fight to Bott by one point and Ivor's fans erupted into an intimidating wave of vocal pandemonium, their aggression firmly directed at the referee. Sitting there with me all these years down the line, Ivor shook his head again, this time with the look of a man who has just sucked a lemon. "He was a Bott, an' all! Of course, I would have loved to have fought him again."

In March 1983 Ivor was set to box John Dorey for the second time, this time for the vacant Southern Area Bantamweight Title. Seven days before Ivor's challenge, Charlie Magri won his World Flyweight Title against Eleoncio Mercedes at Wembley. As part of Magri's preparation, Terry Lawless asked Ivor to come to the Royal Oak Gym in Canning Town as Magri's chief sparring partner. Lakey grinned as he told me, *"They used to laugh at us, because one minute we were arguing and the next we were laughing. It was a great atmosphere up there."* However, one day Terry Lawless decided Charlie needed a day off, so Ivor and Lakey went to the Thomas A' Beckett gym to have a look at Eleoncio Mercedes in training.

"Yeah, I sparred with Mercedes and all, and he was good. He was a very good fighter. We got there and Lakey said, 'Do you want to spar?' His corner-men, they looked at me and they went, 'All right,' and then they said we could go three rounds, and it was good; really good. Then, at the end, Mercedes said, 'Another round?' Anyway, apparently that day was press day. All the press were there. So then Eleoncio said, 'You spar tomorrow,' in broken up English. I said, 'I can't. I'm sparring with Charlie tomorrow.' So all the press, they were all over me then, and they called me 'The spy.'

"Ivor was getting ready to box John Dorey for the Southern Area Title and it was a blinding spar. It suited us down to the ground. Harry Carpenter was there and he interviewed Ivor for the BBC and, when they found out that he was going back to spar with Charlie the next day, the Sun called him 'The Mole.'

I asked Ivor if he felt then, sparring with Magri, that he was going to win the World Title? "Yeah, I did actually. And, you know, everything I said to Charlie, he done the opposite, but he was right in the end, because he won the fight."

A few months after this interview, I asked Charlie Magri about his memories of those sparring sessions. He smiled wryly as he replied, "Oh yeah, Ivor. He drove me mad, he did. He was tough, hard as nails, and he wouldn't keep off me!"

Magri stopped Mercedes in the seventh round to become the WBC Flyweight Champion. Two and a half years later, Eleoncio Mercedes sadly died at the terribly premature age of 28. It was a few days before Christmas and he had been reportedly drinking in a bar in his native town of La Ramona in the Dominican Republic. He was shot by a policeman during an incident in which Eleoncio was said to have allegedly pulled out a gun. Ivor nodded sadly, "And he was a lovely man."

During his boxing career, Ivor sparred with all the top boxers of the time and, in his typical intrepid fashion, he was never very fussy about who he got into the ring with. "I had a go with Lloyd Honeyghan. He didn't try and knock me out or nothing, but we just had a little move around. And Jimmy Flint, I had a move around with him, and with Jim Watt as well. I sparred with loads of fighters. I even sparred with Lakey a few times. I mean, I was light-fly in the amateurs, and I had to spar with him!" Lakey grinned happily, *"Yeah, that's where he got his sneakiness from! I had to give him a little clip every now and again."*

With all the sparring and training done and dusted, on the 22nd March 1983 Ivor climbed into the ring at York Hall to box John Dorey for the vacant Southern Area Bantamweight Title. It was a blazing battle between two good friends who both wanted the same thing so badly. Both of them ended up cut and bleeding, and there was a fair bit of head clashing going on, but Ivor was adamant that there was no foul play afoot. "That was accidental. Definitely."

Dorey boxed well, but he could not keep Ivor off and the seventh round was so exciting that the fans could barely contain themselves, the singing, roaring and stamping of feet reaching a deafening fervour. Dorey smashed Ivor's gum-shield out of his mouth with a wicked right uppercut as he was coming in, crouching, but 'The Engine' refused to come off the rails and, in the second half of the round, he turned things around, forcing Dorey to visibly cringe as he lashed away with body punches. Dorey came on strong in the final round, once more knocking out Ivor's gum-shield, but when the end came Ivor felt that he had certainly done enough to win fair and square, as did Lakey.

Then the referee, Roland Dakin, raised John Dorey's hand. He had scored it to the Eltham man by one point. Ivor had not won the fight in the eyes of the man who mattered. As Ivor stood bewildered in his own corner, his green eyes clouded over with tears as he came to terms with the decision. "You see, the Southern Area Title was, for me, just a steppingstone. It was a starting point. I was looking ahead much further than that. When the referee raised John Dorey's hand, I couldn't believe it. It was unbelievable really. I think I won the second fight easier than I won the first one, when I beat him on points."

"I've watched it so many times. So many times. He won nine out of ten rounds. Nine out of ten rounds! It was unbelievable when John got the decision against him. But these things happen in boxing, don't they? You know, you've just got to get on with it."

Roland Dakin's decision was met with fierce reaction from the crowd. While Ivor and Lakey stood by in stunned disbelieve, the ugly mood outside the ropes boiled over. One of Ivor's fans climbed up onto the ring apron and tried to get at the referee. Dorey's corner-men managed to intercept him at the ropes, but the fan lay in wait and, as Mr Dakin was returning to his ringside seat, the fan punched him in the face. Dakin suffered a cut across the bridge of his nose and had to be taken to hospital for stitches. When we got to this part of his story, Ivor was as honest as the day is long. "Actually, the guy that done it is a good friend of mine, and he can handle himself and that, but he's really not that sort of person. But something clicked, like, 'cos he was such a great supporter of mine. He was a big, big fan. I was his idol, sort of thing, and something just clicked."

"We didn't want any kind of things like that, but they got so frustrated. Don't get me wrong, I'm not saying that it's right, but they must have got so frustrated that things just boiled over. I mean, they think he's won the fight and then ..." I reminded Lakey that Roland Dakin was not the only casualty that night. As the result was being announced, a large group of stable lads had gathered at ringside and began banging on the ring apron. Another ringside fan picked up a spit bucket from one of the corners and threw it all over the MC, Billy Jones. The perpetrator of this act was then punched and kicked to the floor for his trouble. *"Oh, I don't know about that. All I was interested in was getting Ivor out of the way. I don't know who done what, or anything. All I was interested in was getting Ivor out of the way. I mean, it was solid. The place was bursting."*

Some boxing fans are pure boxing fans, people who attend a show and watch every fight because their interest lies in boxing. Then you have fans of a particular boxer, and sometimes, when controversial decisions happen, those partisan fans can tend to take matters into their own hands. I put this concept to Ivor and he thought for a moment before commenting, "Yes, that can happen. Your family and friends will always support you. It's like me supporting, say, a swimmer. I wouldn't support just any swimmer, but if it was a friend I would support them." Ivor is the first to acknowledge that his fans could get a bit lively. I asked him if the trouble after the second John Dorey fight was the worst he experienced during his boxing career. "Well actually, when I was an amateur, when I fought Robert Hepburn, I think it was at the Cambridge Leisure Centre, and the pool table went right out of the window. Somebody jumped on the judges. Oh, it was a riot! Honestly, it was a riot! It was the ABAs and I think all the later fights were put off. They went right into one." I asked Ivor how he used to feel when he could see this commotion going on outside the ring. "Well, you know, I wasn't even thinking about that. I was mad because I didn't get the decision, and that was all I could think about."

Two months after the disappointment of the Southern Area Title fight, Ivor was back in the ring. He appeared at the Albert Hall and he stopped Wolverhampton flyweight, Gary 'Rocky' Roberts, in the fourth round. Ivor suffered a cut over the left eye in the opening minutes and, as the fight went on, the injury worsened. "Yeah, and it was a bad cut as well. I wouldn't say I suffered badly with cuts but, once you do get a cut, they always open up. Anyway, Harry Gibbs, I think he let it go a bit further because I was so far in front." It was a smashing left hook to the body that put paid to Roberts that night. He sat down heavily and took an eight count, and then he got up to fight on. He tried valiantly to fight back, but Ivor knocked him onto the ropes with a sadistic combination from both fists and Harry Gibbs jumped in. It was an excellent bit of refereeing. Ivor nodded keenly and declared, "Harry Gibbs was a genius, and you can say that I said that."

It was February the following year before Ivor was back in action. He fought talented Swansea featherweight, Peter Harris. This is a man who also features in the story of the other 'Jones boy' in this book, Colin Jones, who would go on to become Peter's trainer. Ivor drew with the red haired Welshman (that is Peter, not Colin) over eight rounds at York Hall. Ivor told me, "It was close. It was very close. He was quite a lot heavier than me." Lakey confirmed, *"It was very close. It could have gone either way. The thing was, he was such a cagey, intelligent fighter. It was hard to score really. It was touch and go. I thought Ivor just nicked it, but that's the way it goes."* A couple of years after boxing Ivor, Peter Harris went on to become Welsh Featherweight Champion, and he later went on to win the British Title. He also made a brave challenge against a 'top of his game' Paul Hodkinson for the European Featherweight Title. Harris regained the Welsh Featherweight Title again before he retired in 1996.

On the 6th November 1984, exactly nine months after his last fight, Ivor knocked out Kelvin Smart in two rounds at the Albert Hall. The Caerphilly man was former British Flyweight Champion and he and Ivor could match each other for aggression any day of the week. Smart was a fast fisted, accurate puncher and there were those who felt that he was a tall order for Ivor, but Ivor wasn't taking any notice of that sort of talk. He started off on the attack and just kept on coming until one of his left hooks connected with Smart's chin. The Albert Hall was filled with the sound of raucous elation as Smart lay flat on his back with his eyes closed, possibly trying to shut out the nightmare, and then he bounced back up again at the count of nine. Ivor told me, "My favourite shot was my left hook to the body, and I really wanted that win. Because, do you know what he said when we was out in the middle of the ring? The referee called us together to touch gloves before we started boxing and he said, 'You Welsh bastard!' And I wouldn't mind, but when he won the British Title I went and congratulated him. I went and shook his hand and said, 'Well done.' When I knocked him down, he jumped back up. I think it was just reflexes, but he was gone. So then I had to knock him out again."

"Well, Ivor had to knock him out. We weren't gonna stand no points decision. And with Ivor, when you get his back up, when you rattle his cage so much, he explodes. Kelvin Smart went down the first time and it looked like Ivor had knocked him out, and then he sprang back up. And then Ivor knocked him down again. But the thing is about that fight, Ivor cut his left hand on a Stanley knife a week earlier, and it was that left hand that he knocked Kelvin Smart out with. It was a left hook. Ivor was on fire that night. Let me tell you, no one would have beat Ivor that night, no one!" Ivor quietly reminded me, "Like I said, the night I fought him, my uncle had just died, and I announced that my win was dedicated to him. The promoter was saying 'No, you can't,' and Lakey went, 'Go on!' So I did."

Ivor's next two fights were against Billy Hardy, an outstanding boxer from Sunderland. During Hardy's professional career, which spanned nearly 15 years and 48 fights, he won the British Bantamweight and the British, Commonwealth and European Featherweight Titles. He also made three challenges for World Titles. Hardy had his two fights with Ivor when he was a relative novice, and Ivor is clear in his own mind about the outcome of both. "I know I won the first fight, and the second fight, I know I didn't."

Their first clash came in February 1985 at the Albert Hall and Ivor lost on points over eight rounds. After his sensational stoppage of Kelvin Smart, this decision was all the more disappointing for Ivor. The referee, Nick White, scored it to Hardy by one and a half points, preferring his cleaner punching and correct boxing to Ivor's aggressive style. Hardy speared with his jab while Ivor played his usual game and visited the downstairs department with gusto. In the middle rounds Ivor's work looked as if it was going to pay off. He piled on the layers, pinned Hardy to the ropes and bashed away to the ribs. Hardy was hurt but he kept himself together, refusing to wilt and give in. Ivor punched Hardy's gum-shield out in the seventh, which evoked a ringside remark from Harry Carpenter, who likened Ivor to "a miniature steamroller." In the eighth and final round of the fight, the crowd applauded both gloved gladiators as they fused together with mutual aggression. Hardy's hand got raised at the end of the fight and the crowd booed loudly and ominously, but there was no trouble that night.

Ivor boxed Hardy for the second time two months later, on top of the bill at York Hall. Once again, Ivor lost on points. Ivor was not in the right place mentally that night, but he kept his thoughts to himself. Today, Lakey has his own thoughts on the matter. *"When he didn't get the decision the first time, when he should have won, it really got Ivor down. He didn't feel really sharp for the return, but he didn't tell me because the tickets were sold and he didn't want to let us all down, the promoter and his fans and me. I wish he had told me, because I would have pulled him out if he had."*

Despite his less than perfect emotional state, Ivor never took a backwards step throughout the fight. He knew that this match was going to have a vital impact on his future British Title dreams. The only problem was that Hardy felt exactly the same way. He out-boxed Ivor and his strength on the inside surprised everybody, the general consensus being that Ivor might prove too strong for the Sunderland man at close quarters. Ivor tried his best and traded with Hardy fearlessly, particularly in the fourth round, when 'The Engine' came on strong with a surge of energy that forced Hardy backwards. Ivor's fans were as vocal as they ever were that night, their singing voices strong and their love for Ivor 'The Engine' Jones even stronger but, as the fight went on, it was Hardy who seemed to become physically dominant. Referee, Roy Francis, scored it three points in Hardy's favour and, today, Ivor has no problem with that. "The hunger was gone actually. You know, I had so many promises when they said, 'You do this and you'll fight for the Title.' And all the dodgy decisions; the first Billy Hardy fight, that was the big one. I think I lost heart really. I just lost heart. I was fed up. I was getting older. I was 32. It was all politics and promises."

Ivor 'The Engine' Jones had his last fight on the 16th December 1985. He lost a points decision over eight rounds to West Bromwich boxer, Shane Sylvester. They fought on a National Sporting Club dinner show at Mayfair and it was a fast and furious eight rounder. Ivor tried his best and gave it all he had left. For the first few rounds 'The Engine' was in fine form, looking like his old self, marching forward, clubbing away. And then, in the middle of the fight, he let Shane in. The tables turned completely and Ivor had a painful seventh round, at the end of which he walked to the wrong corner after the bell. Ivor still managed to pull out all the stops for a fine finish to his final fight. "But it was gone then. I already knew that. I wasn't the same fighter. I never told Lakey at the time, because he would have said 'That's it.'"

"I would have, yes. But I knew it after that fight. I said to him, 'Right, there's no point carrying on.' I mean, he never got smashed or anything like that. It was quite a close fight really. But I just knew that was it. Because, when you know the person, and you know what he could have

done ... I said, 'Right, you don't need this no more. You're never gonna fight again as far as I'm concerned.'"

"And I respected his decision because, to me, Lakey is the best trainer in the world. He knows. But I knew as well. I knew it was over. And the money was nothing to me anyway. The spark had gone away, and I always said to myself that I really wouldn't want to become a steppingstone. To tell you the truth, the same thing happened to me when I was an amateur. I fought the best and I know I beat them, and the same thing happened, exactly the same. I mean, how do they rule the decision against you when you've knocked a fella down five times in three rounds? I knocked the same fella out on his own show and his missus jumped on my back!" Ivor laughed at the memory. "She said, 'You fucking hit him in the bollocks!'"

Making that decision to walk away from the ring is often the hardest thing a boxer ever has to do and I asked Ivor how he coped with retirement. He replied after a moment of quiet contemplation, "It was hard." So 'The Engine' had pulled into his final station, but the journey had been a sweet one and that Saturday afternoon, when Ivor and Lakey took a step back in time with me and reflected on what they achieved together, they glowed with pride, and perhaps also a little from the beer we had all enjoyed during the day! Lakey's chest expanded slightly as he declared, *"When he was boxing, he was the biggest ticket seller in the country."* Ivor unpretentiously confirmed, "Yeah. There was one fight, I think it was on a Frank Bruno bill, and it said in the paper that it was a good job for Ivor Jones, because otherwise there would have been no interest."

Indeed, eminent boxing journalist, Colin Hart, once wrote of Ivor in the Sun: *"The biggest box-office attraction in boxing isn't new heavyweight hope, Frank Bruno, or any of our six British and five European Champions. He's a former apprentice jockey, virtually unheard of outside the racing fraternity, but odds-on favourite around the Newmarket and Epsom stables."* Strong recommendation indeed.

If you search Ivor's face at close quarters, there is not a lot of evidence that he once punched for pay. He did suffer from his fair share of lacerations but, as any boxer will tell you, being cut is something that comes with the territory. Ivor once got cut in a sparring session that cost him a few months out of the ring, and a visit to hospital for an operation on the resulting abscess that developed near his left eye. "Yeah, I got cut a few times, but it all started with an elbow. Who was that fella I was sparring with? I can't remember. I'll tell you who it was who sorted it out, it was Dr Pat Whitfield. He was brilliant."

Lakey searched his memory for the identity of the sparring partner involved at the time. *"He was from Uganda, wasn't he? He stopped Ray Gilbody, you know."* His name was Sandy Odanga and I asked Ivor, "Was he a Ugandan?" He replied, "I dunno. He was definitely something! When I was sparring with him, it was getting a bit hard for him for a while. I think that's why he elbowed me. But Dr Pat Whitfield, he was terrific. He cleaned it up and everything brilliant, he did. He cut me and got all the stuff out. I was awake at the time, but I had local anaesthetic so all I could feel was a little tickle." Pat Whitfield is indeed a fighters' friend. He is the plastic and reconstructive surgeon whose expertise has saved the careers of many boxers over the years, including Colin Dunne, Alan Minter and Alan's son, Ross. Mr Whitfield is a genius at his trade and, having had around 100 amateur fights himself, he is a man who knows how it feels to put his face on the line in the name of sport. Ivor declared, "And he never charged me a penny, or nothing."

While I was doing my research for this chapter, I came across a lovely little photograph in the Boxing News of Terry Downes taking Lakey on the pads when they were both a fair bit younger. Lakey explained, *"Yeah, Terry used to manage me when I was boxing."* The piece was published in 1990 and it stated that Lakey and his former protégé, Ivor 'The Engine' Jones, were currently training the boxers at Angel ABC in Islington. Sixteen years down the line, these two boxing fanatics are still there, working away with the boys at the Angel, trying their best to teach them the skills that are necessary to protect themselves at all times in the ring. *"Ivor's put ever such a lot into that club. He's an asset to those kids down there."*

Ivor became suddenly animated at the mention of this subject. "Well, I train amateurs now. We've got a nice little club at the Angel ABC. I enjoy it. We train them like professionals really. We've got this kid, right, he's a lovely kid. He's only 17. He's had five fights, and he's won four since he's been with us, and I will guarantee you, this kid is going to be a World Champion. I think it would be a brilliant thing if they brought boxing back into the schools today, as long as it's well instructed, of course."

Although I am proud to be a Welsh woman, I have now lived in England for over 20 years. I enjoy visiting my family and friends back in Swansea immensely, but living so close to London, I have fallen in love with the big city. In truth, I consider myself to be as much of a Londoner as a Swansea Jack. I asked Ivor if he feels the same about his Welsh roots. "Yeah, I suppose I do really. I mean, I've been living in London a lot of years now. I left home at 15, I was in Newmarket for six years, and then I came to London. For about a year and a half now, I've been with a lady called Judy Bergin. She's as good as gold."

Lakey rapidly confirmed, *"Jude's great! She deserves a mention. She looks after him, anyway. She's as good as gold, a lovely woman."* I had the pleasure of meeting Jude for myself for the first time shortly after my interview with Ivor, and she is one of those people who it is so easy to take to. We were all supporting Colin Dunne's boxing charity, Triumph Over Adversity, and the event was held at Charlie Magri's pub. Talk about keeping it in the family! I have since met Jude on several other occasions and she is definitely a top woman.

The time came for us to wrap up our interview and, as Lakey went to order a taxi to drop me back off at the tube station, I asked Ivor to sum up his relationship with his dear pal. "He's my best friend and, you know, I'll always stick up for Lakey, no matter what. We'll argue; it don't matter where we are, but we'll argue. But, at the same time, we're best friends. I wouldn't have been a fighter if it wasn't for Lakey, and that's definite. Everything I've learned has been off Lakey, and I think Lakey's the best trainer in the world. He gives everything. He did it with me. He done it with Colin Dunne. Lakey used to train them all."

And finally, as Lakey arrived back at the table, I asked him to sum up his feelings for Ivor. *"He's a typical Welsh throw-back. He could easily have gone 15 rounds, and you wouldn't want him in front of you, I'll tell you that. He's like a son to me and I think the world of him. I'd die for him, and I can't put it no better than that. They don't realize what he went through. He fought the best. I've worked with some great fighters and he was one of them."*

As I travelled home on the train that day, a friend rang me on my mobile. "Where have you been?" she asked. "Oh, I've just been to interview Ivor 'The Engine'" came my earnest reply. My voice tends to carry, and I can tell you that I got some strange looks from some of my fellow passengers in that packed carriage, even a few blatant smirks. But, in all fairness, I doubt that my strong Welsh accent helped my case very much.

Anyway, it did not matter to me because, in my heart, I was the one who was smiling. I sat back and thought smugly to myself, 'If only you lot knew.' Indeed, if only they knew about this 5' 5" beacon of light who radiated so much hope and happiness to all those who followed him. For nearly two decades, he was their Champion and they became a sea of faces, shining with elation when he won, and contorted with shock and anger when they saw him get handed questionable decisions. But that was never Ivor's fault. He is a peaceful man. In fact, Ivor 'The Engine' Jones has never been in trouble with the police in his life. But, if a man could be arrested for stealing a show, I think they would have locked him up and thrown the key away.

CHAPTER NINE - TONY BOOTH

***He's a bit of a joker and he loves to play to the crowd. But at the same time, he's a true professional at what he does. He knows exactly what he's doing.* (Peter Buckley)**

Tony Booth is certainly a survivor, not only in the boxing ring, but in life. There are no flies on him - they could not afford the rent in a million years. Tony is one of the very top journeymen in this country and, as the 'opponent' rather than the 'prospect', it is often the way of things that he does not emerge the victor, but at the same time he is the ultimate entertainer. His sense of humour whilst under fire is legendary and his fistic antics never fail to delight the audience. If the money is right, Tony will take a fight at the drop of a hat. Over the years, he has saved so many shows by coming in at impossibly short notice to box an endless list of heavily touted house-fighters when their original opponents have pulled out at the last minute for one reason or another, and occasionally, when the mood takes him, Tony will turn the apple-cart clean over.

When I met Tony for this interview he was on the verge of a 150-fight record. As this book goes to print he has surpassed that milestone, and he made sure that his 150th fight was a win. "There's no way I'm losing this one!" he adamantly declared when I rang him up to wish him luck. He has been boxing for 16 years and, along the way, he won the Central Area Cruiserweight Title and issued brave challenges for the British and Commonwealth Light-Heavyweight and Commonwealth Cruiserweight belts. His last title challenge was for the WBF Cruiserweight Championship in August 2004 when he fought Bash Ali in Nigeria, and the Africans fell in love with him.

Pinning Tony down to an interview was not the easiest job in the world. He is fast on his feet and you have to be quick to keep up with him. Eventually, in May 2006, I travelled to Hull to meet up with him. The chapters in this book have been placed in a certain running order for various reasons, but this was actually the last interview that I was to conduct for *'Sweet Fighting Man – Volume II'* and I felt very excited as I embarked upon my journey.

As the train headed North through the countryside, I stared out at the patchwork of fields, brilliantly highlighted by the stunning yellow of the 'sunshine crop,' the name bestowed upon the flowering rapeseed that lights up our farmland at springtime. I saw a train-spotter sitting on a deckchair on the platform at Doncaster. Living around London, one does not tend to see that sort of thing and, for some reason, it gave me a warm glow inside. A few minutes before the train reached Hull Railway Station there was the magnificent Humber Bridge. This splendid feat of engineering was, at the time of its construction in 1981, the largest suspension bridge in the world, and it retained that title until 1998. The bridge dominated the estuary with majestic ease and the sight of it took my breath away for a moment.

I got off the train with a spring in my step and rang Tony's mobile phone. "I'm here," I told him. "What exit shall I use to leave the station?" He replied, "Come out by the taxis and keep walking. You'll see us standing across the road." I did as instructed and, sure enough, I looked over the road and there was Tony with his friend, Wally Walsh, both waving to me with welcoming smiles on their faces. Wally, who is one of Tony's good drinking pals, came along to ride shotgun for the day and he was a pleasure to have around. The three of us rapidly reached a unanimous decision that a pub with grub would be a good place to get to, so we strolled down the street and into Yates Wine Lodge. We settled ourselves down in a corner, ordered some drinks and some food, and proceeded to make a tape.

Initially that day, Tony was not in the most talkative of moods. This tough Northerner is not a man who readily lets his guard down with strangers, perhaps not a bad way to be in this changing world in which we are all living. Tony is a naturally funny man and his boxing brain works quickly. He cracks jokes with the split-second timing of a stand-up comedian, but at the same time he keeps such a straight face that it is sometimes difficult to tell whether he means it or not. At first, I found his demeanour a little unnerving. I felt a bit like the straight one in his double act. However, as the day passed by, he eased right off on the power and I now realize that, maybe, this is Tony Booth's way of keeping the world on its back foot.

Anthony Paul Booth was born in Hull on the 30th January 1970. He stands at nearly six foot and he has blue eyes. His made his professional boxing debut at light-middle, but these days he boxes at cruiser or heavyweight and he walks around at about 15 and a half stone. Boxers who compete at the heavier weights often look much sleeker in their clothes than they do in the ring, and Tony is a classic example of this. His hair, which he has dyed various colours over the years, is thick, greying and cropped quite short. He has the look of a man who is not to be messed with, and then he smiles, and his face lights right up.

Tony is very much a family man. "My mum and dad are still alive, they're doing all right. Their names are Mike and Margaret. I've got two sisters. And I've got a partner, Jane. I've been with Jane for ten years and she's great. I've got a little girl called Jaye. She's two and a half. And I've got a little boy called Harry. He's nine and he's a brilliant footballer." Later on in the afternoon, Tony proudly showed me video clips of both his children that he had saved on his mobile phone.

Boxing has always been a part of Tony's life. "I started boxing at Kingston Boxing Club in Hull when I was ten. I started because my dad always liked it. It was either boxing or the army barracks, so I went boxing! I had about 65 amateur fights." I asked him, "Did you win any titles?" "Just North East and Yorkshire," came the matter of fact reply. Tony turned professional at the age of 20 and, in order to cover the entire career of this veteran battler, I would have to write a separate book. Therefore, I have picked out some symbolic moments in his life which I hope will show you just who Tony Booth is and what he stands for.

THE FIRST TIME ...

Tony had his first professional fight way back on the 8th March 1990 against Paul Lynch, who hailed from my hometown of Swansea. They boxed in Watford and Tony was a light-middleweight in those days. His opponent, however, was closer to middleweight and Tony lost on points over six rounds. Tony got knocked down from a right hand punch to the chin in the fourth round. He took a count of six and remained cautious for the rest of the fight. He looked a bit puzzled as he asked me, "Who were that? Paul Lynch? I can't remember him putting me down. He beat me on points, but I can't remember going down." I asked how he felt going in for his first professional fight. "I was a bit nervous, but that was it. I weren't too bad."

The first stoppage win is often an important memory in a boxer's mind. Tony's first finish inside the distance came in his seventh fight, on the 8th October 1990. He stopped Bullit Andrews of Birmingham in three rounds at the Winter Gardens in Cleethorpes. "It was all right, but about three weeks later I had TB. I was getting all these chest pains and that, so it's a good job I *did* stop him, 'cos if I'd have gone later into that fight I would probably have been in a bad way. I had to go to hospital for about a week and I signed myself out. I had to take tablets for a year and a half, about 15 tablets a day."

Equally, a boxer's first stoppage loss will usually remain a lasting memory. On the 17th May 1991 Tony lost his first professional fight inside the distance. He was challenging 'The Bury Bomber,' Glen Campbell, for his Central Area Super-Middleweight Title. I commiserated, "He knocked you out in the second round, didn't he?" Tony was quick to quietly correct me. "I've never been knocked out in my life. I was stopped, but I've never been knocked out." I put it to Tony that, when he fought Campbell, the Northerner in the opposite corner was unbeaten in eight fights and he was a hard hitter. "Yeah, but to be honest I wasn't really hurt. I boxed his head off for the first round." This was Tony's first experience of training for a title fight I asked him, "Did that have an affect on you going in, or did you take it in your stride?" He shook his head. "I'd seen a video of him. I was still a bit young, and I think I was a bit nervous. I don't think I should really have watched the video, because I boxed his head off for the first round." Tony was well ahead on points when Campbell suddenly turned things around. Tony got slammed to the canvas with a huge, poker-straight right. He got up and fought back bravely before the referee, Mickey Vann, stepped in to stop it with eight seconds left of the second round. Afterwards the promoter, Jack Doughty, declared that some of Tony's punches would have knocked out most men. When I told him this, Tony raised his eyebrows and answered with a wry smile, "Did he?"

MONTELL GRIFFIN

Montell Griffin was the first man to beat the fabulous Roy Jones. Griffin was challenging the then brilliant Pensacola puncher for his WBC Light-Heavyweight Title and he won the fight, albeit by disqualification, back in March 1997. Jones was unbeaten in 34 fights and I was reading about his progress in the Boxing News every week. I could not believe it when I discovered that, during an over over-zealous attack in the ninth round, Jones caught Griffin as he landed on one knee and, as a result, lost the fight. Five months later, Jones came back to destroy Griffin in one round and regain his title.

Two years before his fights with Jones, Montell Griffin, who went by the nickname 'The Ice Man,' came over to England from Chicago to have four fights. He was IBF Intercontinental Champion at the time, a title he had recently won by upsetting the heavily favoured James Toney. Griffin was unbeaten in 15 fights and Tony Booth was the first man to face him on British soil. On the 4th June 1995 at York Hall, Griffin stopped Tony in two rounds, putting him down at the end of the first. Tony came out for the second, but he was way out of his depth. The American concentrated on a brutal body attack for most of the time and he gave a beautiful boxing display, taking his time and landing with relative ease. When Tony went down again in the second round and landed on one knee for the count of eight, the referee, Ritchie Davies, smiled at Tony and said, "I think you've had enough."

There were no complaints from Tony, then or now. "To be honest, right, I was only there for the money. They rang me up and they said 'Ten rounds.' I hadn't had time to prepare to go ten rounds, so realistically I was just there for the money, do you know what I mean? It's different if you're there to win, but I was there just to get a payday." I asked Tony if he got to know Griffin at all while he was here. "No, but he was only small, wasn't he? Only small." The renowned trainer, 82 year old Eddie Futch came over to England to be in Griffin's corner and I asked Tony if he got to meet him. "I didn't get to talk to him either, but he was little as well." For the record, Montell Griffin is still boxing. He has been fighting since 1993, nearly as long as Tony Booth.

SPARRING STORIES

Over the years Tony has sparred literally thousands of rounds in hundreds of boxing gyms. In 1993 he was a regular sparring partner for the WBC Super-Middleweight Champion, Nigel Benn, who was in his prime at the time. Every sparring session is unique; sometimes it is extremely hard going and sometimes it is a little lighter, a more intricate process. I asked Tony what approach Nigel Benn used to take. "He was good. He was a good boxer and that. He didn't take any liberties. I was in Tenerife about seven times with Nigel and, just before he beat Gerald McClellan, I was over there with him then, sparring. But he only did a few days sparring, and then it was all pad work, but it was good.

"But the best person I've been in the ring with is when I sparred with that Joe Calzaghe. He hits the hardest, but if you watch him on telly he looks as if he slaps. And I sparred with Carl Thompson in Moss Side in Manchester for a couple of weeks, but I didn't stay there; I travelled back to Hull every night. Anyway, in the last round, he catches me with a good uppercut and as I got out of the ring I said to him, 'Can you wipe that Vaseline off my eye?' But it wasn't Vaseline. My eye had just come right up. But he's a nice kid though, Carl Thompson. On the Friday night after that, I'm flying to Belfast to spar with Darren Corbett. So I'm at Belfast Airport and I bent over to pick me suitcase up, and I come up and I banged me head. So when Darren's trainer comes to pick me up from the airport, I've got me eye massive and me head's bleeding. So I just done three weeks of body sparring, which was better for me really, because he's a big puncher, Darren Corbett, and he's a nice bloke. They looked after me well in Belfast. It was nice being there. It's a nice place."

FOREIGN INVASIONS

I ran through a quick checklist with Tony to establish every foreign country he has ever fought in. I came up with: Holland, France, Belgium, Denmark, Germany, Finland, Algeria, Nigeria and Spain. The man has certainly been around. I asked him, which country was his favourite. "I think Germany. They just look after you well, the Germans. After I had the fight, I was playing golf with this German, but he wouldn't come out of the bunker." I gullibly asked, "Why?" Tony laughed, "Think about it! Bunker!" I realised at that point that I needed to seriously sharpen up my act if I wanted to stay in the game. I then swiftly steered the conversation in the direction of some of the men who Tony Booth has mixed it with abroad.

Eddy Smulders:

In October 1991 Tony fought Dutch banger, Eddy Smulders, in Holland. Smulders was twice European Light-Heavyweight Champion and undefeated in 15 fights, 11 of those wins coming inside the distance. He stopped Tony in the sixth round. "He was all right, Eddy Smulders. European Champion, wasn't he? He punched hard, and I was still a baby, see, fighting them all. I mean, how old was I at the time?" We worked it out. "See, I was still only 21 then." I ventured, "So it was like a boy fighting a man?" Tony nodded, "That's it, yeah. It were like that all the time, and he was a good fighter, that Eddy Smulders." Tony liked him so much that in May 1992 he travelled out to Holland to fight the Dutchman again. This time Smulders stopped Tony in the first round.

Ralph Rocchigiani:

In May 1993 Tony travelled to Berlin to box Ralph Rocchigiani and I was under the impression that this was the only time he was ever awarded a draw abroad, but I was incorrect. "No, I drew two actually. I drew with an American in France." After a quick inspection of Tony's record, I discovered that the American in question was Roy Ritchie, who was undefeated in 14 fights when he boxed Tony. But, getting back to the Rocchigiani fight, he was the current German Cruiserweight Champion when Tony scored equal with him over eight rounds. "He went on to win a title, didn't he?" I confirmed that Rocchigiani did indeed win the WBO Cruiserweight Title, which he defended successfully six times before losing it to Carl Thompson on a split decision in 1997. Tony continued, "It was in front of about 10,000 people and, I mean, if you get a draw with a German in Germany, you've won, haven't you?"

Franco Wanyama:

Tony boxed Belgian based Ugandan, Franco Wanyama, twice; both times in Belgium, and the first time was on Christmas Day 1992. When I saw that on Tony's record, I initially thought, 'There must be some mistake. Nobody boxes on Christmas Day, surely!' But there was no mistake. "Yeah. They rang me up and I were a bit skint, so I boxed him. There was about 5,000 people there. I was managed by Brendan Ingle in those days. On Christmas Eve, I went out with Brendan and it's their tradition to have a big meal on Christmas Eve. Anyway, Brendan doesn't eat meat so I was eating all his meat, and he's eating all my vegetables, and I'm drinking all his wine, 'cos he doesn't drink." I asked Tony what time he got to bed that night. "About half-one, half-two, something like that; and we went early as well, otherwise we would have been there all night. So no wonder I got beat on points!

"I boxed him again, and I think he stopped me for some sort of reason." Tony boxed Wanyama for the second time for the Commonwealth Cruiserweight Title in January 1994. This time, he stopped Tony in two rounds. "Like I say, half the time with me, I haven't been there. My head just hasn't been at the races, to be honest."

Bash Ali:

On the 15th August 2004 Tony stepped through the ropes on a steamy African night to challenge the exceptional WBF Cruiserweight Champion, Bash Ali, for his World Title. They fought at the National Stadium in Lagos, Nigeria, which was the hometown of the Champion. Ali had a record of 65 wins and 14 losses. He had his first professional fight in June 1978, 26 years before this battle with Tony. To put it in perspective, Tony was just eight years old when Ali threw his first punch for pay. By the time he fought Tony, Bash Ali was: former USBA Cruiserweight Champion, a challenger for the WBC Cruiserweight Title, former NABF Cruiserweight Champion, former Nigerian Heavyweight Champion, a challenger for the WBA Americas Cruiserweight Title, former WBC International Cruiserweight Champion, former African

Heavyweight Champion, and finally, a challenger for the WBO Cruiserweight Title.

Tony travelled to Nigeria with Eugene Maloney's right hand man, James Russell. I have met James when I have attended some of Eugene's shows in the past, and Tony agreed with me that James is one of the good guys. "He's all right, James. Yeah, nice." When Tony and James arrived at the airport, they were greeted by a vast and colourful welcoming committee. "It was all right, yeah. All the chiefs were there with their scantily clad women. They were all there." I asked, "Were they dancing and singing?" He replied, "No, they were just hanging about."

All too often, Tony Booth appears from nowhere to box a prospect on a small hall show. He makes the crowd happy and then disappears back to Hull with no fanfare. This time, things were very different. The African people really took this Englishman to their hearts. He had come to fight their Champion on their territory and they seemed to like that. Tony took part in television appearances and radio phone-ins, and the fight itself was shown on African Independent Television. He was treated like an international superstar. "Oh, all sorts, yeah. I was like David Beckham. Everywhere I went, there was cars escorting you along and all that." As Tony and James turned up at a television studio to do an interview, Tony fell down and hurt his leg. "Oh yeah. It were pitch black, and I fell. They said they'd put the fight back two weeks I said, 'You can't put the fight back because I've got to get back to work.'" Tony knew he had to be back on his forklift truck at Hull docks the following week, so he fought with the injury.

The big night arrived, and the crowd loved it as Tony entertained them by winking solicitously at the ringside crowd. "I give them one or two, yeah. There were about three and a half thousand there and it were funny, 'cos they were all shouting 'Tony Boot!" Then Tony suddenly became serious. "But, when you go to these places … I mean, I only had about a week's notice. They kept saying, 'You're going there.' So the next minute I'm going over there but, when there's only you and someone else there, you're just there for the money. It's one of them sort of places."

In the second round of the fight it looked like Tony was going to cause an upset. He caught Ali and the old African was all over the shop. "Yeah, I could have even stopped him, but it's hard to explain what goes on when you're fighting in them sort of countries." I asked him to *try* and explain. "It's just that, when you go over there, you're more or less under orders not to win, aren't you?"

It was reported in the Boxing News that Tony's leg injury caught up with him in the fourth round and, as Ali was closing in, the referee stopped the fight. I asked Tony if that was true. He hesitated for a moment before replying, "Yeah, it was something like that. It was just more or less, like, you're there to get beat in a certain round, aren't you?" For the record, Ali was 48 years old at the time he fought Tony and it was his ambition to go on to become the oldest man ever to challenge for a World Heavyweight Title. After boxing Tony, he never fought again.

THE BEST OF BRITISH - *Crawford Ashley:*

Former British, Commonwealth and European Champion, Crawford Ashley, was one of our top fighters during the 1980s and the 1990s. Tony has boxed Crawford twice. The first time Tony was matched with the 6' 4" Rastafarian, Crawford stopped him in one round at the Elephant and Castle in December 1996. The Leeds puncher put Tony down four times in that first round before the referee, Mark Green, stopped it in the last ten seconds. Tony laughed, "And then, when I boxed him the second time here in Hull, I nearly beat him!"

But, sticking with their first fight for the moment, when a man goes down four times in the first round of a fight, I tend to question the referee's 'bravery' on behalf of the boxers in his charge. Once or twice, maybe, but four times is, in my opinion, too much. I asked Tony how he felt about referee Green's handling of that fight. "Yeah, I were just fighting him for the money and I took a dive in the first round. To be honest, when you go down, if you get up at eight, they usually don't stop it, but if you get up at nine, they usually stop it. So I kept getting up at nine hoping he was going to stop it, but he didn't, so I had to keep on going.

But I was there for the money in that fight, and I wouldn't mind, but I'd been practicing my dive on the dog for a week!"

The second time Tony boxed Crawford, it was a completely different story. They boxed in Hull on the 9th June 1998 and on the line were Crawford's British and Commonwealth Titles. Even though Crawford emerged victorious with his titles intact in the sixth round, Tony took him to hell and back first. Tony was coming in off a string of five wins, including those against Martin Langtry and Bruce Scott, both of whom he turned the tables on [see below]. When Tony engaged in battle with Crawford that night before his home fans in Hull, it looked for all the world as if he was about to cause another upset. He had a rare home advantage and he was seven years the younger man. However, despite the age difference, it was Tony's 79th professional fight in contrast to Crawford's 38th. "Hull City Hall, that holds 2,000 people. When I fought Crawford Ashley there, I sold £4,500 worth of tickets in two weeks. But I don't think it was an advantage fighting him in Hull. It's just more pressure, isn't it? I'd sooner fight him in Leeds."

I remember watching this fight on the television with a friend of mine. I was a huge Crawford Ashley fan in those days (I still am) and this was the first time that Tony Booth really captured my attention. The first bell went and gone was the funny man. Humour had been replaced by ruthless defiance. In the first round, Crawford caught Tony with a vicious left hook, one of Crawf's favourite shots. There were gasps from the audience, but Tony just beckoned him in and shouted "Come on!" The battle lines had been deeply drawn.

Tony nodded proudly. "That were a good fight, wasn't it?" I confirmed that indeed it was. Even in the face of Crawford's hardest punches, Tony maintained a dangerous glint in his eye. "And when I went down, I went down in that fight for, like, a standing eight count. It were just one of those things, 'cos I wasn't hurt. I was just going down for a breather, and he was fucked an' all, wasn't he?" Tony even managed to out-jab Crawford at times, even though the Leeds man had the longer reach by six inches. "He put me down twice, and then, when he put me down, Mickey Vann - who was from Leeds as well, so they shouldn't have really had him refereeing - he said 'Break,' so you're supposed to take a step back. Well, when he said 'Break,' Crawford whacked me twice, which I thought were a bit out of order. I remember the ringside commentators were saying, 'He should keep his hands up' and all that, but at the end of the day you're supposed to fucking step back, aren't you?"

Tony gave it everything he had that night, sometimes fighting like a man possessed by a devilish desire to win but, when the end came, in the sixth round Tony unravelled and there was nowhere left for him to go. Mickey Vann came to his rescue and the fight was over. Crawford was still the Champion. I informed Tony that the Boxing News wrote that his performance was: *"one of the bravest British Title bids in recent history."* He raised his eyebrows. "Oh, it said that, did it?"

Directly after the fight Crawford commented to the ringside television cameras, "Every fighter who boxes for the Lonsdale belt gives 120 per cent. When I caught him in the second round I thought he wouldn't get up. Certain fighters run and hide from me, but he didn't. He did catch me, but you get caught in the boxing game. If he fought all his fights like that, then his record would be much, much better. He's a class fighter. I'd tell him to train as hard as he did for me, because it won't be long before he wins lots of titles." This, Tony did remember. "Yeah, I know. I appreciated that. He spoke well, yeah."

As a result of interviewing Crawford for my first book, he and his wife, Hayley, have become friends of mine. While I was working on Tony's interview I rang Crawford and told him that Tony was to be in this volume. I asked Crawf' if he had any contribution to make towards this chapter and he thought for a moment before replying. "Tony Booth, I just wish he'd trained a little harder for each one of his fights instead of taking them at short notice. I think he could have beat a lot of fighters that he lost to. I think, later on in life, he'll probably regret it, but he's a lot better than his record says he is." I read Crawford's words to Tony and he nodded his head and smiled. "Well, yeah, it's right what he says, and I'll take that from him 'cos I've got a lot of respect for him. He's all right, Crawford."

UPSETTING THE APPLECART

Every so often, Tony does the unexpected and wins a fight against the favourite. I was interested to learn what motivates him to pull the cat out of the bag and rewrite the script. "I don't know. I mean, you're expected to lose, aren't you? And sometimes, it depends who's there. I mean, if I've got all me mates there, I don't like to let them down, do you know what I mean? But when you get a week's notice and the other kid has been preparing for five or six weeks, it's a bit different.

"But I have got to say that I've been with my partner, Jane, for ten years now and I do think that, if I'd have met her ten years earlier, I probably would have done a lot more, because she's the one who got my head sorted out. It was when I got together with her that I started winning all those fights against the likes of Martin Langtry and Bruce Scott. That all started happening when I met her."

Martin Langtry:

In September 1997 Tony won a six round points decision over Martin Langtry at the Winter Gardens in Cleethorpes. Langtry was Midlands Area Cruiserweight Champion at the time and he was undefeated in 12 fights. Tony changed that and, at the same time, finished Langtry's career. He put the man from Lincoln down in the second round and promptly got told off by the referee for gesturing to Langtry's fans instead of retreating to a neutral corner. Langtry came on strong in the last round and trapped Tony into his own corner, but Tony simply nodded over to his trainer, Geoff Rymer, as if to say, 'Don't worry, he's not hurting me.'

"I mean, Martin Langtry had had about 12 wins then, hadn't he? All his mates were shouting for him. All his supporters and that, they were shouting 'Wanker!' so I knocked him down and did like that to them." Tony then demonstrated what he meant with the gesture that goes with the word 'Wanker.'

Bruce Scott:

Two weeks after Martin Langtry came Bruce Scott. Tony fought the Hackney based Jamaican at the Alexandra Pavilion in Muswell Hill. Scott had a staunch record of 19 wins against 2 losses when Tony beat him on points over eight rounds. This was sweet revenge for Tony, as Scott had stopped him in three rounds in November 1995 and beaten him on points in July 1996. For Tony, it was a case of third time lucky and, on the night, the adrenaline of surfing a winning wave gave him the extra edge that he needed to take the decision.

"I boxed Bruce Scott for the first time at Halifax. I got knocked down and he knocked my tooth out. Then I fought him at Bethnal Green and he beat me on points. So he stopped me, he beat me on points, and then they offered it to me again when I beat Martin Langtry. They rang me up at short notice to fight Bruce. I'd been to Majorca with my partner, Jane. I'd been doing a bit of running over there, but that's all. And somebody said, if you'd been stopped and already beat by him, a lot of kids wouldn't have boxed him again. But I beat him the third time, didn't I?"

Omar Sheika:

Omar Sheika was a hot young American prospect from Patterson, New Jersey. He was 21 years old, unbeaten in 14 fights, and what really set him apart from the rest was that he was handled by Mike Tyson's old team, consisting of manager, Bill Cayton, and trainer, Kevin Rooney. In July 1998 Sheika's team brought him to England and he fought our very own Tony Booth at Ponds Forge Arena in Sheffield. "I'd been on the piss for about three and a half weeks, but I said I'd fight him, and I beat him on points over eight rounds."

I have only seen this fight in bursts of a few seconds, but the limited footage I have witnessed shows Tony boxing with relative ease. However, Sheika's excitable and highly vocal trainer, Kevin Rooney, was still raging at the Board of Control officials about the decision for an hour after the fight was over. My good friend and veteran house-second, Lenny Lee, was working in Tony's corner that night and he told me of his memories. "I remember Kevin Rooney more than anything else. He went potty! He went absolutely crackers! He even came to me, because he saw I was in Tony's corner and he obviously thought I was more important than I actually was, and I tried to explain that to him. I think Tony deserved to win it, because he sort of mugged him out of it."

I asked Tony if he feels he won it fair and square. "What I did, I just jabbed and moved, jabbed his head off, and in the last round or two he started unloading one or two body shots. I could feel them, like, but I think that I had him boxed and gone by then. After the fight, the Daily Telegraph rang me up and asked, 'What was it like fighting Omar Sheika?' I said, 'It would have been harder fighting Homer Simpson!'"

Scott Lansdowne:

In April 2002 the applecart took another tumble at the hands of Tony Booth. This time it was Leicester southpaw, Scott Lansdowne, who fell amongst the fruit. When we got onto this one, Tony was straight in with, "I can't stand fighting southpaws. I don't want to fight any southpaws unless I get good money." Lansdowne was unbeaten in six fights at the time and referee, Billy Aird, stepped in to stop the fight in Tony's favour in the fourth round at the Elephant and Castle. Referee Aird did a great job that night, because Lansdowne was in big trouble. He had already been on the canvas in the first and he had been cut in the third. "Yeah, and he's won the Southern Area Title now at heavyweight, hasn't he? [It's actually the British Masters Title that Scott Lansdowne held at the time that I wrote this.]

"My partner, Jane, was down there, and she wouldn't watch the fight. All my mates were down there as well. He hit me and started waving to his fans, so then *I* hit *him* and I started waving to *his* fans, and the next minute I went and stopped him, didn't I? I didn't knock him out, but he was out on his feet." I asked Tony, "Have you ever been out on your feet?" The answer came loud, proud and adamant. "No, no, no. No, I've only ever been stopped more or less on me own accord, to be honest. Even in that Crawford Ashley fight, I went down for a breather because there was no standing eight count."

THE JOURNEYMEN

Not everybody Tony boxes is a prospect. He won the vacant Central Area Cruiserweight Title on the in April 1995 from Art Stacey of Leeds. Tony took the ten round points decision at the Royal Hotel in Hull. "Yeah, he were a journeyman. He were a tough kid though." Things got very heated in there, and in the third round the referee had to take time out to warn both of them for dodgy headwork. They touched gloves and there was no more trouble after that. The last round was the best of the fight and, as they stood and had a proper punch-up, they brought the crowd to their feet.

I put it to Tony that he doesn't mind having a scrap in the ring, which put him in mind of another journeyman who he traded punches with. "That was one of the funniest though, that Nigel Rafferty, when I boxed him here. [They boxed at the Ennardale Leisure Centre in Hull in July 1995.] Yeah, he bit me, and all sorts. I had a bite mark on my shoulder for about three weeks!" Tony stopped Rafferty that night in the seventh round at Hull, and he obviously didn't object too much to the chomping factor because he boxed Rafferty three more times after that, earning a draw and two points wins for his trouble.

THE LATEST CALL

I asked Tony how many shows he thinks he has saved by coming in at short notice. "I dunno. Maybe about 40 or 50, something like that. One time, Eugene Maloney rang me up at half-ten in the morning. I had to get a train down to London and all the trains were off, so I got a taxi." I asked him, "What do you think was your latest call?" He thought about it briefly and replied, "Actually, I think it were the last time I boxed your friend, Tommy."

At the time of this interview, Tony had boxed Tommy Eastwood twice. The first time was Tom's professional debut at the Elephant and Castle in September 2001. Tommy won on points over four rounds but the fight was not without its drama. In the second round Tommy knocked Tony down with a right uppercut on the chin. Tony shook himself and rose from the canvas after a couple of seconds to surge forwards and survive the round. As the round ended, somebody threw an illegal punch. I'm not sure who the guilty party was, but I strongly suspect that it could have been Tommy. They continued to trade heavy headshots to the sound of the bell, which rang urgently and persistently until they were eventually parted. I will always remember the referee (who was, by comparison, of a small build) trying desperately to force himself between these two big men and prize them apart. Near the end of the third round, Tony (who was the heavier man by at least a stone and a half) lifted Tommy off his feet with the same sort of action as his forklift truck and waltzed the Epsom man back to the ring post. While this was happening, Tommy threw back his head and laughed, all needle forgotten now. Tony has had so many fights and I wondered if he remembers individual moments such as this. "I remember fighting him, but I don't remember getting knocked down, to be honest."

The second time they fought (the time that Tony refers to above) was in October 2005 at Heathrow. For Tony, this really was a last minute affair. "I was supposed to go to work, two 'till ten. What happened was, I went in this café over there and I had a big breakfast. Then I went in Diva's over there and had two pints of bitter, and that's when Roy Hilder rang me up. He said, 'I've got a fight for you if you want it.' So I've just had a big breakfast and two pints of bitter. But the money was right and I said I'd take it, so he said, 'All right, I'll see if I can get it.' So he rang back and said, 'Right, you're fighting.' With that, I got a taxi from here all the way home, got me gear, got the train, and I went straight to Heathrow Airport. And Tommy beat me on points, didn't he?"

One of the enduring memories I have of that fight was a conversation at the bar afterwards. I was standing with Tommy's mother, Sylvie, and Tony had joined us for a drink. Sylvie was never overly keen about her son boxing, but at the same time she recognized that it helped to keep him on the straight and narrow. That night, however, she made her feelings clear on how she saw the brutality of her son's chosen sport. She told Tony, "I don't know how you can do it." Tony gently replied, "I've just been paid nearly two grand for that fight. That's how I can do it." But Sylvie stuck to her guns. "So you got paid nearly two grand, but you just got battered in there. Is it worth getting smashed up for two grand?" Tony retreated behind his guard at this point, with the air of a man who has had this conversation many times before, and we duly changed the subject. In fact, I think it was at that point that I saw and took my opportunity to powerfully persuade him that he should make an appearance in this book.

Now, months later, we were actually doing the interview and I reminded him of that conversation. I said, "You were very gentlemanly and polite that night, but if you were to answer Sylvie's question straight from the hip, how would you word it?" His no nonsense tone of voice accentuated his reply. "Look love, I could have worked on the door that night for £60 or £70, and some idiot could come at me with a broken bottle. Instead, I travelled to Heathrow and had an organized fight and, for that fight, I probably got paid more than Tommy." I can confirm that he did.

Two months after this interview, Tony and Tommy completed their trilogy. Tommy was originally scheduled to box another fighter, but that fell through and Tony Booth was the only man who would agree to come and fight him at short notice. They boxed at Goresbrook Leisure Centre in Dagenham.

The first time I laid eyes on Tony that day was as he walked through the hall towards the ring. As soon as I saw him, I knew that something was not quite right. Tommy was in a highly focused frame of mind that afternoon and his body attacks would have stopped many a lesser man. However, Tony simply clowned around and did his Ali shuffles. At one point he turned around whilst in a clinch and shouted to the crowd "I'm knackered!" The audience laughed, but my heart went out to him, because I could tell that he really meant it. Tommy found it hard to keep a straight face at times during that fight, such are the comedy skills of Tony Booth. But, from my seat at ringside, I cringed every time one of Tommy's fists sank into Tony's midriff.

We had to move on rather quickly after the fight, so I did not get to see Tony before we left. The following day I rang him up to see how he was. I told him that, to me, he had not looked very well the day before, and I was concerned. That gallant and tough man explained, "I'd been to a wedding on the Friday and I think I ate something dodgy. The night before I came down to box Tommy, I was up and down on the loo all night. And his body shots didn't help either! But Tommy is looking really sharp. You make sure you give him my regards." What a man!

A JOB WELL DONE

More often than not, Tony is only too aware of his brief before he steps into the ring. He knows why he is there and he knows what he has got to do. But somehow, he always manages to make it an entertaining fight. "Well, obviously, you just go in there and just get stuck in, don't you? I mean, they've offered me one for next week. He's 17 stone, a bit too big, but anyone else, I don't mind fighting anybody. Like my dad said years ago, 'They've only got two arms and two legs.' I boxed a kid last year, Carl Wright from the Midlands. He hadn't been beat yet. I got in there and I wasn't fit, so he beat me on points. See, when I boxed for the British Title, I was training three times a day. I'm lucky if I train an hour and a half a day now. So, if they can't beat me then?" He shrugged his shoulders." I mean, if I'd have had three or four weeks notice, I'd be standing him on his head, wouldn't I?

"I boxed James Cook twice and he beat me on points. One time, I'd been training really hard to fight him, and I came home on the Friday night and I went on the piss. I got into a street fight and dislocated my thumb. So I boxed him eight rounds just with my right hand, and he still only beat me on points!" For the record, there was a mischievous gleam in Tony's eyes as he said that, and I know that he respects former British and European Super-Middleweight Champion, James Cook. Everybody does. James was another of my subjects in '*Sweet Fighting Man*' and, having recently been awarded the MBE for Services to Youth Justice in Hackney, he has made an appearance in this book also. Incidentally, when I told James what Tony had said, he threw back his head and treated me to one of his lovely, deep and rich Jamaican laughs.

FUNNY MAN

Tony is a born comedian. When he is fighting, he can be right in the thick of it one minute, and seconds later he will trap his opponent against the ropes and he'll start chatting over the other man's shoulder to the people sitting in the safe seats at ringside. Or he might get caught with a particularly hard shot and, instead of buckling, he will perform one of his favourite moves; a nifty little Ali shuffle. I asked him what is going through his mind when he is doing these things. "Well, you're not bothered, are you? You just go with the flow, don't you? And I like a laugh.

"When I was boxing in Bethnal Green last week, I kept saying to the bloke, 'Are you gonna ring that bell?' 'Cos I was knackered, you know? But you've got to have a laugh, haven't you? I've always liked a laugh. I just flex me arms and that, and I do the Ali shuffle and all that, and then I start panting over the ropes if I'm out of breath. And then I grab their arms and the referee says, 'Stop holding,' and I say, '*He's* fucking holding *me*. *I* ain't holding *him*.' Do you know what I mean? Just daft things."

It took a few phone calls to set up this meeting and the first time I heard Tony's voicemail message on his mobile it made me chuckle. He starts off like a heavy breather and then he gasps: *"This is Tony booth. I'm running the London Marathon. If you leave your number, when I finish I'll ring you back,"* punctuated with more heavy breathing. I left a message and when he rang me back I asked him, "Were you really running the London Marathon at the time you recorded that message?" "Oh, I've done loads," came his nonchalant reply. So I diligently wrote up questions on how many marathons he has run and which charities he has raised funds for. However, when I met him for this interview, I asked him again. This time he confessed with a cheeky grin, "I haven't done any, no."

At this point Wally Walsh interjected, "He had one voice message on there, it said: *'Hello, it's Tony Booth here. I'll have to ring you back because I'm going to be up the gym training. I could be fighting any time.'* That was the funniest one!"

Tony continued, "I mean, to be honest, I've thought about going on the comedian circuit 'cos I've got loads of jokes, and I'm quite a funny guy anyway." Tony tells jokes with a kind of 'Cooperesque' delivery (and that is Tommy, not Henry or George, by the way). He then treated me to a sample of his repertoire, and a few of his yarns I shall not repeat for fear that we might both end up getting sued! Here are two that are printable. "It's like our lass says, she rings me up and she says, 'I've got water in the carburettor.' I says, 'Where are you?' She says, 'I'm in the river.'" When we had all stopped laughing, he went on. "And it's like when I went for my first medical when I started boxing. The doctor says, 'Take all your clothes off.' I says, 'Where shall I put them?' He says, 'Over there, next to mine.'"

One night, when I was chatting to Sylvester Mittee, he summed up this side of Tony's nature beautifully. "Well, it's Booth by name, booth by nature isn't it? I mean, in the days of the boxing booths, the fighters were all professional journeymen who took on all comers. They entertained the crowds, but they always kept themselves safe. Self-preservation was at the forefront of their minds. It seems to me that Tony is keeping this tradition in place."

HOSTILE TERRITORY

The typical crowds that Tony faces are largely there to support the man he is fighting at the time, and I had to ask him if he ever feels intimidated in a packed hall. "When I boxed in Algeria it took them half an hour to get us out of the ring. There were loads of bodyguards and that." I asked Tony who he was fighting that night. "I can't remember his name now. [It was actually Mohamed Benguesmia and he stopped Tony in the fourth round in January 2003.] All the crowd were making cutthroat gestures. I think there was a war on over there at the time or something. I was advised not to go over there, but I went anyway.

"Colin Hart says to me, 'How can you go to all those places?' Because no one else does, do they? Sometimes, what I do, I go out there and, like, I've got a little girl of two-and-a-half and a little boy of nine, and I think to myself, 'Why am I in these sort of places?' Do you know what I mean? Because your kids are the main people, aren't they?" "What about before you had the children?" I asked. "Did you used to care so much about your safety then?" He shook his head, "Not so much then, no. But now, I don't want to die young because I just want to see my children grow up."

FIGHTING FIT

When Tony first started boxing he might be out two or three times a month. These days he boxes, on average, once a month. For a man who is in the ring as often as he is, I was interested to learn how much time he spends training. "Well, to be honest, all I've had this week is a sauna. But next week I'll be back in training on Monday, just in case I'm fighting on the Friday. Wally Walsh tries to take me on the town for a beer, but I don't have it! I am a professional!"

Still on the subject of Tony's training regime, we got onto the youth of today. "I think they should at least bring the boxing training into schools, keep them fit. I think it would teach them respect, and there's a lot of, like, fat kids about, isn't there? So it would get them fit. I mean, when I was boxing for the British Title, I used to do circuits. It was eight exercises and they were half a minute each. If you could do three of them, you was fit. But it was hard. You get all these big bodybuilders, but they couldn't do all that.

"Before, when I first started, I was running eight miles a day. These days, I do about three or four mile, fast. Like, next week, if I've got a fight, I'll do that four times in a week. But I live just outside Hull now, so maybe I'll just have a run into Hull and that." I asked him, "What do you think about when you're out there on the move?" He thought about it for a moment. "All sorts. I don't know really. Money, work, I don't know what I think about. Sometimes, you can just go out into the country and I just chill out, just looking at the fields and that. That's nice, to go running out there. Otherwise, you're in all these main streets and it just does your head in."

BRINGING HOME THE BACON

Often when we come across a true character in this world, it is often easy to forget that there is a human being behind all the bravado. When we watch our boxers in action, behind the all thrills and spills of their ring performances, more often than not there lies somebody who goes out to work every day, just like the next man in the street. Tony Booth has never been a man who is afraid to get his hands dirty. He has worked on the Hull Docks as a forklift truck driver for many years. "It's all right. It's a good laugh on the docks, but you just can't guarantee the work, you see. I'm not working at the moment, but I'm hoping to work in the next week or so. It's in Liverpool on a building site. It's just a few months work, a bit of labouring. At the moment, I don't know what to do. I might start working with kids or something, I don't know. I just want a job that I know I like doing.

"I work the doors and all that. I work in the pub across the road, and I used to work in this pub we're in now when I was 18. I was working the doors in the clubs as well when I was 21. So that's why I've got a lot of respect in the town, you see." I asked him if he ever gets challenged when he's working the door of a bar or club. "No. I've got a lot of respect. I used to have to fight a bit, but I've got a lot of respect, so it's not so bad."

DIRTY TRICKS

Boxing is a notorious playing field for dirty tricks and I presumed that Tony must have experienced his fair share of liberty takers over the years, but he shook his head. "Not really. Nowt' much. Mind you, I was supposed to box this fella in Belgium once. I were gloved up ready. I were in the ring, and that, and they said, 'No, no, he won't be in yet.' So he didn't get in there 'till about three hours later! I thought that were a bit out of order." These words were delivered with an impeccably solemn expression and, what with the combination of his quiet voice, his

Northern accent and the background music in the pub, I have to confess that the joke went totally over my head. I answered him earnestly, "That's right out of order." It was only when I listened to the tape that I got the joke. I have to say that, at the time, Tony was very kind about it and let the moment pass by quietly.

"I mean, like, the other day I boxed a heavyweight and he'd probably been training four or five weeks for a fight. They rang me up a week before the fight date. I'd been on the piss and all that, and he beat me on points. I mean, half the time, they just fucking use you. They ring up to give you a fight at short notice but I've never, ever been knocked out by anyone. I've only ever been stopped." I asked him, "And what about you? Have you ever played any dirty tricks?" He grinned as he replied, "Oh no. Not at all, no." At the same time, he gave me a cheeky little wink of the eye. Enough said!

IF THE PRICE IS RIGHT

All too often in the sport of boxing, what the fighter wants and what the fighter gets paid are often considered low down on the priority list. The Champions and the highly rated fighters normally get paid what they consider to be decent money, but the boxers on the bottom end of the bill are often at the bottom end of the food chain. One of the things that strikes me about Tony is that he is a boxer who knows his worth. "Sommat like that, yeah. They have to pay me decent money if I'm fighting for them now. I'm supposed to be fighting this Friday and they're paying peanuts. It's one of them dinner shows and they're all sitting there, pissed up and having a meal. I mean, I'd sooner be sat there pissed up myself and watching the boxing. During my career, my biggest payday has been about five and a half grand, I think.

"To be honest, I haven't earned a lot of money out of boxing, 'cos if I've been boxing I haven't been working, so it's what I would have earned anyway. I'm self-managed these days. Roy Hilder's been getting some fights for me, and that's all right. [Hilder is one of the coaches at the Peacock Boxing Gym in Canning Town.] If they ring me up, they ring me up. And no one's forced me to do it, have they? At the end of the day

I've still got my health, and my mates and that. I've got a great partner and two beautiful children. You can't buy that, can you?"

TONY's HEROES

So who are the boxing heroes of this warrior from the North? "Thomas Hearns, mine was. I went to a do about a year back with Thomas Hearns and it were good. I went to one with Sugar Ray Leonard, but he were a bit of a boring bloke, you know. But Thomas Hearns was good. And Emanuel Steward, I never realized what a clever bloke he was. He's just so knowledgeable.

"I thought Nigel Benn was brilliant. He was good to watch. And I used to like Tony Sibson years ago. All of them. Mark Kaylor, I used to like Mark Kaylor years ago. And Prince Naseem, he's in jail now [at the time of this interview], but Prince Naseem, I thought he was brilliant. I used to train with him in Sheffield, and when he hit you ... I mean, he was only nine stone and he used to knock them out for fun! That lad, he fought good people and he made them look ordinary, and they all slag him off.

"And Mike Tyson, when he was in his heyday I thought he was brilliant. I'll tell you somebody else who I thought was brilliant, and that was Larry Holmes. He boxed them all when he had to, Larry Holmes. He didn't duck anybody. He nearly beat Marciano's record, didn't he? These days, nobody knows who the Heavyweight Champion is any more. Do you know who the Heavyweight Champion is? I don't. And the man who beat Alan Minter, Marvin Hagler, he was one of the best, so it just goes to show how good Alan Minter was."

THE HARDEST SPORT IN THE WORD

I have always thought that boxing is the hardest sport in the world, but Tony begged to differ. "To be honest, I think rugby is the hardest. I think rugby league is hard. I mean, Hull's one of the top places in the North for rugby. When I was playing once, I was defending and all the big kids started running at me, tackled me easy, you know, three of them kids diving on you. There's one or two people in Hull played for Great

Britain, and they've got plastic hips and all sorts, do you know what I mean? I only played rugby once or twice.

"I used to play football. I used to play for City boys, and that. I started boxing when I was ten, and then I started football and I was doing both. But I thought I could do better at boxing, so I went with the boxing."

JUST CHILLING

"To relax, I like to watch my horse racing. And I watch Only Fools and Horses, and the film, The Long Good Friday. But Fools and Horses is the one. I've got all the tapes. When I boxed Christmas Day, there were a big double spread about me in the Daily Mirror. They says, 'What will you miss the most on Christmas Day?' I said, 'Nowt' much, as long as me dad tapes Fools and Horses.' I'm a big fan of Del Boy.

"I enjoy going out for a drink in the afternoons with Wally. I mean, I can go around town at night time and all that, but I prefer going out with Wally and a few of the older ones. We just have a good crack. He hasn't got a bad bone in his body, Wally. If everybody was like Wally Walsh, we'd be all right. He's sound as a pound. And you wouldn't think he was 50 would you?"

CONCLUSIVE WORDS

At this point Tony had to do a body swerve for a few minutes, and Wally Walsh took the opportunity to tell me what he thinks of his friend. "Tony Booth, the journeyman, what can you say about him? You pick the phone up, ring him up, ask him to fight anybody and he'll be there. He's a proper fighter. He's a street fighter and a professional fighter. God bless him. The Warrior of Hull. He's a nice person as well. He's got a lovely family, which he looks after, and he's a very good man. And I'd just like to say that if there are any footballers reading this, can you sign something and send it to Tony's son, Harry. Because his lad's football mad. Tony is a journeyman, a working class man and a working class boxer, and he's struggled and fought for his family. He's one of the old school." [Any footballers who do read this and would be kind enough to send Harry a signed photograph can post it care of the publishing company address: Sweet Touch Publishing Company, Studio 221, 61 Victoria Road, Surbiton, Surrey KT6 4JX]

Tony returned to our company and time was getting on. It was really time for me to be heading back to London but, in the verbal sense, Tony was really starting to blossom and I felt reluctant to leave. So we ordered another beer, which Wally Walsh kindly provided, and I just sat back and let him talk.

"I've boxed heavyweights and never been hurt. If I was getting hurt like that, I wouldn't be doing it. Of the best boxers I've been in with, I don't know, it might have been David Haye. He's talented, isn't he? And Enzo Maccarinelli is a good boxer. And Eddy Smulders, I liked him. Eddy Smulders was about the best I've boxed.

"To be honest, I think you've just got to live your life. They say, 'Don't do this. Stop doing that.' But, if you're gonna go, you're gonna go, aren't you? My partner's dad, right, he was Chief Inspector in the police and he was 76, and you couldn't have met a fitter bloke. He dug our garden and did all sorts. Then he got cancer, and he was gone. It was terrible."

After a quiet moment of reflection, Tony suddenly burst back to life. "I think I'm joint-first for the most wins though. I might have the most losses, but I'm joint-first for the most wins, with Lennox Lewis." In fact, Tony has actually left Lennox Lewis far behind in that respect. At the time of our interview, he had had eight more wins than the former World Heavyweight Champion, and since then he has notched up a few more. "To be honest, I never rated Lennox Lewis, and I'll tell you why. 'Cos he got hit twice by that Rahman and he got knocked out. Oliver McCall hit him and he got knocked out. His best fights were before he really got going. People say to me, 'You've had the most losses,' but they forget, I've had the most wins as well.

"I'm feeling really good at the moment and I'm training hard, so I'll see how I get on in my next few fights. But, if I stick to cruiserweight, I think

I could go on for another few years yet. When I finish altogether, I'd like to get some sort of job training people, or hopefully doing something with kids, just helping some sort of kids. But, before all that, I've got to make sure my own kids are all right."

The boxing career of Tony Booth has been a fine one. I had one last question for him. If he could sum it all up, who would have been the biggest influence, the most important person to stand out in his mesh of memories? "I don't know. My dad always liked boxing. I always wanted to please my dad. I enjoyed sparring with people like Prince Naseem. And Herol Graham, he was a gentleman. One of the best things in my career was sparring with Nigel Benn. I got picked to spar with him and they kept asking me back, and that meant a lot to me. And when I met my partner, Jane, she was a big influence on me, and she still is.

"I ain't got a lot out of boxing. All I've got is good memories, and that's all they are. I've enjoyed myself and no one's forced me to do it. I've took one or two daft fights that maybe I shouldn't have done, for the money. I might have been a bit skint, but that's life, isn't it? If we could all had our lives again, we'd change things, wouldn't we? I mean, from a boxing point of view, if I could do it all again, maybe I wouldn't have taken the daft fights and I would have knuckled down more.

"When I started, when I was in Sheffield, they got me there when the season was closed. I was earning no money and I was in a bed-sit. Well, that's no good to me. I want to be earning. In other ways, I've done all right. I mean, I always say, you can do whatever you want, but the main thing is your health. The last few fights I've had, I've been getting punched and it don't hardly bother me. I mean, I know kids that have had 30 or 40 fights and some of them are fucking punchy, to be honest. I've had 150 and I'm bang on, do you know what I mean?"

Our interview drew to a close and I switched off the tape-recorder. Before I returned to London on the train, Tony and Wally treated me to a few beers in some of the pubs around the town. Everywhere we went, these two men were well known and well liked. I checked my watch and realized that time was getting on. "I really must go," I regretfully informed them. Wally Walsh also looked at his watch and frowned with the sort of old fashioned gentlemanly concern that never fails to move me. "Hey Tony," he reminded his friend, "I don't like to think of her going down that tube in London, not when it's late at night." Tony's blue eyes twinkled as he replied, "She's all right. She's tougher than us!"

CHAPTER TEN - COLIN JONES

***"Colin Jones was one of my heroes. When I first started boxing, I used to watch him on the telly and I loved his modesty, his fighting style and the way he went about his life. He was a great role model. He was a fighter's fighter."* (Colin 'The Dynamo' Dunne)**

"He should have been World Champion." Whenever I am engaged in a conversation about boxing, which is one of my favourite pastimes, I have heard those words used to describe Colin Jones so often. When I met the man himself for the first time, I told him so, and his modest answer was delivered with slightly raised eyebrows and some surprise. "Really? That's nice." Colin Jones, the red haired one from Gorseinon in South Wales, won the British, Commonwealth and European Welterweight belts and fought three times for World Titles. He never achieved his ultimate goal, but two of his World Championship challenges, both against Milton McCrory of Detroit, were extremely close and many boxing aficionados, including the late, great former editor of the Boxing News, Harry Mullan, felt that Colin had done enough to win both.

A friend of mine, Nigel James, spoke to Colin on my behalf at the Boxing Writer's Club Dinner in 2003. At the end of that year, Nigel sent me a Christmas card with Colin's phone number written inside. What a Christmas present! I got on the phone to Colin and he said he would be happy to let me interview him. We met up at his Gorseinon home in May 2004. As I parked my car outside his house, Colin came to the door to greet me. On his face was a smile of welcome, but he still has that tough look about him. These days he weighs in a healthy looking 12 stone. He told me that he walks five miles every day before he starts work at his building business. "As soon as I get up I go for a walk, and I do physical work as well, so it keeps me quite fit." He has intense blue eyes and he wears his hair cropped close to his head. The red is faded now, showing signs of grey, but it still looks healthy and strong, just like the man himself.

As we settled down in Colin's conservatory the heavens opened, which gave me that cosy feeling of being inside a warm and comfortable home, shielded from the elements, the sense of security accentuated by the sound of raindrops beating against glass. As Colin's wife, Debra, made us a nice cup of tea, we switched on the tape-recorder and began this interview. As he shared his memories with me, Colin's words, spoken with the smooth Welsh accent of a man who has never lived away from Gorseinon, were always calmly measured and honest, sometimes brutally so. In this respect, nothing has changed since his fighting days, when this eloquent young man always conveyed his thoughts to the television cameras so fluidly and intelligently. He always thought before he spoke and he was always serious, sometimes critical, but never emotional. No snarling insults or pre-fight stunts for him. He would never have tolerated any of that. It was simply not his way.

Colin Jones was born in Gorseinon on the 21st March 1959. He was one of eight children, five boys and three girls. "My mum is still alive. My father passed away ten years ago." While Debra pottered around in the kitchen, she told me that she and Colin have been together since she was 15 years old. They have three children, Simon, Bethan and Scott.

Colin started learning to box at the age of eight, which was only natural as all the Jones boys boxed. Colin's younger brother, Peter, was 1981 ABA Bantamweight Champion and had seven professional fights. His brother, Ken, was Welsh Light-heavyweight Champion. Colin nodded, "That's right. We all fought, all the boys." I asked if he still remembered his first amateur fight. "Yes, I can remember. I was 11 years of age and, well, because I'd already previously had two or three years in the gym, it wasn't so bad for me, because I was well schooled. I'd go and do sparring and I'd been in the gym solid for three years, so I had that bit of an edge over everyone else who started at 11."

Colin's amateur days were spent at Penyrhoel Amateur Boxing Club, where he went on to become twice ABA Welterweight Champion in 1976 and 1977, and he boxed for Wales on several occasions. "Yes, but do you know, it's amazing how most people jump the most important years of your boxing, which is the Schoolboys. I had my first Schoolboy fight in 1970, and I think it was in '71, '73 and '74, I was British Schoolboy Champion. I think people tend to forget about the Schoolboys and, of course, you had the Welsh Schoolboy Championship. You've got to win them to go on to the British. Those Schoolboy days were probably the best learning process of my career really. You was only a kid, like, and you was travelling to all different parts of the country. Tremendous experience, that was. You would have all the different counties and you were more or less guaranteed a fight. No walkovers."

In 1976 Colin was chosen for the Montreal Olympics. He was the youngest member of the British team. "Being so young, 17 years old, it's hard really to put a value on it. But it was a tremendous experience, to go away for five weeks with the Olympic team, and I was still a kid. I have some tremendous memories of some great characters, like Robbie Davies. I buttied up with him, you know, and he was a great character. We didn't come home with many medals. Pat Cowdell was the only one who came home with a medal."

There are two other members of that same Olympic team who also appear in this book. One of them is Clinton McKenzie. When I interviewed Clinton, he told me, "Colin Jones, to me, was a very personal human being. We used to talk serious, but he had a funny side to him. He was someone you could have a good chat with, very mature for his age. And boy, could he bang with that left hook of his! We sparred once and he was devastating. All respect to Colin. He was just a lovely sort of guy." Colin smiled fondly as I read those words out to him.

Memories of the other fellow Olympian who makes his mark within these pages, Sylvester Mittee, kept Colin smiling. "He was from the West Indies wasn't he, Sylvester? There was something about those people. They didn't have a chip on their shoulder about this black and white issue. Sylvester was genuinely a naturally funny person, you know, a lovely sense of humour, lovely character. There just wasn't a bad bone in his body. He'd rather laugh than be nasty; that's the type of character he was. And to be honest with you, Clinton was on the same par as well. Very joyful people, you know."

Sylvester Mittee was happy to reminisce with me about a conversation he had with the serious 17 year old way back then. "I remember sitting with Colin while we were out in Montreal. We were talking about life and he said to me, 'You haven't *seen* life. You haven't been down the pit.' I said, 'What the fuck do I want to go down the pit for, man? I'm black as the ace of spades already!'"

Colin reached the Olympic quarter-final and lost a brave challenge against wily Rumanian, Victor Zilberman. I asked him if he felt pleased with his performance at the time. "Yes. Zilberman was a very experienced fighter. He was older, mature, and I think that was what separated it. I think if I'd have come along in the next Olympics, it could very possibly have been a different story. I'd have been mentally stronger, more mature.

"I must have had a hundred and odd amateur fights, which is a lot for an amateur boxer, and I did it properly. I trained as hard as an amateur as I did when I turned pro. I only lost about four fights as an amateur. Other than the Olympic Games and the European, I won every title fight I fought as an amateur." These days, Colin still takes a healthy interest in amateur boxing. "I watch a lot of the amateurs. I think they've spoilt the game a little bit with head-guards and the points system, which has taken the art out of marking a fight, and of scoring a fight as well. Unfortunately, you can train a monkey to press a button, and not only that, but it takes the knowledge away from the game. You don't have to have knowledge any more. You don't have to be able to spot a good fighter." I was deeply involved in amateur boxing myself for seven years and, to my mind, one of the biggest failings of the computer scoring system now widely used is that the judges never register body shots. When I put this to Colin, he nodded in agreement. "And that's the hardest shot to throw, the body shot, but they don't seem to value it in the amateurs."

When Colin was 18, he made the decision to become a professional boxer. He signed up with Eddie Thomas, 'The Merthyr Marvel', who himself won the Welsh, British, Commonwealth and European Welterweight Titles. Eddie trained and managed Colin and when I mentioned Eddie's name Colin was swift to interject, "The *great* Eddie Thomas. Oh, he was a good man. A *great* man."

The age of 18 always seems to me to be so young to become a professional boxer. I was surprised that Colin did not remain in the amateur ranks and possibly compete in the next Olympics. "I'll tell you what happened. I came home from the Olympic Games when I was 17, and the following year I was picked for the European Games, out in Halle in Germany. There was only three of us selected for the Welsh team, so we was representing Wales and we virtually had to fund it ourselves. The club didn't have no money. It was a very poor club we was in, but they did help because I was working underground, not earning massive money. Then, when I came home from the European Games after boxing out there, I'd lost the Welsh tracksuit. And they billed me then, for the tracksuit. I think it was about 40-odd quid, and I was only earning that a week! I said, 'No, I'm not going to pay that,' and I didn't pay it, and I decided then that I was going to turn pro.

"I had a couple of good offers from London. A lot of the London promoters and managers made offers, and quite nice big figures, you know. But indeed, Eddie Thomas came down and he said, 'Well look, turn pro with me, but I won't be giving you any money.' He said, 'I'll give you £1,000 in order for you to pack in underground and I want you to train flat out, become a full time pro.' It wasn't a lot of money, £1,000, but it tided me over for my first few fights, and he rigged me out with kit. Of course, there was a big discussion with my father and myself, and my father said, 'Look, the man's got a great background as far as boxing is concerned. He is Mr boxing,' and I wasn't a great traveller away. I didn't want to go to London. So I turned over with Eddie and it was a good fighter-manager relationship, which are hard to come by."

Colin's ring name was 'The Gorseinon Gravedigger', which prompted me to ask him if he ever was, in fact, a gravedigger. He smiled, "Well, I worked in the cemeteries, yes. There were different schemes that you was on in those days. One day you'd be out in the parks; another you'd be in the graveyards. It was all for the local authorities. I went there from underground. I was underground for a couple of years."

The coalmine was Colin's first place of work when he left school. "It was all right. It was good. With the other men, there was good camaraderie there. I think it's a good place for anybody to start their working life, underground. I don't say *all* their working life mind, but to *start* their working life, I think it was a good thing." Quite a few years ago I interviewed prominent Welsh trainer and manager, Dai Gardiner, and he told me some harrowing stories of working down the mines in his day. I put it to Colin that things down there must have changed a lot by the time he worked underground. "Yes, possibly. But underground is underground mind, immaterial of what era you're looking at. Conditions are always bad. It all depends where you work. Some pits are dry, some are wet, so it all depends, you know."

Colin made his professional debut on the 3rd October 1977 at the Afon Lido in Aberavon. He stopped Mike Copp of Swansea in five rounds. "Because of the type of fighter I was and the type of person I was, I didn't drink and I obviously didn't smoke, so I was always in 100 per cent condition. If I didn't have a fight I'd still be in the gym, and the day after I'd had a fight I'd be back in the gym the following day, immaterial of what condition I was in. That was because of my love for the game, and when that love run out, that's when I retired. I called it a day. And fighting in Aberavon was a bonus as well. Because you could always fill the Afon Lido. Even if I was only fighting six rounds, you know, I'd virtually sell it out myself. Eddie didn't need a big top of the bill. I had a good army of supporters. They were always loyal through thick and thin, and they were very sporting supporters. They'd come to watch the boxing show and they showed as much interest in who was on the bottom of the bill as who was on the top of the bill."

Two months later Colin stopped Bradford southpaw, Martin Bridges, in four rounds at the Airport Centre Hotel in Heathrow. Colin knocked Bridges down twice before the referee, Paddy Sower, stopped the fight. "I had no problem boxing southpaws, because I had so much experience as a kid, fighting all types of fighters. You get modern fighters today saying they're only sparring a couple of rounds a fortnight before the fight, and that. I'd been boxing 15 or 20 rounds a night in the gym, even as a kid, and fetch anybody on, you know; orthodox, southpaw; I could adapt to 'em."

Colin was boxing back in Aberavon the following January, and he stopped Alan Reid of Edinburgh in just 30 seconds. "Alan, aye. Ken Buchanan fetched him down. My memory of that fight is that Eddie Thomas missed the punch that I knocked him out with. He was always missing the punch, Eddie. Because he was always busy doing something in the corner, and by the time he had done that, bang it was over, gone. So many of the lads would say, 'Oh, Colin's on next. Right, we'll nip up to the bar now, get a round in and come back.' Well, by the time they got back, it was all over." Looking back at Colin in those days, he always came across as so clinical, both before and after a fight. "I *never* got close to any of the lads I fought, from Alan Reid right up to Milton McCrory and Don Curry, *any* of them. It wasn't a social event. It was business. I don't think I've ever spoken to any opponent before or after. It's business."

Two weeks later Colin was back in business with another stoppage victory inside one round. He took slightly longer than the half a minute duration of his previous fight but, in all fairness, he only took 89 seconds. This time the man on the receiving end was Belfast's Willie Turkington. The place was the Sobell Centre, Islington. "And you don't see a lot of that these days either, boys fighting so close together, back to back, you know? On the John Conteh bill, that was."

At these early stages of his professional boxing career, Colin was starting to suffer with a plague of hand injuries, but he was very matter of fact about that. "Well, that's part of the trade, that is. When you hear a fighter say he can't fight because he's got a bad hand, to me that's a load of bloody poppycock, because you're in a business where you're *gonna'* get injuries. You'll be lucky if you get three or four fights a year if you keep pulling out because 'injury this' and 'injury that.' So I used to tell Eddie, 'Don't worry about my hands. We'll tape 'em and get on with it.' You'll never avoid it, because it's part of the trade.

"I mean, we used to go running up the Brecon Beacons, mind. They're landmarks in Merthyr, the Beacons; not only the run itself and the gradients, but it was the time when you was running them. It was difficult underfoot because there was probably snow up there in the summer. It was very bleak. Not only was the run hard, but the conditions were hard when you were running. It was freezing. But I think it paid off in the end, because it really did toughen you. As Eddie Thomas said, 'There'll come a time when you come back to the corner after 15 rounds and you won't be able to blow a candle out.' Now, I thought that Eddie meant that you wouldn't have enough wind to blow it out, but what he actually meant was that you'd be so fit and your breathing would be so perfect that you wouldn't blow a candle out. You wouldn't be puffing. I didn't realize 'till years after what Eddie meant, you know. Just sitting down talking, like we are now, and then it came to me what he meant."

Colin kept up his busy schedule with a March victory over Tony Martey of Ghana on points over eight rounds at Aberavon. This was the first time he had to go the distance as a professional and I put it to him that the Ghanaians are, in general, a tough bunch of fighters. "Yes. I boxed a couple of Ghanaians, and he was clever as well, Martey. I've got to give him credit for that." I reminded Colin that Martey was a former Commonwealth Games Gold Medallist. "I didn't know that at the time. I only learned that last weekend. I was at the boxing and somebody told me, and I could see why. He was a good, competent fighter, but I don't think he was a serious enough fighter to beat someone like myself.

"You'd probably get a better idea if you spoke to people who knew me at that time. You'd probably get a more honest opinion. I was not a nice person to be around. You know, when you're that far into the game, you're so involved in it, the will to win is greater than anything else. You're *not* a nice person to be around. To stay married as long as I have is a bloody feat in itself, because you're not a nice person to be around. You can't help it. It's in your makeup. You can't put that into somebody, that win at all costs. You've got to be *born* with it." Although referee, Wynford Jones, scored Colin's fight with Martey 80-72 for Colin, the tough African was always in it. "Well, a lot of people thought he won it on points, to be honest with you. You always get an element like that in boxing, which I think is good for the game. To be honest with you, winning like that gets you back on the right track again, because you can't bang everybody out. There are clever fighters out there, which Tony Martey *was*. Give him his respect, you know."

In July 1978 it was indestructible Belgian, Frankie Decaestecker, who stepped into the lion's den that was Aberavon and Colin beat him on points over six rounds. It was a very close fight and when the referee, Adrian Morgan, awarded it to Colin by 58-57 the crowd booed and jeered for some time. Decaestecker received a standing ovation all the way back to his dressing room. I asked Colin, "Did you think you had won it fair and square?" He hesitated slightly before giving his answer. "Everybody marks a fight differently. It's subjective really, because one of my left hands was worth three of anybody else's. When I used to hit them with it, they used to shudder from head to foot. You know, you'd get these fancy-Dannys, I used to call 'em, they'd flick three left hands and it looks lovely when they're on the go, but they're not hitting you. They're on the gloves and all that. If you look at the pictures after the fight, he was bumped up to hell and there wasn't a blinkin' *mark* on me, not even a little scratch! I look at things like that, you know?" I asked him again, did he think that he had won the fight; yes or no? "It was such a long time ago. Those were fights that have come and gone. They're just part of coming on through boxing, so there's not really that much importance attached to them."

On the 3rd October 1978 Colin scored a points win over Horace McKenzie. This was the first of two fights these two would have as professionals. McKenzie was Welsh Welterweight Champion at that time. For the record, this was exactly a year after Colin's first professional fight and he was still only 19 years old. "Well, I'm not sure, but I think you had to be 20 or 21 to be able to box for a title in those days." Colin's fought McKenzie, who came from Cardiff, at Aberavon and this was a much more popular decision than his last fight. In today's politically correct world, one could say that these two had 'issues' and a fair bit of rough stuff went on between them. In the second round punches were thrown by both boxers after the bell. Later in the fight McKenzie was warned for other offences, including another shot thrown after the bell at the end of the sixth round. "Well, it just goes to show what it means to win really, and there was no love lost between me and Horace McKenzie, even as amateurs. I boxed him three times as an amateur and I beat him three times. So obviously, there was going to be no love lost, because he wanted to have one over on me as a pro, and I think that more so with me and Horace, him being from Cardiff and me from Swansea."

Colin finished 1978 with a December win against Johnny Pincham, who he halted in his tracks at the Mayflower Leisure Centre in Plymouth. Colin needed reminding, "Did I stop Johnny Pincham?" I confirmed that he did indeed, in four rounds. "In four was it? Well Johnny was an old pro, wasn't he? From the Joey Singleton's, that type of breed of fighter." Indeed, both Pincham and Singleton were the sort of boxers who would go in with anybody at any time. Both were Champions of their respective areas and Singleton also won the British Title, which he defended twice before losing it to Dave 'Boy' Green, when the 'Fen Tiger' was just on the rise.

Colin crushed Pincham mercilessly, putting him down with a huge left hook to the head for a count of eight early in the first round. Pincham recovered well, but Colin's relentless surge of aggression told it's own story and, in the fourth and final round, Colin sent through a left hook to the head to shatter the brave battler from Crawley. Pincham rose on wobbly legs at the count of eight, but Colin was straight back in, forcing the referee to stop the fight. "He was brave, yes. But also, I don't know how many fights he'd had, like, but he could have been on the way down." Pincham only had two more fights after Colin and both were points losses.

Springtime arrived and in April 1979 Colin stopped Sam Hailstock in four rounds at the Double Diamond Club in Caerphilly. Hailstock was from Philadelphia and he was a late substitute, coming in at 24 hours notice. "He wasn't a bad boy, but coming in at short notice he obviously wouldn't be knowing what he was up against. I think I probably took him a bit by surprise."

The following month Colin stopped Cornish-Italian, Salvadore Nuciforo, in four rounds back at Plymouth's Mayflower Leisure Centre. Nuciforo was actually a light-middleweight and the match was made at 10st 12lbs to compensate for the weight difference. The Boxing News was now hailing Colin as the best welterweight prospect in the country. Six weeks earlier, Nuciforo had stopped Sheffield tough guy, Mick Mills, in five rounds at the Albert Hall and was firing on all cylinders. He certainly had the heart and the stamina, if not the skill. They fought on top of the bill and it was a hell-raiser of a fight. It was scheduled for eight rounds, but it was never destined to go the distance and, in the fourth round, Colin landed with a left hook to the body. Nuciforo landed on his back. Long after the referee had finished his count, Nuciforo was still on the floor. "Oh yes, he put up a good fight. He was a big, strong lad.

"You know, kids today moaning 'cos of two or three pounds difference, Eddie Thomas would take the fight if the boy was seven to ten pound over, as long as he knew in his mind that you could beat him. 'Don't worry about the weight. Can you *beat* him?' *That's* what he was worried about. He weighed up all the pros and cons, how he thought it would go, and nine times out of ten he was spot on. I often used to get a far bigger fighter than myself, and that stood out on the night because people were in awe, you know. Good God! Your opponent would jump on the scales and you'd look up and say, 'Christ 'Ed, are you sure you've got the right opponent here? He's not for somebody else, is he?' And Eddie would say, 'No, no, don't you worry now. You do the fighting; I'll pick the opponents,' and I'd trust him. Obviously you *can* come unstuck, mind, but I think it's better to take those chances early on than later, and that's what Eddie done."

In July 1979 Colin returned to the Afan Lido to box Alain Salmon and it took him two minutes and five seconds to swipe the Frenchman from his path. Salmon had severe problems standing up to Colin's vicious body shots and he had to take three counts before the referee waved the fight off. Colin had now stopped eight of his opponents in 11 fights. I reminded him, "You were still only 20 years old, and that kind of sustained success might surely make most men feel invincible?" He thought about it for a few moments before replying, "Well, to be honest with you, from the first fight onwards, you've got to have that self-belief. You could call it self-belief, or you could say invincible. I think when you have fights with the Tony Martey's and the Frankie Decaestecker's, then you get your feet back on the ground. I think that's what Eddie was clever at. If you were starting to bulldoze and walk through a couple of fights, all of a sudden there'd be a little stiff one slung in, just to level you out again, so you'd think it's not all a bed of roses, you see?" And I think to be a top pro you *need* that added pressure. You need to keep your standards up. Because I think, once you let your foot go off the gas, that's when things start going wrong then. I've seen so many great young fighters over the years, and they have nine, ten fights and they take their foot of the gas because they think they've made it, and you've never actually made it until you bloody retire. That's the time when you realise what you've done, when you look back."

In October 1979 Colin produced another stoppage win, albeit a late one, against Joey Mack. The St Kitts born fighter, whose real name was Jerome McIntosh, lived in Birmingham, and he had lost more fights than he had won. He had been around the clock a few times, but he was supremely fit and he had earned the right to box Colin in this eliminator fight for the British Title by becoming the first man to stop Mick Mills (who was previously undefeated and had stopped 13 out of his 17 opponents), and then winning the Midlands Area Title against Achille Mitchell. They fought at Caerphilly's Double Diamond Club and the stoppage came in the tenth round; not a moment too soon. Despite the longevity of the fight, Mack was outgunned from the first bell. He went down no less than ten times and many people who were there felt that it should have been stopped much sooner. "He'd had a good run of wins, I think; Mick Mills and people like that. Joey Mack come along and beat him in an eliminator, and then he come along and fought myself, which was *another* eliminator, which you don't see any more. We had so many eliminators. Jesus Christ, I don't think I've heard of an eliminator since I don't know when.

"I've got a lot of respect for Joey Mack. But I don't think it went ten rounds, did it?" At this point, I am afraid that the apprentice became the master as I confirmed to Colin that it did indeed go ten rounds. Colin and I diligently checked our records and we both discovered at the same moment that I was correct. Colin was astounded and exclaimed, "Good God! You're right. I *never* thought I done ten rounds up till now. Good God! I'd have lost money on that!" When I spoke to Colin about the bombardment that Mack absorbed that night he told me, "Well, to be honest with you, every time I hit him with a good shot, sometimes when he was hurt he went down anyway, just to shake his head, you know? He took a bit of a shellacking that night, but he was a gutsy performer to keep getting up and having a go." In the sixth round Colin knocked Mack down five times. Sitting talking to me, 25 years later, it was obvious that Colin still held his old opponent in high esteem. "A lot of boys would have said, 'I've had enough.' They weren't shots that were sort of semi-hurting him. They were *really* hurting him."

In January 1980 Colin was back in the ring, this time with Cardiff's Billy Waith. Colin stopped him in six rounds on a World Sporting Club dinner show in Mayfair. "No love lost with me and Billy." I chuckled as I pointed out to Colin that Billy Waith was the second boxer that we had talked about where there was 'no love lost', and both of them were Welsh! "That's right. No love lost. There was more hatred in those two fights than probably *any* of my earlier fights because, well, Wales, we're a funny old nation, aren't we? 'Who's the best in Wales?' sort of thing. Never mind the British Title and things like that, let's get Wales sorted out first, you know? And Billy wasn't a bad talker in the press anyway. He kept saying that he had forgotten more than I'd ever learn." Waith complained throughout the fight to the referee that Colin was kidney punching him. "It was his own fault. He was warned on several occasions. He kept turning into the shots, and eventually one of them was going to, well, *seriously* hurt him, to be honest with you, and the next thing he's kneeling on the floor."

Colin's next fight was the first of two classics that he would have with Kirkland Laing. They called Kirkland Laing 'The Gifted One.' His boxing style was quite unorthodox and awkward, but at the same time he possessed every weapon that a boxer needs. He had fast hands, lovely footwork, massive power, lightening reflexes, and a supreme physique, despite his notoriously sporadic approach to training. This Jamaican born pugilistic artist was well known throughout the boxing world for his insatiable lust for everything that a boxer should stay away from. He was an intriguing character and the crowd loved to watch him, because he often took risks in the ring, dropping his hands and messing around when he should have known better.

Colin and Kirkland fought for the first time on 1st April 1980 at Wembley Conference Centre. Laing was undefeated in 19 fights and he was British Welterweight Champion. His was defending his title against Colin. "As you say, an awkward fighter, but gifted. But he was also very disrespectful. We weighed in on the day of the fight and he came on to me. He was very disrespectful. I was never a big welterweight anyway, I never had no definition, and he was in good shape. He had great muscular definition, which I never did have." I remarked that if you get two boxers of equal fitness, one black and one white, the black boxer often looks more muscular. Colin chuckled, "Yes they do, but even if I was black, I *still* wouldn't have had it."

Colin and Kirkland fought a thrilling fight. A lot of the time, Laing looked to be dominating the action with flashy counter-punches, while Colin patiently stalked his pray. Colin's first big impression came in the third round when he knocked Laing's gum-shield out, which drew a roar of approval from the crowd. Laing must have had big problems with that gum-shield because in the fourth round it flew out again, and he was, by now, cut nastily inside his mouth. The crowd chanted Colin's name as he had to weather a strong attack from Laing in the fifth. The sixth round was a great three minutes for Laing, but Colin kept up his relentless and dogged pursuit, always menacing. By the eighth round Laing was looking battle-worn. His mouth was bleeding freely and he kept pawing at the injury with this right glove. Colin sensed his man was in trouble now, vulnerable. In the ninth, Colin saw an opening and took his chance, thumping Laing's gum-shield out again, sending it spiralling out into the crowd. Kirkland clutched the top rope in a desperate attempt to stay standing, but Colin shoved him backwards and battered him around the ring. Somehow Laing remained on his feet but the referee, Roland Dakin, had seen enough and jumped in to stop it. Colin had done it. He was the new British Welterweight Champion. In the Boxing News, Harry Mullan described the outcome of this fight as one of the most dramatic turnabouts he had ever seen, and Colin agrees, "It probably was." Certain boxers touched Harry Mullan's heart in a special way, and Colin Jones was one of them. Colin responded to this thought reverently. "I liked Harry too. He was a nice guy."

But, back to the fight, we discussed that dramatic finish. "It was the start of the ninth round, and it's funny how you overhear things. Don't ask me how, because I don't think I was anywhere close to my own corner, and I was moving round, still chasing him. It was a bit of a repetitive fight, you know, walking on, walking on. It was strange really, because that's when I overheard Eddie Thomas saying in the corner to Gareth Bevan, my trainer - and don't ask me how with all the noise there - but I could hear Eddie saying, 'Oh my God,' he said, 'I hope I haven't put the kid in too soon.' And I thought, 'Jesus Christ, we're in the ninth round of a title fight and he's making a comment like that!' I thought, 'I'll show him now!' That was the little bit of a boost that I needed and, of course, Laing was doing his rat-a-tat, up on his toes, doing his prettier stuff. Indeed, I thought, 'Only once I've got to nail him and that will be the end of it.' And, fortunately for myself, I *did* catch him with a good right hand then. It was lucky really that Dakin stepped in when he did because, if he hadn't have stepped in, Laing wouldn't have been fighting me the second time. He'd have been hurt, *badly*.

"There's a very fine line between stopping a fight too early or too late, a very fine line, and the referee has got a hell of a job to do, to find that fine line, you know; it's hard. That's why it's so important that these referees who are picked by the Board, especially when they're given title fights, it's important that we get the best in there to look after the boys, and don't let anybody slip through the system and allow an under-par ref."

In any event, Colin was now British Welterweight Champion. When I asked how he felt when they wrapped the Lonsdale Belt around his waist, he was rather nonchalant about it. "It meant more to *win* than to get the Lonsdale belt. Because, to be honest with you, at that stage I never really thought about the British Title. Belts meant nothing to me. My dream was a World Championship. That was my dream, which I never attained, but winning the British was part of the process of getting there. So it wasn't as if you took it for granted, but I was *expecting* to win it. I had so much confidence, and it was knowing that, if I couldn't win the British, I couldn't get to my goal. It was a great achievement along the way, but I think winning the Lonsdale belt outright was the one. That was *the* one, not so much the first one of winning it because, if you lose your next fight, you ain't got no Lonsdale belt."

Two months after his British Title win, Colin stopped American import, Richard House, in one round at the Albert Hall. Despite the brevity of the fight, Colin remembers the man. "'The Spook,' that's what they used to call him." It was a nasty stoppage. The man from Missouri was down and unconscious for almost a minute before being helped back to his corner. A minute seems such a long time in a situation like that and I asked Colin if he ever felt worried when they took a long time to get up. His reply came like cold steel. "Not really. It never even crossed my mind. And I've had some really *nasty* knockouts, you know. I've hit boys, and the way they went down and the period of time they were down... You think about it more *now*. Afterwards, when you've had years of retirement and you see so much going on, people getting hurt, you think, 'God, how did I do that?'

"But it didn't matter at the time. Whether it's the hardness bred into you, I don't know, and the lack of concern, if you like. I think there's an element of that as well, if you're really honest about it." I responded, "So it's either you or him?" He nodded, "That's right. It could be me on the deck there. That's without being ... That's how I felt at the time. Winning was everything and, fortunately for myself, everybody came through it okay. Nobody actually got hurt. With Richard House, it was probably one of the most clinical performances. Got him in the right position and made the shot."

On the 12th August 1980 Colin defended his British Title against Peter Neal. They boxed at the National Eisteddfod Pavillion in Gowerton and Colin stopped the Swindon man in round five. It was Colin's first Welsh appearance since winning his title and the crowd was charged with emotion. "Yes, the National Eisteddfod had just finished. We had a voluntary defence after beating Kirkland Laing and, well, Peter Neal was next in line anyway, so we had Peter, who *deserved* a shot at the title, because he thought he should have had a shot at Laing before I did. The poor fella took a bit of a belting, didn't he? He was in a bit of a mess at the end, but he was a game fighter. Should he have been around today, without a doubt he would have been British Champion, because he was a tough old cookie."

Ten days before the Christmas of 1980, Colin gave the crowd at the Rhybycar Leisure Centre in Merthyr an early gift when he stopped Clement Tshinza of Zaire in three rounds. Tshinza used his experience to stay out of trouble before Colin caught him with a left hook, which damaged a blood vessel in the African's right eye. Tschinza could not see and the fight was stopped. In any event, he impressed Colin, who told me, "He boxed well. He boxed very well."

Colin's first fight of 1981 was a re-match against Horace McKenzie in February. Colin won it inside seven rounds. "Horace was always going to be the type of fighter who'd give anybody a good fight. He had a strong will to win, Horace did, but unfortunately for him it wasn't strong enough. But he was a good, solid, sound fighter. And the second fight being in London then, in the Grosvenor, and boxing for Jack Solomons, it added a bit of extra spice, you know? But he was a good, solid, sound fighter."

The Commonwealth Welterweight Title was vacant. On the 3rd March 1981 Colin challenged Mark Harris of Guyana for the belt, and won the title in nine rounds. "Well, as I say, belts and trophies didn't mean a thing. Money did, there's no doubt about that, and the purses started getting better, which made life a little bit easier. But, unfortunately for myself, it didn't make *boxing* any easier. You were up to the next level again. But it's nice when you can do the right thing and prepare the right way. You've got a bit of money in the bank, so you don't have to go to work for one thing, and you really become what's known as a full time pro."

Harris was very tough and extremely stubborn in the face of Colin's blows to his ribs, which resounded around the half-empty Wembley Conference Centre. Harris went down at the beginning of the second round, but came back soundly enough to have Colin under pressure in the fifth, despite the fact that his mouth and eye were bleeding. But Colin was back on top in the sixth, and knocked the man from Guyana down three more times before the fight was stopped. "Aye, that's right. He took some good shots. To be honest with you, I never done any homework on any of the fighters we got. I never done any reading up on them, or looking at them on the videos; nothing like that. He was a good, solid fighter, but I don't think he was built for the welterweight division, to be honest with you. He was a bit short, a bit squat, but he took some good shots. He was brave."

On the 28th April 1981 Colin had his second fight with Kirkland Laing. They boxed at the Albert Hall and Laing was challenging for Colin's British and Commonwealth Titles. The previous July, after their first fight, Laing had declared in the Boxing News: *"I still can't believe how he beat me. How could I lose to a guy so far below me in terms of skill?"* Before they met for battle the second time, Kirkland took another shot at Colin in the trade paper, when he stated: *"I was beating Jones out of sight before he caught me. No boxer in England has more skill than me, and you can't deny that."* 'The Gifted One' obviously felt that he had a score to settle. Colin, on the other hand, was not happy about the lack of respect that Kirkland was showing him and, instead, it was *he* who settled the score, with his fists. This fight was almost a carbon copy of the first one, with Kirkland ahead on points and Colin turning everything around with one big shot in the ninth round. This time it was a left hook, and Laing's feet went from under him. He went down. He struggled back up. He teetered back to the ropes and the referee jumped in to rescue him. "I've always said, if you can't fight at the Albert Hall, you can't fight. Because, number one, the way the hall was built, the acoustics and everything is there, it's *all* there. That place, even half-full, created an atmosphere. Fortunately for myself, again, I had a tremendous following, and I think that reflected in the fight as well, especially in the eighth round when I was down twice."

The eighth round was indeed a dramatic one. Laing was going for Colin's body when Colin dropped to the canvas, his gloves cupped around his groin. The referee, John Coyle, gave Laing a warning and Colin time to recover. But, as soon as Colin was up, Kirkland hit him near the hipbone and he went down again. John Coyle didn't begin a count and Colin got himself back together and rose to his feet. As the round progressed,

Laing chased Colin around the ring ruthlessly and it looked for all the world like 'The Gorseinon Gravedigger' was about to be stopped, his winning run teetering on the edge. Right at the end of the round, Colin produced from somewhere a second wind and finished with a cluster of hooks to the body and head. "When I got off the stool for the ninth round, something was telling me, 'That's it! He's having it in this round again.' Because right at the end of the eighth round, I hit him with a shot, it must have only went about six inches, right as the bell sounded. Bang! I've hit him. A little short left hook. His gum-shield was buckled in his mouth. He nearly went back to the wrong corner because of that shot, and his mouth just burst. You could see he was gone, and I thought, 'I've got him.' I was still in trouble myself, but when you've got the crowd coming behind you then as well, which is like an extra round, I knew I was going to have him in that ninth round. There was nothing going to stop me. I think that was classic, Harry Carpenter saying, 'Oh my God, he's gone and done it again!'"

I believe that the fighting styles of Colin Jones and Kirkland Laing were always going to fuse into something special and Colin agreed. "Made for the classic fight really, wasn't it? I've got to be honest with you, mind, I think because they were 15 round title fights in those days, if it had been 12 rounds he would possibly have beat me on points in those two fights. But, because I knew I had 15 rounds to do it in, I could afford to be patient. Again, because of a tremendous will to win, I actually came through in the end, and the conditioning, the running over the Beacons, it all added up. I had so much confidence in my stamina, my staying ability and my chin that it don't matter what he would have done to me." And the icing on the cake was that Colin had now won his Lonsdale Belt to keep.

Today, the mention of Kirkland Laing's name can still wipe the smile off Colin's face. "Yes, well again, there was no love lost between us. He was very disrespectful during the weigh-ins and things, putting me down and things like that. I think it was the first fight when he come up to me during the weigh-in and he said, 'Tell me. Why is your manager taking this fight? He *knows* you're gonna get a whupping tonight,' he said. 'I'm gonna ping your head back with the left hand tonight,' he said. 'Oh, there you are then,' I said. 'As long as you think like that, it'll be down to me to see about it.' And that always put that little bit of edge on the fight again. He'd probably have been better off saying nothing, but he had to come and talk. He was very confident and, obviously, I was the underdog going in; that was obvious. But not in *my* mind." I was amazed that Colin felt that way the second time, now that he was the Champion. "Yes indeed, and that's what *other* people thought, you know, that I was the underdog. But, when you've got that confidence that you've done all your preparation, you *can't* do anymore, then you've given yourself 110 per cent chance to beat him. To me, that was good enough to beat *anybody*, as far as I was concerned. I may not have looked good doing it, but I'd get to them in the end."

For the record, Kirkland Laing kept on fighting for another 13 years. Eighteen months after his second loss to Colin, he caused the Ring Magazine 'Upset of the Year' by beating Roberto Duran, and then he went on the missing list for almost a year. He returned to the real world and went on to regain the British Title (against Sylvester Mittee) and win the European Title. Sylvester recently described Kirkland to me as "a likeable rogue", an opinion that is widely shared by those who knew him. Kirkland finally hung up his gloves after being stopped by Glen Catley in November 1994. After his retirement from the ring, Kirkland's life took a sad turn. He ended up living virtually on the streets of Hackney. In 2003 he barely escaped with his life when he fell from the balcony of his high-rise council flat. However, having made some enquiries, I am pleased to report that Kirkland is now living back in his hometown of Nottingham. He is in far better shape than he was, and he is close to his family. It should never be forgotten that he was 'The Gifted One', and he will always be remembered for his sublime skills in the boxing ring.

On the 3rd September 1981 Colin experienced the first blemish on his professional record. The loss came by way of disqualification against American club fighter, Curtis Ramsey, at the Sophia Gardens in Cardiff. In the second round, Colin caught Ramsey with a swiping right hand as he was falling to the canvas. The way the referee saw it, Colin had hit Ramsey when he was on the floor. Colin remains quietly adamant that he was not guilty of this offence. "If I *had* have connected when he was on the floor, I would have said to myself, 'Okay, you might have asked for that,' but I didn't connect. I connected with a body shot before he backed off, but not when he was on the deck." The referee that night was Adrian Morgan. His decision was greeted with boos from 2,000 of Colin's supporters and there was almost a riot.

Colin was a Welsh hero, Adrian Morgan was a Welsh referee, and the fight took place in front of a fiery Welsh crowd in the capital city of Wales. I asked Colin, "When you think back, do you think Mr Morgan's decision was brave and right, brave and wrong, or brave and stupid?" Colin replied with no hesitation. "I think the last one. That's probably a little bit of a letdown with the Welsh, in general. They try to be too fair and too accommodating. In boxing, if you're going to play away and you're on to a shellacking, it's a shellacking you'll have. There'll be no compassion. It's a winning game. I think Adrian Morgan made a big mistake that night, without a doubt. There's not really a lot you can say about it, other than it was a silly decision.

"My world had caved in. It had! You know, to lose an unbeaten record through something as silly as that, it was unbelievable. If Adrian Morgan had had any idea what it took to get to that stage of being unbeaten and to go through the Kirkland Laing fights, and fights like that. I mean, we come back then to the Board of Control having competent referees for the occasion, which I don't think he was, to be honest with you. And the day after, the building fell down! There was snow on the roof and it all came down! That's what prompted them then to knock it down and put the National Sports Centre there, so at least some good came out of it."

Just 12 days later Colin was back in the ring. He stepped in as a late substitute for Pat Cowdell and stopped Milton Seward of Michigan in three rounds at Wembley Arena. "I think it was a good managerial decision from Eddie to put me straight back in, and he could have put me back in with *anybody*." Colin's next fight was in November 1981, back at Wembley, to stop another American in three rounds, this time Nevada southpaw, Gary Giron. Giron was a late substitute and he looked as if he simply did not want to be there. In the third round, Colin knocked him down. He got up, but he was under fire without retaliation when the fight was stopped. "Oh no, he was just diving in. I think he was just waiting for the big shot and, to be honest with you, if I hit him with a tidy shot, he would have been only too glad to be out of it. I can't really say a lot about Giron, because I don't think he was a brave fighter."

After a break of nearly ten months, Colin defended his Commonwealth Title against Sakaria Ve at the Empire Pool, Wembley, in September 1982. The Fijian lasted less than two rounds. "Well, I've got to be honest with you, the way he come out fighting, he was just begging to be knocked out and, unfortunately for him, I hit him with a good body shot. I think I took him off the floor when I *did* launch into him. I was probably up for that fight as much as any fight I ever had in my career. Don't ask me why. I was so focused that night, it was just one of them nights I felt great, you know. Pity it wasn't a better opponent."

On Guy Fawkes Night 1982, Colin challenged Hans Henrik Palm for his European Title at K.B.Halle in Copenhagen. The classy Dane had collected quite a few British scalps on his record, until he ran into Colin Jones. That night, the red haired Welshman gave the Denmark audience a firework display of his own, stopping Palm in two rounds to become the new European Welterweight Champion. This fight had originally been scheduled for the previous February but, having actually flown to Copenhagen for the fight, Colin went down with appendicitis and had to pull out with hours to spare. "That's right, because I'll never forget, we'd just moved houses, we had, from the first house we bought together to a bigger house, which was almost double the value. I was relying on that purse to pay for the house, and on the day of the fight I even tried to cover up that I *had* appendicitis, but I was in agony to be honest with you. I'd gone yellow! I tried to waffle the doctor, but the doctor shone the torch in my eyes and he knew straight away, just by looking at me. He pushed his fingers in my appendix, and whoah! He said, 'I knew they weren't right,' and he told me I couldn't fight. They wanted to operate on me out there and I said, 'No, you won't operate on me out here. I'm going home.' So they flew me home and within 24 hours I'd had the operation. I think, within about three weeks, I was back in the gym then, ready to prepare for him again."

Colin prepared well and this was to be one of his best ever performances. "I had a great build-up to that fight, great preparation. I developed an infection in my chest when I was over there, but nevertheless, I think that night was probably the night when I should have had a World Title fight. That was my night. I'd have given *anybody* trouble that night, because I felt so good." I asked Colin if it bothered him, going to fight a Dane in Denmark. "No, to be honest, it didn't bother me, because it very rarely came down to the judges. You know, if they're going to outsmart me and outwit me, then so be it, they're going to beat me, because there weren't many top class fighters who I was going to beat on points. It would have to be an exceptional thing if I went the distance in somebody else's country to win something on points." To Palm's credit, he had publicly acknowledged the fact that, since winning the vacant European crown against Georges Warusfel the previous February and defending it once against Pierangelo Pira, he had only ever been the 'interim' Champion and could not consider himself the real thing until he had beaten Colin Jones.

While the preliminary announcements took place, Colin looked so unconcerned. Palm, in contrast, looked restless, jogging up and down on the spot. The boxers met at the centre of the ring and, as the referee issued his final instructions, Colin's face remained impassive, the perfect poker player. At the sound of the opening bell, Colin was straight on his opponent like a magnet, surprising the Dane with hard, punishing left jabs. Palm was an upright sort of fighter and he used his boxing skills and his extra height to make it a tactical battle, both boxers trying to lure the other on to dangerous ground. The crowd were loud throughout and Colin's supporters made themselves heard, regardless of being the away fans. Just before the end came, a Welsh voice could be heard clearly above all the others crying out, "Come on, Jonesey Boy!" Seconds later, Palm got caught as he was swaying away from Colin's punches and a left hook to the chin laid him out on his back.

That would possibly have been a good place to stop the fight, but Palm managed to rise and the Dutch referee, Karel Klijnot, allowed the action to continue. Palm looked to be out on his feet and, when Colin saw the glazed look in his opponent's eyes, he steamed straight into him, throwing hooks and uppercuts from every direction. Palm tried to cling on, but he folded under fire like a damp sheet of paper, his gloves sweeping the canvas. As Colin turned away to walk to a neutral corner, Palm's right knee buckled and he fell to the floor. Amazingly, that brave man dragged himself up at the count of three and took a standing eight count before Colin swept him back across the ring with another ferocious attack. When the referee finally stepped in, Palm fell forward again and Klijnot caught him under the chin to support him.

Thankfully, Palm recovered very quickly and, after the fight, his features swollen and marked, he shrugged his shoulders and declared, "These things happen. That's boxing." The Danish crowd were sporting enough to reward Colin's performance with an honourable ovation. At the same time, the Welsh fans joyously chanted their hero's name as the new European Champion raised his gloves in triumph. Colin then turned his attention to Palm. He put his arm around the beaten man's shoulders and spoke compassionate words into his ear. I asked Colin to describe his feelings about becoming European Champion and again, he refused to get carried away by his newly elevated status. "It was a steppingstone. I never dreamt of winning those titles so quick to get to my goal. It all happened reasonably quick, you know." For the record, Hans Henrik Palm never fought again.

The following year, on the 19th March 1983, Colin got the chance he had been waiting for and challenged unbeaten Milton McCrory for the vacant WBC Welterweight Title that Sugar Ray Leonard had vacated. In order to focus solely on his purpose, he relinquished his British and European Titles. "That's right. I just give them up."

They called McCrory 'The Iceman,' and this would be the first of two fights that Colin would have with him, both being for the World Title. The Detroit boxer was trained by Emanuel Steward at the legendary Kronk gym, where he regularly sparred with Thomas Hearns in the fabulous days when 'The Hit Man' was on top of his game. In the Boxing News, Hearns once said of McCrory: *"He ain't even 19 yet. He can box like a veteran and bomb you out with either hand. Every fighter down at the Kronk likes to think of himself as a 'bad' fighter. Well I'm tellin' you, McCrory is more than 'bad.' He's 'super bad!'"*

Colin fought McCrory at the Convention Centre in Reno, Nevada. "Well, it's the pinnacle of your career, isn't it? Everything you've been working for since you was nine years of age. It was a dream, a dream which you thought would never come true until you was actually there and doing it. You never thought it would materialize. After I won the European Title, people like Hugh McIlvanney, Ken Jones and Reg Gutteridge all started talking World Title fights. I thought, 'Christ, I'll have to defend my European a few times, the Commonwealth, the British; I'll have to defend all these titles before I even get up there.' I didn't realize until after the Palm fight that I'd arrived. It didn't really sink in until we were out in America preparing for it, but I thought I deserved it at that time. It was only a pity really that it didn't come when I won the European Title. That was *my* night.

"It's a long preparation for a World Title fight. It's not just the last four weeks, but there's a gradual build-up to it. But everything went well; the preparation was fine. When we got out there, I didn't have no family around me, as such. We didn't have no entourage with us. There was only Eddie, myself and Gareth Bevan. Three of us went, and we were out there for four weeks the first time. The fans, the boys, they came out later then, about two days before the fight. So really speaking, it was a good build-up, because there was no fuss with anybody.

"Obviously, when you're having your first World Title fight, you don't know what to expect. It was the first time I'd fought in America. Being out there made me feel great. 'I've arrived, I'm here, I've done it.' Perhaps that was a little bit of the wrong attitude, because you're only 75 per cent of the way there. The final hurdle, which was the last 25 per cent, was actually winning it. I think I was about 24 years old then, and I could have taken it a little bit more seriously. I think today I'd change things, most certainly, if I could go back." "Swept away by the occasion?" I asked. "Yes," he replied. "I think that's probably a fair assessment of it. I did get a little bit swept away. It was a tremendous build-up to it. You'd never get anything like that in a British or

Commonwealth or European, or any other fight that you ever have. Nothing is like the build-up to a World Title. You feel so important, and you *do* tend to get swept away by it. I don't know about other fighters, but I know *I* did a little bit, and it possibly could have been down to my age."

The night of the fight arrived, the first bell rang, and McCrory, who was the taller man at 6' 1", immediately started piling up points with his long jab. "Yes. I think, the first time, he fancied having a bit of a fight, and with success, you know, for the first six rounds. It was one of those fights, because there wasn't really a set pattern to it. He didn't really back off me until I started getting to him. When he realized then that he couldn't blast me out of there, he give me a bit of respect and he started backing off. I think he realized that, if he'd have tried to stand toe to toe in the later rounds, I might have had him. And it nearly come close to it; it nearly paid off. But he was a good fighter, Milton McCrory."

Prior to the fight, McCrory had predicted that he would knock Colin out in the third round. When the end of the third round came, Colin smashed into him with a big right hook, as if to say, 'Well, we're going into the fourth round now, and I'm still here!' As he returned to his corner, Colin grinned at the British ringside reporters. "Well, nobody should make predictions, should they? It's disrespectful, isn't it? I mean, I could have said that against all the boys I fought in the early days. Perhaps they weren't quite up to the same par with you and you could, I suppose, pick a round. But, its not very nice, is it, for the opposition?" As if, maybe annoyed that he didn't stop Colin in the third as he predicted, McCrory gave it everything in the fourth, but Colin never looked hurt. He seemed, instead, to be constantly looking for the big haymaker punch, instead of combinations and body shots. In contrast, McCrory's punches were thrown in clusters and eye catching for the judges.

Before every round began, Colin was out of his corner and half way across the ring before the bell had sounded. "The reason being is because I wanted to keep backing him up all the time. I didn't want him to build up any momentum at the beginning of a round. You're up and at 'em. Psychologically, when you're half way across the ring, you ain't got so far to get to somebody to form a momentum, so I had him moving on his back foot all the time that way."

In the sixth round Colin started to turn things around. He started landing with body shots, and a left hook staggered the American, though McCrory managed to remain standing, while his corner-men looked on with worry etched into their faces. Colin won the round and took some of the wind out of McCrory's sails. Colin continued to regain ground as the rounds went by and, in the ninth, he dug a brutal left hook into McCrory's stomach. McCrory's painful grunt could be heard from the press seats, and he spent the rest of the round on the run, which prompted the crowd to start booing.

During the final rounds, as Colin continued to impose himself on the rapidly tiring McCrory, the crowd became less impressed with their own man and more enamoured with the Welshman with the red hair. "Yes, in all fairness, you'd swear I was fighting at home. But, at the end of the day, it's all down to the officials, isn't it?" During the twelfth and final round, the promoter, Don King, left his seat and stood beneath McCrory's corner, screaming at him to finish strongly as the exhausted boxer battled away valiantly, his trunks splattered with blood from his nose.

And then the final bell rang, and it was over. The fighters stopped fighting. Tension mounted as the judges' scores were tallied. The result was declared a draw. "When I got the draw, I knew then that I'd been given another chance, another lifeline.

"After watching it on TV, I thought about how I could have changed things." I asked him how he would have changed things. "I don't know, but I think I would have gone for gold early. I showed him too much respect." During the fight Colin neglected to throw many of his trademark body shots. "No. I've got to give him credit for that, because he was a good puncher himself and, if somebody doesn't allow you to throw body shots, then they don't allow you; if you can't get in and they're clever, they know there are certain ways to nullify it, and he was good at doing that. So you've got to give him credit for that as well, a *lot* of credit.

"And another thing with the build-up to that fight was the purse offers. I was offered ex-amount of money to have the fight here, at Wembley, and I was offered a much larger amount of money to take the fight in America. In all fairness to Eddie, he said, 'You can have the fight here or over there, it's up to you.' But the gulf in money was so great that I said, 'Well if I hit him on the chin in America, or I hit him on the chin in Wembley, we'll have the same result, so we'll take the money and go to America.' So we did, and I'd have still done that. I'd have still gone to America anyway, even if it was today."

Five months later, on the 13th August 1983, Colin fought Milton McCrory again, for the still vacant WBC Welterweight Title. This time Colin lost a desperately close split decision to the American at the Dunes outdoor arena in Las Vegas. The heat was unbearable and Colin later regretted travelling to America to fight McCrory for the second time. "I should have taken the second one in London, because where they stuck it, you know, it was ludicrous for a white man, especially me being fair anyway." The boxers began to do battle beneath the sweltering sun and, in the first round, McCrory caused a sensation when he knocked Colin down with a left hook, right hand combination.

As we sat in Colin's conservatory that day, he smiled grimly at the memory of that shot. "Yes. It was a good shot. A funny story came out of that. I'd never been put down before, only once, as an amateur with Lloyd Lee in the semi-finals of the ABAs. And again, similar type of shot, first round, quick left hook. I'll never forget, it was so warm out there and it was about 20 seconds before the end of the first round, and it was totally alien to me. I was *never* on the deck. I thought, 'What the hell am I doing here?' I came round a bit quick, shook my head, looked at the corner and got up. I had everything about me. When I got back to the corner I said to Eddie, 'Ed! I can't see. I've lost my vision.' I said, 'I'm frightened. I think I've gone blind.' And he said, 'Well, how the fuckin' hell did you find your way back to the corner then?' Because I had to come a fair distance back to the corner, like. And it broke the ice, that did. That was the answer I got, you know, and I thought, 'Well, this is what it's all about, like, innit?' But I got over that okay though, mind, considering - and it gave the fight another twist."

As was the case in their first battle, McCrory took the earlier rounds but Colin continued to storm forward. "I had him in the seventh and I think I had him again in the ninth, but the fear that I had in the seventh was what was said to me by Eddie in the corner. He said, 'Look, don't go out all guns blazing, because otherwise you could blow up.' Because it was so *warm* there, and if you assert yourself for the full three minutes, like I normally would have, and you didn't do the job, then you would have been there for the picking after. It was that warm, especially with my colouring. Climatically, it would have suited a coloured man better than myself, and so we had to take that a little bit into consideration.

"Looking back now, I think it was the *wrong* decision. Because Gareth Bevan, who knew me and had me since I was nine years of age, said, 'Go and get him.' But Eddie said, 'No. You wait for your next chance,' and, of course, it never came. I should have gone for gold. That's one of the things I would change now." McCrory fought back valiantly in the eighth round and Colin seemed to be letting him back into the fight. There again, stopping a fighter like Milton McCrory getting back into anything would be far easier said than done. Colin dominated the ninth, tenth and eleventh rounds but then, in the twelfth, as in their last meeting, McCrory put on a dazzling show. Emanuel Steward was watching like a hawk from McCrory's corner. He knew that they were both too tired for a knockout, so he reasoned that the man who threw the most shots in that final round would win. He was right. McCrory threw the most shots. He won. Afterwards Steward confessed, "I really didn't know which way the fight was going to come out."

And so, Colin was to return to Wales without the World Championship belt. I asked him how he felt when they announced the decision. "Devastated. Totally devastated." I asked him if he cried when he returned to his dressing room. He hesitated for a split-second and gave me a sideways look. "I think inwardly, yes. I don't know about outwardly. There's nothing anybody can say to you. It's the loneliest place in the world. Nobody wants to be in the loser's changing room. It's sad really, because it's not just one fight on one night. It's a build up of 16 years of fighting. When you realise that your chance is gone, it all hits you in one night. That very second after that fight, you know it's all gone out the window." "Almost like a state of shock?" I asked. "Well, there you are!" he replied. "And I've got to be honest with you, it takes you a long time to get over it. I wasn't right for, Christ, I would say weeks, if not *months* after that. You keep thinking, 'If only, if only,' depressing yourself all the time. It could drive you round the twist.

"But, lucky for myself, Frank Warren come on the scene and he give me another chance. He treated me right. He gave me two warm-up fights before the big one. And well, I didn't think that I would have another chance, to be honest with you. When you've frightened a lot of people off, you're not going to have another chance." "You become one of the Who Needs Him Club?" I enquired. "That's right," he replied, "and there were so many tidy fighters in that club. To be honest with you, to have a third chance was very, very fortunate."

But, before that chance would arrive, Colin had two more fights. On March 1984 he stopped Allen Braswell. They boxed at the Afan Lido, the scene for so many of Colin's earlier fights, and it was now a far cry from the glitter and the glamour of travelling to America and fighting for World Titles. As if to emphasise the contrast in the events, Braswell, who travelled over from Brooklyn, put up a distinctly average performance. Colin stopped him in two rounds. "Just basically a nice warm-up, innit? Obviously, I was being steered towards a third World Title fight."

Colin's next fight was in June 1984 with another American, also at the Afan Lido, but that is where the similarity ended. Billy Parks of New Orleans was tall, slender and statuesque, a very proud looking fellow. His features were handsome, chiselled and he sported a neat moustache. He looked like a boxer on top of a trophy, all arms and legs, with a sort of Tommy Hearns thing going on. He had previously boxed at lightweight and remained unbeaten as a welterweight, until he met Colin. Before the fight, Colin was interviewed in his dressing room and he quietly and reasonably explained that, although Parks was being considered the underdog, Colin was taking this fight as seriously and importantly as if it were for the World Title. Colin reasoned that, if he could not get past Billy Parks, then how could he expect to be given a shot at the World

Title? It was almost as if he had received some sort of premonition about the hard night ahead.

Colin and Billy Parks thrashed it out for nearly ten brutal rounds, before Colin finally stopped him. "I was quite pleased on the day when I seen him at the weigh-in. I thought, 'Oh, I'll cut this fella in half, you know, but indeed, take your hat off to him, he took the shots. He was a very resilient fighter." When the boxers were announced in the ring, the Welsh crowd gave Parks a sportingly respectful cheer. Colin's introduction raised the roof. The action began and Colin made the American wilt with the force of his strength, first to the body and then, when Parks made a move to protect his lean torso, Colin went for his chin. But Billy Parks was a dangerous fighter and, before the fourth round was over, he had inflicted a bleeding slash across the top of Colin's right eyebrow. Colin returned to his corner, his face a mask of blood. As he sat on his stool, he stared anxiously up at Eddie Thomas, who was busily tending to the horrible gash, before the referee walked over to the corner to inspect the damage.

Colin marched out for the fifth, undeterred by his injury. As Parks used his jab to try and worsen the cut, Colin was more than prepared to take the risk to get back on the inside, where he knew he could wear the American down with more body work. At the end of the fifth, the referee came back to Colin's corner to have another look at the cut. Eddie Thomas looked on silently, anxiously. Reg Gutteridge was commentating from ringside that night and he said you could feel the tense atmosphere emanating from the Welsh crowd.

The fight was allowed to carry on and, in the sixth round, Parks warmed to his task, having more and more success with his fine boxing skills. But, as the crowd got behind their man, singing and stamping their feet, they gave Colin's boxing boots invisible wings and he reasserted himself strongly. Parks was so tough. Some of Colin's body shots bent him, shook him, but did not break him. He simply wasn't that sort of man. When Colin walked out for the eighth round, he was now swollen under the left eye. Parks met Colin's aggression with aggression and, although Colin looked to be ahead, the score would still have reflected a close thing. Colin's face was a in a sore and sorry state as he returned to his corner at the end of the round. Parks sat in his own corner across the ring, completely silent. In fact, he never uttered a word in his corner throughout the entire fight.

Colin waded in with big winging shots from both fists at the beginning of the tenth round. Still, Parks stood and fought. Then suddenly, Colin got through with a devastating right hook to the chin, followed with a right uppercut that sent Parks' legs bandy. His knees buckled and he looked about to fall as the referee jumped in and stopped the fight. As Colin was making his final mark on that brave man from New Orleans, Reg Gutteridge inadvertently told their fortunes when he declared, "What a finish *that* would be." Colin laughed. "That's right. I remember those words. But, you know, you can't beat pulling out quality shots in the last round. I don't know how long there was left of the fight but, if there was over a minute and the ref would have let it go, again that was a borderline decision only he could make. Because, a couple more heavy shots and he would have been ... You know, he was in trouble anyway. He'd gone. He was vacant. I think that's a great decision, to stop somebody being seriously hurt. I mean, at least he walked away with his life, didn't he?

"The thing is, the only saviour you've got in that situation is the referee. Your corner can always throw the towel in, but they're not always going to pick that up, are they? Some boxers are too brave for their own good. It seems as if you're quitting, see, and nobody wants to be known as a quitter. Billy Parks was a very confident opponent and a gutsy fighter. Anybody with less courage than he had would have swallowed probably in three or four rounds, but he showed great resilience and he was still there at the end. I said to Frank Warren afterwards, 'Don't get me any more warm-ups!' It was unbelievable. He was as far as anything from a warm-up fight as you could get.

"Anyway, at that time, how can I say? Life got a bit easy. I'd had a couple of World Title fights. It was my second fight for Frank Warren. I started having a few bob in the bank and life probably was a little bit too easy. And I don't think the love for the game was there. It was starting to ebb away. I knew that after that fight."

On the 19th January 1985, Colin Jones stepped through the ropes to fight for the final time. In the other corner was WBA and IBF Welterweight Champion, Donald Curry, the man they called 'The Lone Star Cobra.' In those days, Curry was a fighter who looked to be destined for all time greatness. He had never been beaten as an amateur or professional, and in four years of punching for pay, he had notched up 20 wins, 14 inside the distance. Curry was tall and lithe and, at the age of 23, he had a poised air of self-assurance about him that belied his youth.

When he came over to England to fight Colin, he prepared at the Fore Street Gym in Birmingham city centre. The other boxers in the gym would stop what they were doing so they could watch him at work, and Curry went about that work with no fuss or sense of superiority among his British contemporaries. He was simply a World Champion who had come over here to defend his titles against the man with red hair who came from a little place in Wales called Gorseinon.

These were indeed Curry's peak years and Harry Mullan once called him in the Boxing News: *"One of the finest and most complete performers I have ever been privileged to watch."* Colin agreed. "He was probably at the top of his career. He was exceptional, without a doubt. He was so accurate, and he was powerful with it. It was a shame that I got cut, because I would have liked to have tested him for eight, nine or ten rounds. I would have liked to have seen what he had left after that, because that's when he started having a little bit of a weight problem as well. We knew about that obviously, but there again, he was so accurate. He knew what he was going to do and he done a good job."

They fought at the National Exhibition Centre in Birmingham and on the line were Curry's WBA and IBF Welterweight belts. The first three rounds belonged to Curry and, as he came out for the fourth round, he looked to have not even warmed up properly. Colin was never hurt. He remained as determined as he ever was, firing away with left hooks whenever the opportunity arose. Suddenly, The Cobra struck out and sliced a vile slash over the bridge of Colin's nose. In the first minute of the round the referee stopped the action and took Colin by the arm to lead him over to his own corner so that the doctor could inspect the pitiful mess. The doctor placed his thumbs above and below the cut and it opened right up. There was no way that the fight could be allowed to continue.

As the doctor said the words, Colin sagged against the ring post, physically and mentally exhausted. There was nothing left. "Well, there's not a lot you can say about that really. When you're beaten so emphatically like that, there's nothing you can say. Once you get cut that bad, it's the right thing that you get stopped. I don't think he would have cut me like that earlier on in my career, but I think, once you get a bit older, you do tend to get a bit soft. I think it's the early days that catch up with you."

As soon as the fight was stopped, the first of hundreds of plastic beer bottles came hurling into the ring. Mindless thugs with too much alcohol inside them took over and a massive punch up followed, during which Curry remained unruffled. He paraded around the ring in a crown, which Colin also tried on for size as they laughed together afterwards. As Colin stood beside his victor, he gazed longingly at Curry's World Title belt and, on impulse, he bent over and kissed the belt, a symbolic gesture as he was kissing his dream goodbye.

And so Colin Jones made the decision that comes to face all boxers in time. He decided to hang up his gloves and retire. "Well, in all fairness to Eddie Thomas, he knew more than anyone what a World Title meant to me. He knew more about what I thought about it than I knew myself. So he said, 'Don't make any rash decisions tonight. We'll have a little think about it now. Go away on a holiday,' he said. 'Go away and have a little break away in the sun, and come back and we'll see how you feel.' I hit a rough patch then, after that fight. Frank Warren felt there were still a lot of good fights left in me, but he didn't *know* me like Eddie knew me. He hadn't been *with* me. And neither did he know me like Gareth Bevan, my old trainer. They *knew* me. They knew that, on the build-up to the last two or three fights, I just didn't have that little edge that I normally had.

"When I came back from holiday then, I decided that I didn't feel like it. I was tired. I was burnt out. Frank Warren offered to send me away and I did go away to train. I went to Almeria in the south of Spain. We went down there for two or three weeks. We took a couple of sparring partners over with us. I said to Eddie, 'Ed, I'm out here now, and I don't know *what* I'm doing here. I don't love the game no more.' And do you know the sparring partners? I didn't want to hurt them. I *didn't* want to hurt them! If you'd have talked to me three years before that, I would have wanted to take them to bits. Eddie said, 'It's your decision. It's up to you.'

"When we came home, I had a bad back problem as well, and Frank paid for me to see Dr Bush at Harley Street. I went through a course of injections for six weeks while I was training, and the Doctor said, 'I'd like to be at ringside for your next fight.' You see, I'd even got round to thinking I could have another fight. Because of this course of injections I was having, my back was coming a bit better, but my heart wasn't in it. I was doing it specifically to please others, not myself, 'cos the money didn't come into it. So I asked the doctor why he wanted to be at ringside for my next fight, and he said, 'Well, if you get a nasty bang and you twist on what you've got, it could very well end up naughty for you.' I said, 'What do you mean by that?' He told me, 'Well, these injections, they haven't *cured* your problem, they're just *covering* the problem.' I think it was steroids and I forget the name of the other drugs. It meant nothing to me. I said, 'Are you serious?' He said 'Yes,' I said, 'Thank you. You've just made my mind up for me. Thank you very much.' So I come home, I rung Eddie up, because I'd been going back and forth to London three or four times a week on my own, you know. And I didn't mind that. If I thought it was going to get me better, it was all right.

"Anyway, I said to Eddie, 'Ed, I've finished.' 'Good for you,' he said, and that's how it ended and we were big butties forever after. Because, you know, he didn't put up any sort of resistance. 'I'll be down on the weekend,' he said, 'me and the missus, and we'll have a little drink and a nice little meal, and that will be a parting gesture,' and that's what happened. And Frank Warren, I still see him about. I think he's got the utmost respect for me."

After he finished boxing, Colin decided to turn his hand to training and managing boxers. To begin with, he found it very rewarding. One of his success stories was another red haired Welsh boxer, Peter Harris of Swansea, who boxed at featherweight. Harris drew with my friend, Ivor 'The Engine' Jones (the other 'Jones boy' in this book), and won the Welsh Featherweight Title twice (he lost it the first time to future World Champion, Steve Robinson). He also won the British Featherweight Title, which he lost in his first defence against hardy Liverpudlian and future World Featherweight Champion, Paul Hodkinson. Harris fought Hodkinson again for the British and European Titles, but was stopped in the second round. Colin remembers Peter Harris fondly. "He was a good little fighter, Peter, and he was a nice kid. In all fairness to him, he adapted to the training regime. He give Paul Hodkinson a bloody good run for his money. Twice he fought Paul. Paul Hodgkinson was at his peak then.

"The thing was, after I retired, I thought it was a good idea to go into management, and I was training a couple of boys as well. But it wasn't for me for the simple reason that, what I asked of a fighter as a pro, he couldn't come up with the goods, and it was so frustrating. I was expecting them to do what *I* did, and that's probably the wrong way of looking at it, because everybody is different. But I was the type of bloke that, if you *didn't* do it my way then we didn't get on, and it's wrong when you're managing a fighter. I honestly had the fighters interests at heart 100 per cent, because obviously I wanted them to succeed, and there's only one way to do it and that's the *hard* way."

These days, Colin's two sons are both showing an interest in boxing themselves. "I find it a little bit concerning really, because they *want* to do it, and they're always on to me to come up the gym and see if they're doing this right or that right. And I say, 'No,' because I think it's the wrong place for a father to be. That's my personal opinion. But if they want to do it, that's up to them, you know. Leave them do it. If they decide to fight, I'll definitely be following them then, but I still don't think I'd get involved as far as training goes and things like that, because I don't think it works."

They say that time flies when you are enjoying yourself, and before I knew it two and a half hours had passed by. Outside, the rain had stopped falling and the sun was shining. Inside, my interview with Colin Jones was drawing to a close. All that was left for me to do was to ask the customary questions that I have always put to my boxers. "So who was the biggest influence on your boxing career?" I asked him. He answered with no hesitation. "Eddie Thomas, without a doubt." Of his favourite boxer of all time, again there was no contest. "Cassius Clay, without a doubt. Greatest athlete, never mind boxer, that ever lived." I asked him who the biggest influence has been on his life and he told me, "I've never had time to think about that."

Finally, before we switched the tape-recorder off, I asked him, "Are you a religious man?" He replied emphatically, "No! Not in any form or way. I only wish there *was* a God, mind, to stop all this nonsense that's going on today, all the killing. Because if he *is* there, I don't know where he's hiding. Because there's a lot of atrocities going on in the world." When I put it to Colin that maybe the problems that the human race continue to face are down to the misinterpretation of the meaning of God by unscrupulous, self-serving and fanatical people, his one word reply was quiet and thoughtful. "Maybe."

* * *

Since we did this interview, Colin has become deeply involved with the training of the Welsh National Squad. I rang him up to speak with him about it and he told me, "Yes, I've been doing that for a while now. We take them up the Brecon Beacons to train at Derring Lines Barracks, and also to the National Sports Centre in Cardiff. This weekend I'm with the Great Britain Squad in Sheffield. They're youngsters, they are, going up for an assessment. The squad is already structured for the Beijing Olympics, but they are probably looking at 2012.

"There's a great guy in charge of the Welsh Squad. His name is Tony Williams and he's the National Team Coach. He's starting to turn it around now, and he really does deserve all the success because of the time and effort he's putting in. He was a very good friend of Howard

Winstone's. They boxed around the same time. He was just after Howard, but they were from the same stable. I'm one of his Staff Coaches.

"The funding for all of this is coming from the Sports Council of Wales, which is why the Welsh lads are doing so well. Indeed, because of all this funding, Wales are doing very well. It means they can go away and pull themselves together, which is great, and it's all down to the Sports Council of Wales funding it. They're ploughing in a lot of money. We're nowhere near the funding that England, Ireland or Scotland get, mind, but we're starting to show the results with the youngsters coming through. And I'm enjoying it, that's the main thing."

THE LAST WORD

CONGRATULATIONS TO JAMES COOK MBE

There is a part of the London Borough of Hackney which goes by the chilling name of 'the murder mile.' This is a place where drugs, gangland warfare and muggings are not considered the exception to the rule, and it is a sad fact of life that guns and knives are often considered rudimentary tools of the trade. Those crime statistics that we see reflected by the media are merely the result of the ones which are actually reported. Several go unreported for fear of retribution. This place, which is virtually a stone's throw from the affluence and opulence of the City, was once described by the *Daily Telegraph* as being "more dangerous than Soweto."

Nestled between three colossal housing estates there is an oasis of hope. It is called the Pedro Club and it is situated in Rushmore Road in the Lower Clapton area. The club was founded in 1929 by Katharine Elliot, who went on to become Baroness Elliot of Harwood DBE. The Baroness was a childhood friend of Elizabeth Taylor's. Passing on the baton, so to speak, that famous diva of the silver screen went on to become the Pedro Club's Vice-President in the 1960s. To this day, there is photograph on display at the entrance to the Pedro that was taken of Taylor laying a brick on a new wall, something that she did to symbolise her support and commitment to the Pedro Club.

During this time, Elizabeth Taylor and Richard Burton put on a gala premier of their film, The Sandpiper, at London's Empire Theatre and they donated the £5,000 proceeds to the Pedro for the rebuilding costs that were necessary way back then. Taylor and Burton were refreshingly prepared to become involved on a hands-on basis. They arranged an event at the club to raise its profile, and that day they met and talked to several of the children who were to become the beneficiaries of their kindness. But time moves on and a few years ago it looked like the Pedro was about to close its doors for good, which would have been a tragedy. Thankfully, this was not to be.

James Cook was British and European Super-Middleweight Champion in the 1990s. James came to live in England from his native country of Jamaica when he was nine years old. Jamaica's loss was England's gain. As James said in my first book, "Jamaica is still every part of my roots. I won't forget that. But now I am British, because obviously, I was British Champion." These days James has a very different type of battle on his hands. He puts his heart and soul into fighting the forces of crime, deprivation and delinquency in Hackney, the place where he has made his home.

Just as the doors of the Pedro Club were about to be closed for the last time, James walked in and decided that that was simply not going to happen. James' official title at the Pedro Club is Treasurer, but more appropriate job descriptions would include Role Model, Peace Keeper and Father Figure. James has made it his life's mission to guide the young people who populate the streets where he lives towards a positive and constructive path in life. Thanks to James and people like him, the young people of Hackney continue to have somewhere to go, somewhere to be, somewhere they can call their own.

James is not a man who feels comfortable behind a desk, so he makes it his business to patrol the streets on a daily basis, seeking to help those that he can reach in an endless endeavour to catch the ones who are in danger of falling, before serious trouble catches up with them. Weighing in at a mere few pounds over his fighting weight, strolling down the road, sleek and muscular in his street garb (including shades and string vest) he poses a formidable sight, and then his face breaks out into the sunniest smile and he puts one in mind of an urban warrior on the side of everything that is right. To the young people who James looks out for, he is a 6'2½" guardian angel. In their lives, which in many cases are destined to be uncertain and ever-changing, they know that James Cook is always there for them, always dependable, always the same.

James does not see anything out of the ordinary in the work that he does and the sacrifices that he makes. To him, it is simply a job that needs doing, and he's the man to do it. As he earnestly explained, "My main thing is to be out on the street, trying to get the young people into some form of education, to learn a trade or something. I want to teach them that they've got to earn their money. They've got to go out and work for it."

I am delighted to report that James was awarded the MBE in this year's Queen's Birthday Honours List for Services to Youth Justice in Hackney. As it started to dawn on this unsung hero that he was about to have letters after his name, he greeted the feeling in his typically laid-back fashion. "There was a letter come through the post, which I didn't take any notice of. I just chuck it down. Then, the second letter come through the post asking for some detail, and it had 'Downing Street' or just something like that. I thought, somebody is writing me and saying 'My servant.' I thought, 'I never had a servant in my life!'

"Anyway, I read a bit more and, funnily enough, on the day the Birthday Honours List came out my brother phoned me, 'cos he's a computer whiz kid and he'd been looking it up on the internet. He said 'Do I call you 'Sir' now?' So I said 'What are you talking about?' He said 'Your name is on it'. So I shot over the road and went inside the shop and I said 'Could you check the Birthday Honours List?' They said 'What you looking for?' I said 'Never mind that, just check it. Go through all the names.' So they did go through all the names and my name was on there, and then they start screaming. So I thought 'Mm, maybe there's something in this.' I didn't take no notice until the official letter came with 'MBE' on it, and then I thought 'Okay.' Then obviously, the press and the Boxing Board got involved. I got a letter from the Boxing Board saying 'Well done', and then I started taking it a bit seriously.

"Southern Area Champion was my first title as a professional. I thought winning any title as a pro was good, so that was great. Then came the British and then the European, and I thought that was good enough. But, yeah, they're saying for Services to Youth. I've always been working with the youth, and that's why, to me, it's such a great idea when somebody come from any area, and go back in the area and do something. This is why I love a guy like Ricky Hatton, 'cos he's natural. He's with his friends all the time. He doesn't show off. He's just natural in the area. No matter how much money he's got, he's just with his friends and he don't go to no private party. He mix with everybody and, guys like that, I love. This is why I say, no matter who you are, I don't care if you're David Beckham, Posh, or whatever, you all started from somewhere, from an area. Go back in there. Don't all of a sudden become bigger than everybody else. Go back in the area and help out the young people in that area.

"Coming from where I'm coming, I didn't expect all of this. It don't matter where you come from, it just shows that you can always achieve. You don't have to be flash and show off, you just need to be natural. Coming from Jamaica, Peckham, Hackney, it just shows that you don't need millions of pounds to live good with people, to love and respect people. It's just great having a normal life now, and you guys calling me 'Sir', that's not bad. I'm getting used to that! When I first got a phone call from the Hackney Gazette, they mentioned it to me. They says, 'Do you know who nominated you?' I says, 'Well, it's definitely not the young people. But I keep telling them that they need God in their lives', so it must be somebody from the Church!"

James started working with the youth on the streets at the age of 16 years old, when he was not much more than a lad himself. "The Pedro club was around then, but I didn't start at the Pedro Club because, as you know, I spent half my time in Peckham and the other half was in Hackney. If I was in Peckham, I would have been finding something to do with the young people. But after coming to Hackney, where I've been for about 25 years now, the Pedro Club was going. It's a famous club, re-opened in the 1960s by Elizabeth Taylor. She gave the club its first donation when she first came into the club, and she's still a Patron of the club. With such a high profile you thought they'd probably never leave the club but, you know, it's time, they're getting on and they leave it to the community.

"I happen to live round the corner from the club and a few years ago the council turned up. They was gonna close it and I thought 'This ain't right,' so I went in there and the council was in there. I started searching the club and found the documents, and I tell the council they can't have it because it belongs to the young people. I just got Frank Maloney, Bruce Baker, Bernard Hart and a few others, and said, 'Listen, will you come and help me with this club and sort out a management committee?' I got Derek Williams, Geraldine Davies, Marvin Stone, I just got these people to come and help."

Another major force behind the running of the Pedro is Ufu Niazi, the manager. Ufu is somebody who James immediately recognised as an invaluable force. "I went and got him, because he know about the club and he know about the young people. I said 'Will you come and help me with the funding and stuff?' So he decided to come and help me with it, and I'm grateful for the work he's putting in. Obviously, he don't get paid as he should, you know, because we ain't got any funding. But we just keep digging at it, just to keep the club running hopefully five or six days a week.

"I just put a sign up saying 'Youth and Community Centre', because I want the youth and the people in the local community to use it. So, I think, my next objective is to keep it going, and maybe get some dance classes in there, so that everybody can come in and use it. Then it will be more multi-functional. It's not necessarily about bringing in funds. It's about getting the community, the young and the old, mixing together because there's a gap between the old people, who stay by themselves, and the young people. It's just to get everybody in the area - everybody's supposed to respect each other, so to be honest, that's my next goal. I think the best way to do that is to getting a dancing class in, where everybody could start a function with dancing, you know?"

To my mind, one of the things that makes this world a wonderful place to be is the fact that, no matter how bad things get, there are always people who are willing to give of themselves to help others, people who spread light where there is darkness, compassion where there is destitution, warmth where there is need. Different people act for different reasons and I asked James straight out what made him choose to tread such a selfless path from such a young age. His reply was matter of fact. "Jimmy Redwell and Ronnie White, my amateur trainers [at East Lane Boxing Club], they was working people, and when they couldn't come down the club they used to say to me 'Will you take the class?' They was all different ages, and that was when I found out that I could teach a class, get everybody smiling, everybody's happy. So I thought, you know, with what's going on, if I could make a young person come and be with me and come out smiling and happy, I think at that time it was a job well done.

"I just carried on like that. I think people have just got natural talent to do things. To me, I think, no matter what, I could just make a young kid smile and be happy. It's just something I find natural to be doing, without a problem. They might come in miserable and fighting but, at the end of the day, they'll sit down and speak to me, and probably listen. I like that feeling, definitely."

Hackney has the largest number of under 16s in any London borough and the Pedro is the only youth club in the area. James' confirmation of that fact was emphatic. "Absolutely. One youth club. One free state." Working in such a potentially hostile environment, I was interested to learn if there has ever been a time when this gentle giant has felt in danger. He smiled and shook his head. "I think the kids will be in danger when they see me coming because, I must admit, the kids, no matter who they are and what they are, there's so much respect. Even if they're smoking out the front and they see me coming down the road, you know, between eight and 25, they start to put it away. The thing about it is, no matter how much the crowd is, no matter how much trouble they're making, once I go over there and say 'What's happening', it will start to get squashed.

"At this moment, the estate and the youth is getting on with this street code, where you can't leave one area and go to the next area. You can't leave one estate and go onto another estate. It's madness. I think personally the government needs to address this by opening up things for the young people to do, like they did many years ago when there was the Girls' Brigade and the Boy Scouts. There was always something to do. Now they're building and closing down everything and there's nothing for the young people to do, so its something that the government are bringing to themselves. But arresting these kids ain't gonna do it. They need to be providing something for the young people to learn."

At the time we made this tape, James was unaware of when he was actually going to collect his MBE, but he has his own ideas on dress code. "Yeah, I don't know yet, but all I'm getting from people is that I have to be wearing these fancy clothes. I just keep telling people, I like to make a change. I like to wear one of my string vests and go give one to the Queen, and say to her 'This is how we do it in Hackney!'" James has this disarming way of suddenly becoming endearingly shy, and this element of his personality surfaced when I pressed him to tell me what he thought he really will say to the Queen when he meets her. "You know me, Mel. When the day come, I'll be bloody shy as anything. I don't like all this fancy dressing up gear. I just want to wear a suit and do what I need to do. I don't know but, when it comes to it, I think I might be shy and probably will just shut my mouth. I don't think I'll say anything. I'll probably be too frightened."

The facilities at the Pedro Club include a pool table, a keep fit studio, a fully equipped computer room, a motor mechanic workshop, an art room, go-carts, a dance floor and they have a five-aside football and basketball pitch. Also, the organisers are in the process of completing a recording studio, which will hopefully be up and running by the time this book goes to print, earning much needed revenue to keep the whole thing going.

Despite the absolute necessity of the Pedro Club and everything it provides, this special and most vital organisation faces a daily struggle to survive. James sadly explained, "We get a quarterly grant from the council of between £3,000 and £5,000. The thing is, it costs about £72,000 a year just to run the building. We're open every night of the week and, when it's all up and running with all staff in place, we get about 100 young people in and out of the door every night of the week. We're looking at opening at the weekends and organising dance nights to get the young and old people together, get some more communication going on."

James starred in the original *'Sweet Fighting* Man' and, as a result of that, has become a treasured friend, so I felt it only right that he should have the last word in this book too. I wanted to close this book with a tribute to James Cook and everything that he stands for. God bless you, James Cook MBE.

Anybody wishing to make a donation (no matter how large or small) in order to assist James and the team at The Pedro to continue their tremendous work can send cheques and postal orders (made payable to The Pedro Club) to the publishing company address of this book at: Sweet Touch Publishing Company, Studio 221, 61 Victoria Road, Surbiton, Surrey, KT6 4JX.